MOVED BY DESTINY

Also by Christopher Schaefer

Re-imagining America
Finding Hope in Difficult Times
(Hawthorn Press, 2019)

Partnerships of Hope
Building Waldorf School Communities
(Waldorf Publications, 2012)

Vision in Action
Working with Soul & Spirit in Small Organizations
(coauthored with Tÿno Voors, Lindisfarne Books, 1996)

Moved by Destiny

Life Stories of Social Engagement

Anthroposophy and Social Reform

EDITED BY

Christopher Schaefer, PhD

WITH ASSISTANCE FROM

Joan Jaeckel

SteinerBooks | 2026

2026
SteinerBooks
An imprint of Anthropsophic Press / SteinerBooks
1 Taconic Place
Ghent, New York 12075
www.steinerbooks.org

ISBN: 978-1-62148-404-2

Printed in the United States of America
by Integrated Books International

Contents

Section IV: People, Land, and Society: Initiatives for a Better World

Section V: Leading with Spirit: Supporting Communities and Organizations

Section VI: Peace is the Way

Preface

We live in challenging times and the question naturally arises: What can a spiritual movement such as anthroposophy, initiated by Rudolf Steiner over 100 years ago in Central Europe, offer us now to ameliorate the suffering of the world? One answer is to look at the many reform efforts which Steiner himself undertook to renew culture and society, which have continued to flourish since his time. These include the more than 1,000 Waldorf schools and kindergartens seeking a renewal of education in many countries of the world, or the therapeutic communities serving the needs of people with disabilities and special needs. We can note the varied efforts to heal the earth through biodynamic agriculture or the many efforts to develop a more holistic approach to medicine, as well as social and artistic therapies. There is also the initiative to renew society as a whole after the enormous destruction of World War I, known as the Threefold Social Order Movement, and new and innovative approaches to banking and investment as well as a host of other initiatives to serve the common good.

This is indeed a continuing powerful and healing legacy but our present times ask for new efforts to heal and transform a world suffering war, environmental destruction, and growing social and economic inequities. The essays in this book on healing social life seek to address this question and need, out of the life stories of individuals who have been moved by social concerns and have integrated these concerns with their spiritual striving and the insights of anthroposophy.

The journey to this book began in July 2024 with friends Carrie and John Schuchardt of the House of Peace, when my wife Signe and I were having coffee and expressing our dismay over the genocide in Gaza. John wondered why the Anthroposophical Society, founded by Rudolf Steiner in 1923, had not expressed outrage and condemnation at the terrible suffering of the civilian population and called for an end to the war. I responded by saying that the Society did not see itself as a body that took political positions but rather as an institution that fostered the spiritual life of humanity. The conversation continued with John asking again why did the Society not take a position calling out the terrible evils of war that were occurring in Ukraine, Gaza, and other parts of the world and that had been visited on the world by US weapons and militarism since the time of the Vietnam War. Didn't Steiner see witnessing and confronting evil as a central task of our time? I agreed and suggested that many individuals connected to Steiner's work did see it as essential to their inner and outer journey to confront evil in themselves and in the world and attempt to do the good. We then moved to talk about the House of Peace and its work with refugees and the sick and wounded suffering from the ravages of war. We also wondered whether more people today are becoming aware of Sophia, the being of divine wisdom who surely spreads her mantle of insight to recognize that we should be beyond war and violence at this stage of human evolution.

Yet John's question stayed with me and as the Threefold Social Order Today Group (3FSO Today) was planning a lecture and conference in the autumn, I suggested asking Gerald Haefner, the leader of the Social Science Section in Dornach, Switzerland, the international headquarters of the Anthroposophical Society, to address the theme of anthroposophy as a movement for peace,justice and social reform. He accepted and gave his talk followed by a conversation with panelists on November 10th. In it he stressed the question of what are we each doing, how is our heart awakened to ameliorate the suffering of people today, what initiatives are we engaged in to make a better, more just and peaceful world? He noted that there are two main pillars which support the life of anthroposophy, of

Anthroposophia, that of inner development and self-transformation and that of being ever more actively engaged with the needs of the world, specifically and actively. This echoes a sentiment expressed by Rudolf Steiner in *The Life, Nature and Cultivation of Anthroposophy,* in which he states,... *kindling the love of humanity, anthroposophy grows creative in moral impulses to action, and in the practice of a truly social life.**

A few days after the lecture and conference I thought, let me ask those who attended the lecture and conference, or had expressed interest in attending, to submit essays on how they have experienced the relationship between their social engagement, their activism, and their involvement with anthroposophy. I sent out the invitation just before Christmas and gave a March 15th deadline for the submission of essays. Much to my surprise, from about 90 people who received the invitation, and with some encouragement along the way, I received 22 essays. The essays are deeply moving as people share their lives, their search for meaning, and their efforts to integrate spiritual interests with their social engagement. From transforming a business, to starting one of the first CSAs in the United States, to working with inner-city youth in Detroit, or working for peace in war-torn countries, each person relates their inner and outer journey, revealing the threads of destiny which led each person to engage with the needs and suffering of the world.

It is interesting to note that the essays are mainly from people of the 1960s generation, although I tried to engage a few individuals from younger generations. I think of this older generation as the institution builders of the anthroposophical movement in the United States, following the generation of pioneers. It is our generation that expanded the Waldorf school movement dramatically, that also supported the growth of biodynamic agriculture, curative education, and the arts, and that led to an increase in the membership of the Anthroposophical Society.

* *The Foundation Stone / The Life, Nature & Cultivation of Anthroposophy,* Jan. 13, 1924, Forest Row, UK: Rudolf Steiner Press, 2011.

While I believe the lives described are representative of a generation who engaged with anthroposophy and social questions deeply, the essays do not cover the full spectrum of initiatives that have grown out of Rudolf Steiner's work, because the invitation was sent only to those who had expressed an interest in or attended the Baumheier Lecture and Conference. I can think of many important initiatives that would naturally be included if I had cast a wider net in the invitation, and I apologize to those who feel omitted.

The essays have been roughly grouped according to subject areas but could easily have been combined differently, as there is much overlap in themes. In combining and editing the essays submitted we have attempted to let each voice retain its unique character and style.

I am deeply indebted to Joan Jaeckel for copyediting the manuscript and providing advice and support throughout the process of arranging this manuscript. Signe Eklund Schaefer has also provided invaluable assistance and encouragement. Most importantly I thank the contributors for their inspiring essays and meaningful, heart filled efforts to contribute to a better, more peaceful, and sane world.

In many respects the biographical journeys described in these essays are an answer to John Schuchardt's question about anthroposophy, peace and social justice in our time. It seems to me that we have all attempted to live with and enact aspects of Rudolf Steiner's Motto of the Social Ethic:

> The healing social life is only found
> When in the Mirror of the Human Soul
> The whole Community finds its reflection,
> And when in the Community
> The virtue and strength of each one is living.

Christopher Schaefer
Great Barrington, Massachusetts, May 2025

Section I

Responsible Business Communities

Building a Company and Finding Myself

Pierre Noack

The first-born of three brothers, I grew up in the Belgian countryside on a small century-old grain mill overlooking a waterwheel. My parents suffered the hardship caused by World War II. My father was conscripted into the German military at 17 and was later a prisoner of war. My mother experienced the German occupation of Belgium. Those experiences taught them to be critical of any authority; they were independent and operated the mill business together for about 30 years until retirement.

With a low income for hard physical work, we lived very modestly yet never lacked anything. My brothers and I would help our father whenever we could; our mother would expect us to help in the vegetable garden, and in all aspects of the household. This upbringing gave me a sense of responsibility, of realness, and the ability to handle a wide range of tasks. We had very slim resources and had to be creative. I joined the Boy Scouts and loved being outdoors in nature. My Catholic upbringing established a spiritual basis that I broadened by reading books on Tibetan Buddhism in my teenage years.

After completing public high school, I graduated with a major in mechanical and electrical engineering from a technical college in Brussels. I then had a wonderful practical learning experience in metalworking and machine building by working for two years in a small smithy and machine building company in Belgium. Driven by my interest in the German language and in my German heritage, I decided to apply for work in Germany and was immediately hired by a family-owned middle-size machinery producer, Aerzen GMBH.

All of my life experiences, combined with physical strength, gave me the confidence that I could handle almost any situation. In 1986, after 6 years as a young engineer at the German headquarters of this company, I was invited to manage its then struggling US subsidiary. At the time, I had no management experience but the trust that I received from the management moved me to accept the post with enthusiasm. Self-confident, I did not hesitate. There ensued many learning-by-doing years.

The US subsidiary was small and embedded in a joint venture with a company that had been established in the US about a decade earlier. Our US subsidiary relied on its partner company for all administrative tasks. However, the joint venture did not work well and the decision was made to dissolve it, reorganize, move to another location, and establish the US subsidiary as a separate entity. Aside from establishing yearly financial targets such as revenues and profit, the parent company did not impose any specific strategy on its subsidiary which therefore experienced a high degree of independence. Our team was small, engaged, young, and motivated. For several years, my initial enthusiasm carried me through the challenges, and hard work compensated for my inexperience.

Facing strong competition in North America, despite working many, many hours, the company under my management barely met its business targets. Our market segments included some that I felt misaligned with my personal values from the point of view of environmental impact or business practices. We were in the early to mid-1990s; and I was in my mid-to-late 30s.

I, my wife, and our two young daughters were living in a rural suburb of Philadelphia. I loved nature, enjoyed the outdoors, and tended to our large vegetable garden. I realized that I was not spending enough time with the family, felt I was neglecting them, as well as neglecting myself. Missing a meaningful purpose in my work and feeling torn between priorities, the inner tension increased and drove my stress level to such heights that I felt increasingly depressed. "Work-Life Balance" seemed to be the solution. I introduced periods of relaxation into my life. However, I wanted to live an integrated life with one purpose: work-life-integration rather than additional fragmentation. I was desperately looking for firm ground, for orientation. I yearned for a connecting principle, a single ideal that could permeate and connect the various segments of my life.

At school age, our daughters soon attended a Waldorf school. During each visit at the school, I felt a refreshing and invigorating sense of deep truth, realness, kindness, and wholeness all at once. This sparked my interest in the source of this pedagogical approach and I discovered anthroposophy. Conversations, reading circles, and participating in school community initiatives were most inspiring. Once, a statement by the class teacher of our older daughter sparked my attention. He mentioned a principle stated by Rudolf Steiner on curative education: What we observe is a symptom that has its source at a deeper level. This wise comment immediately seemed relevant to my situation. I then needed a bridge between that experience of the Waldorf school and my work at the company.

Most thankfully, contacts made at the Waldorf school led me to Christopher Schaefer, whom I asked to help me as a consultant. Together with Chris and with our employees we created a long-range plan for our US division. I learned a lot from him, through the challenging process of engaging the entire staff, by participating in workshops, and from our debriefing conversations. One important insight was that organizations have fourfold characteristics similar to human beings—a physical body, life body, soul, and spirit. Likewise, organizations develop a physical body, a life body, a soul, and spirit in their phases of maturation.

Similar to the fourfold human being, so does a community with its physical body, life body, soul, and spirit mature from birth through childhood, adolescence, to adulthood. Applied as a moral ideal, this has deep, positive, even healing implications for leadership and management. The leaders must not only be in tune with the physical, measurable aspects of the organization, but also with its latent spiritual qualities. I wondered, how can any organization be managed for the long term while ignoring half of its reality: its soul and spirit? This then became my field of continuous learning.

In the early years, we operated with the highest flexibility, trusting each other, having the best for the company in mind. In that phase of development, rules were barely needed; the team was self-managed. After some years however, the company grew organically and our staff increased, necessitating rules and clear standards. I realized that the company passed from childhood and moved into its adolescence phase. We established better structures, and documented work processes. However, we often swung back to the previously more spontaneous work approaches. This challenged the implementation of changes, caused frustration, uncertainty, and called for discipline. Like most managers, I dreamed of an intrinsically motivated staff, a work-community with a strong sense of ownership. I felt that to achieve this, I had to develop management skills.

I took courses, read books on leadership and management, attended seminars, and joined business associations. I was eager to learn and implement some of the ideas. I experienced that removing symptoms did not automatically solve the problems that caused them: It is not the band-aid that heals the wound! Anthroposophical understanding of the human being provided the perspective I needed for addressing the source of the issues by considering all four members of the fourfold organization and its development phases. And as I was searching and trying to understand these processes to reach the "deeper" source of the symptoms, I felt as if something very tender was beginning to germinate, something that gave a sense of a company spirit. It felt indeed very fragile and needed to be tended to. I then wondered if the organization was maturing to incorporate its own Self, a sort of sprouting process.

This beautiful process became increasingly noticeable. I discovered that my task was to remove obstacles that may hinder this becoming, and I sensed that to tune into this development I needed first to work on myself. Viewing the organization from the whole, or from its whole-self shed light onto its daily processes; the issues to be handled became clearer and could be viewed in their whole context. My goal was to build an effective and strong management team and to strengthen the company's culture.

Neil Sicherman, a leadership consultant, and a friend, met me on my path. Immediately, his definition of leadership resonated with me: "Leadership is moving toward Potential." Thus, each one can be a leader in one's own life. Since one cannot properly understand others before understanding oneself, Neil introduced us to the Riso Hudson Enneagram as a tool for a better understanding of one's personality. The same tool helped me to better understand the individuality of the organization as well as its inner workings. And this was only the beginning of a very stimulating journey.

I came to realize that I would never come close to the familiar picture of a charismatic, outspoken, and mighty leader. Once I felt depressed by seeing some of my shortcomings and the challenges to overcome them. Neil's answer was, "Just be present," and I understood that being more fully myself, truly human, authentic, and selflessly moving toward potential frees and empowers others to become more themselves, feeling more human. It is healing and energizing. Two books gave me additional insight and inspiration: *The Fifth Discipline* by Peter Senge and *Theory U* by Otto Scharmer. From this point on, with a better understanding for the dynamic drivers, moving toward potential, and trying to lead as Otto describes "from the future," the organization began to show its own character. Some examples follow.

Design work for the new Aertzen USA company building: The company outgrew its rental space; a plot of land was purchased nearby and we began the design of our new building, a building that expresses the organization's values: a building laid out to foster the interaction between departments and between employees. Moreover, it had to promote transparency, be environmentally friendly, and include elements of organic architecture. All the employees were invited to participate in the design and we hired a team of young, dynamic architects. It became a remarkable building: the materialization of moral values and the expression of a consistent ideal. The building stood as a statement of possibility. Gandhi's "be the change you want to see in the world" became our slogan.

We adopted the concept of the "triple bottom line," coined by the green building movement, that accounts for "People, Planet, and Profit." Defining it in slightly different terms to mirror the threefold nature of social life, we modified it into "People, Planet, and Prosperity." Located near Philadelphia, we referred to "Life, liberty, and the pursuit of happiness" of the Declaration of Independence on multiple occasions, such as at the ground-breaking ceremony and our grand-opening. This triple-bottom-line concept impacted multiple areas of our organization.

We anchored the threefold concept into our quality assurance system as well as in the bylaws of the company, meanwhile trusting that the financials were to be seen as a result and not only as the goal of the organization. This changed the focus toward the long-term evolution of the organization, focusing on doing the right thing for the right purpose. We formulated completely new strategies, developed corresponding goals, and introduced balanced scorecards as a management and transparent communication tool. The annual reports mirrored the triple bottom line.

The effect of the triple bottom line approach became noticeable in our quality assurance; we focused on developing quality in our employees rather than forcing them to comply with an ever-increasing volume of directives. This was particularly valuable to achieve a consistently high level of quality across an infinite number of applications; equipment configurations and combinations; and industry-and-client-specific standards and expectations. An anecdote may be worth mentioning: After a few years, we switched to a different auditing company to recertify our organization to international quality standards. We chose an auditing firm involved predominantly in the stringent aviation sector. On his second visit, the auditor told me: "Pierre, I am so happy to be here; auditing your company feels as good as taking a warm bath. Could you join us at our yearly corporate meeting and talk to us about your approach?" He reported that he had never experienced any organization where the employees so openly showed their work to the auditor and asked for advice to improve on the shortcomings.

The layout of the building also followed a threefold pattern: a large open area featuring wide windows connecting the production to the office section. It fostered encounters between employees since it was the only inside connection between the two sections, successfully lowering the perceived barriers between white and blue-collar cultures in the workforce. It is in that space that we held our weekly all-company standing meeting. At this meeting we mentioned the main orders that shipped during the past week. Since the company provided capital equipment to a vast array of applications in a broad range of industries and utilities, we wanted to raise the employees' awareness of the commodities and services produced with the help of our equipment. The meetings offered continuous improvement opportunities by sharing the challenges and successes across disciplines of the organization.

Next, we addressed the compensation system. This is always a delicate project that raises a lot of suspicion against management. Trust must be earned! A combination of consistency in the way decisions are made and followed through, authentic presence, and conversations with focused listening helped in establishing a basis of trust. The compensation system was redesigned to consist of three parts; the first and larger part was a function of individual skills and responsibilities. It lies in the hands of each employee to develop additional skills or to take on more responsibilities, and, if valuable for the organization, grow this portion of the compensation. The second part, that was equal for all employees, included the benefits such as health insurance, vacation time, retirement savings account, training opportunities, and so on. The third part was a function of achieving the goals of the community, of our company, together.

The design of the HR department reflected the distinction between personnel administration and development of capabilities. In the hiring process we paid particular attention to the cultural fit that included a degree of sensitivity for what the company stood for, and a desire to learn. The company's character became increasingly perceptible and attracted new talent and people in search of meaningful and purposeful work. This in turn had a reinforcing effect on the company's character and quality.

Growing the capabilities of the individual employees through various company-sponsored courses and training programs added to the motivation and engagement and therefore to the company's competencies with the purpose of strengthening the relationship with its customers. As a result, the company successfully developed capabilities in technically challenging areas of high value.

As a logical continuation of this development the company evolved toward becoming an environmentally and socially responsible organization, a "benefit corporation," a B-Corp.

However, the striving for harmony can also lead to a dangerous avoidance of conflict, inconsistencies, and erosion of trust. Mindfulness and a sense of deep unwavering responsibility for the Spirit of the organization provides the orientation and the strength needed for a leadership standing on a firm moral and spiritual foundation.

I became aware that other opposing forces can try to undermine the Spirit of the organization by introducing doubt and distrust, or by distracting from the company's course, for example, some shiny new business ideas that sound appealing and create excitement, but that mask details that should have been a warning. To no avail; do we then invest capacities to the detriment of other projects, or do we embark in a direction that takes us off course? I learned the importance of continually connecting with the community Spirit to evaluate our steps by tuning into its ideals, its spiritual purpose, and its core principles.

I left the US subsidiary about 10 years before this writing. I have had time to reflect and to put things into perspective. I cannot gauge the full impact we have had on individual employees and on their families, or on customers or suppliers. But based on numerous comments, I know that a contribution has been made to a better world.

A few footprints remain that have the potential for sparking more curiosity at a later time. For example, the raised-bed garden where employees can learn to produce vegetables under the guidance of a biodynamic gardener. The gardening team produces over 700 pounds (about 320 kg) of fresh organic vegetables that are donated to the local food bank. Another example is the company building that has since been expanded while retaining its original intent and style. The company however has changed its focus from organic growth to a more rapid growth through acquisitions. The business volume is now a goal rather than a result, and the company has in that sense been growing successfully. However, the soul of the organization has changed.

Before leaving the company, I had tried to ignite in the management team the passion for the spiritual dimension of the organization. I have since realized that a deeper questioning or a longing, coupled with the willingness to work on oneself with moral and spiritual insights, are needed for igniting this passion. This leads to a healthy and inspiring integration of work and life. However, none of this can be dictated. It is a free individual decision.

Most rewarding for me was building a work-and business-community—a model organization that contributes to a stream of evolution toward a peaceful and prosperous society—while embracing the purpose of becoming ever more human. Moving things forward requires fewer political programs and more of an inner resolve and trust in moral, spiritual values. This approach has transformed me and continues to do so as I keep treading my path in the light of anthroposophy. I am most thankful to those who entrusted me with the management of the company. I am also extremely grateful to all the people who showed me the way or accompanied me for a part of it, to those who challenged me and pushed me—knowingly or not—to develop.

How Steiner's Insights Brought Light and Warmth into the World of Work

Robert Michael Burnside

My life has always been centered around the need to work, to earn income, with the goal of doing work in a way that also benefits others. Having a strong Christian upbringing, I always longed to live out the teachings of Christianity in the world. On reflection now at 75 years of age, I see that after meeting the work of Rudolf Steiner in 1985, when I was 35 years old, I had found the strong grounded foundation for conducting life and work in a truly Christian way for which I was longing.

1. Destiny as Preparation for Seeking to Know Spirit

Growing up in a Working-class Family in the US

I was born in 1949, growing up in a working-class family in a small town in the United States. My mother worked as a nurse in a hospital in a nearby large city, second shift in the evening, so she could do her motherly duties of raising children and keeping the house going during the day. My father did a variety of jobs along his way, constantly burdened by paying off the debts left from his father. From an early age it was clear to me I would always need to work to earn money to make my way in life.

Mother Is a Strong Example of Christian Ideals Carried Out in Life

My mother was an active member of the Methodist Church, also singing in the choir. She was a strong example for me of a human being that didn't so much talk about Christianity as live it in her actions. When I was 14 years old, on discovering the new minister had a drinking problem, she invited him to have dinner with our family on Friday nights. Her thinking was that perhaps he could avoid drinking on Saturday if he joined us on Friday night in a family setting. There was never any alcohol in our house. The visits helped him reduce his dependence on alcohol. After a few months she and father agreed to invite him to live with our family. Father and I built a three-room addition on our house for him to move into, which he did for four years. He was a world traveler and taught me much about world religions. When I turned 18, I was preparing to go to a local community college to work my way through. However, the minister, in gratitude to our family, instead paid my full four years tuition at a private university. This experience was an example for me that when someone, like my mother, embodies and carries out Christian values into life, other good can also arise.

Avoiding War, Joining the Peace Corps, Experiencing Cultural Differences

When I graduated college in 1971, America was at war in Vietnam, and all young men were potential draftees to fight in the war. I discovered that, if I joined the Peace Corps, for the two-year tour of duty, my draft would be postponed. So, in 1971 I joined the Peace Corps and was assigned to Haryana, India, in an animal husbandry project which had the goal of helping the cows of the Punjabi farmers give more milk. It was a shock both for me and the village farmers to meet each other's culture. It seemed to them like I was from Mars. I experienced that their culture had its own life and had nothing to do with American culture. Yet, between those two very different cultures, positive, loving, and effective human relationships could still occur. I experienced that human relationships can transcend deep differences.

Joining the World of Work; Facing a Decision

On my return from the Peace Corps, the draft had ended. My first job was with a global jeans manufacturing company where I started as a marketing and merchandising assistant. I worked there until 1984, rising up in the ranks, starting by buying denim in China. In 1984 the company was sold to a leveraged buyout fund. As an outcome of the sale, I was offered the chance to be a member of management of the newly privatized company, which would bring me a lot of money. The CEO made it clear to me that if I joined the new organization, I would become wealthy. He demonstrated this by indicating the many nearby buildings he owned. However, I was 35 years old and needed a break. I had two boys, 5 and 7 years old, that I had hardly seen due to all my world travel for the brand. From a practical side, I knew I had stock options that would allow me to live for six months while I looked for another job, so I declined the offer.

Seeking a Path to Spirituality

While I was looking for another job I also searched for a meaningful approach to spirituality. I had been a member of many Protestant churches, coming eventually to feel that the Christian churches were more of a barrier to knowing Christ than a bridge. During those six months, I explored many different spiritual paths. I went to Eastern Buddhism classes and tried many of the trendy paths coming from California. Nothing seemed just right. Finally, I came across a brochure about a study group reading Rudolf Steiner's anthroposophic works that met during evenings at someone's home. When I went to that group, BOOM! LIGHTNING STRIKE! I knew I had found my path. It was absolutely clear immediately. I then adopted anthroposophy and the spiritual science of Steiner as my path forward and have been reading his extensive body of spiritual-scientific research ever since.

2. Anthroposophy as a Guide in the Working World

Absorbing "Karmic Relationships" and a New Job with a Not-for-Profit

The first serious study I did of Rudolf Steiner's work were the 8 volumes of *Karmic Relationships.* Learning the ideas about karma and reincarnation changed my understanding of and approach to life. During the six months I also found my next job, working for a global not-for-profit leadership development teaching organization. On recruiting me they said they were a strongly idealistic organization that wanted to add a person like myself who had experienced the reality of business. The organization was formed in the 1970s with the mission of developing leadership for the benefit of society worldwide. It had the vision of how leadership might be a benefit, not only to a person, a team or a company, but also to the wider world. This was greatly inspirational for me and for the others working there. It was a strong community of very idealistic people. I was honored to join them and loved the work. Warmed by my study of karma and reincarnation, there was a definite feeling of being a member of a karmically bound community.

Bringing Ideas of the Threefold Social Order into the Work

I taught in the primary program, a five-day face to face event with twenty-four senior leaders, delivered around the world. In 1989, the CEO asked everyone to imagine a new leadership program that could be a follow up. I proposed a program that would address the issue of the spiritual aspect of leadership. My study of Rudolf Steiner's spiritual science had given me the impetus and language, and also the courage to pursue how the spirit in the human being comes to life in developing leaders in the realm of business. I was especially inspired by Rudolf Steiner's ideas about social freedom, equality of all human beings, and the necessity of brotherhood in the economic sphere in his book *The Threefold Social Order.* The new program would go directly at the question of how to help people develop their own spirit and their own leadership in a way that would be beneficial not only to them, their team and organization, but also to the wider world. In 1990 we formed a team to develop it, with the framework of "ideas into action"—that knowing oneself was not enough, one needed to live it out consciously in reality. It was a six-month program where leaders first developed their vision and goals together with other leaders, then went away for three months followed by a coach, gathering three months later to share with the others what had happened, followed by a final three months followed by the coach. The whole idea was to bring their best self through development over this period of time into action so that the act itself is deeply involved with the spirit of the self, yet one that is developed with others and for the benefit of others. The program was built in a way that avoided the idea that the staff had more knowledge than the participants. Instead, it was an approach that said all of us have knowledge and wisdom that we need to bring together and that serves everyone involved. This ideal reflected Rudolf Steiner's threefold social order with its idea that the equality of all human beings, brought together in freedom and united with a brotherly impulse, could be of benefit to the world.

Seeking the Balance of Ideals and Reality

The program ran for two years. Although it was well received by the participants, the organization ended the program after two years because it was difficult to scale internationally. Anthroposophy helped me understand that trying to find the middle ground that balances the beautiful idealism of making the world a better place for leadership with the practicality of making enough money that the organization could grow, is a difficult but worthwhile goal that needs time to be sustainably fruitful. I continued to work in the organization, but over the remaining years, I reached the point in my developmental journey, with the help of anthroposophy, where I came to understand that, as a person, I could be too idealistic and not realistic enough in my approach to life. When I was 50 years old, I added a master's in business administration to balance out my love of ideals with the practical application of how you actually make things happen in the world of work. Ending 15 years with the organization, I chose to go back into the world of for-profit businesses.

Practicing Anthroposophy in New York City

I found work in New York City with a global public relations company. The CEO gave me two tasks: build a professional learning organization, and help build a sales culture. He said the young people there thought that selling was making the client do what the organization wanted, not necessarily what the client needs, therefore they were reluctant to sell. He said we need to change that to where they see selling more as a service. It took three years, but we were able to change the sales culture from one in which people held the view "I will force on this client what I want in order to get the money and power I desire," to "I will provide a service orientation in which I ask the client what is the problem they're trying to solve, understand it deeply, and then bring the client a solution that can help the client solve it." Once people understood that selling was a service orientation, they actively practiced it. Over 15 years at the organization, I developed models that reflected what I was able to understand of anthroposophy. For example, anthroposophy offers a basic understanding of the human being as composed of three separate abilities that need to be brought together: thinking, feeling and willing. I used this to develop a model of how one communicates knowledge to another, "Head, Heart, and Feet." The holistic transfer of knowledge involves three aspects: head, heart, and feet.

Thinking: a *clear concept* for the head that one understands, can share with others, and others can also understand.
Feeling: a *positive emotion*, the thought feels good to both hearts, both the one sharing and the one receiving.
Willing: *movement into action*, the first few steps are clear on what to do to begin to bring the knowledge to life.

Head	Heart	Feet
cognitive	affective	behavioral
thinking	feeling	willing
wonder	compassion	conscience
intellectual	emotional	physical
vision	mission	action
spirit	soul	body

Grappling with the Dragon of the Internet

Beginning in the year 2000, the internet exploded into the world, with learning becoming primarily digital. Seeking to provide digital learning to the employees of the public relations company, I adopted the socially collaborative online learning method of a new digital learning startup to teach an innovative method of client service to the nineteen hundred sales associates who were scattered across sixty countries. In the learning design, we put people in groups of thirty to study the new client service process. They would be together online at their convenience for six hours of learning over six weeks. We tested two types of groups—first, people who were at the same level in the organization and the same country, compared to a group composed of people at all levels, trainee to CEO, and across the sixty countries. The more diverse group with all levels and all countries was ten times more creative and engaged than the group of people who were similar.

The CEO loved the process, as he heard fresh ideas from around the world. We also discovered many colleagues we would never have been aware of because in the online program every voice had equal access to the conversation. This also reflected the threefold social order ideas that, when people are treated as equals who all have something to offer, much more can be achieved. Also, similar to my

Peace Corps experience, this again showed that when human beings are brought into a situation where they're given the chance to build relationships across differences, it brings more than when you work together with others who are similar to you. This truth reflects the knowledge that Rudolf Steiner shared in his book *The Philosophy of Freedom* where he clearly outlines that the freedom for each individual to bring their ideas to the community can bring about the deepest outcomes.

When I left the company, I joined a small socially collaborative online start up, working for a number of years as a senior learning advisor. There again I was faced with how human beings can best make use of technology to enhance their humanity, not lessen it.

Ambrogio Lorenzetti, Saint Michael the Archangel Slaying the Dragon *ca. 1335, Fondazione Musei Senesi, Siena, Italy*

The image of the archangel Michael battling with the dragon has always been a help to me, bringing me courage to deal directly with negative realities. Rudolf Steiner lectured many times about the Archangel Michael.

Humanity Is Merging More and More with Technology

Rudolf Steiner makes it very clear that it is destiny for humanity that in the times we are in, we will merge more and more with technology. My current work is to understand how best to work with the explosion of artificial intelligence, AI, to find an ethical use for it. This continues my work following the archangel Michael's struggle with the dragon. As the famous saying by Melvin Kranzberg goes, "Technology is neither good nor bad, nor is it neutral." It is clear that human-AI symbiosis is happening, and that this, as in nature, can be a highly positive and mutual partnership, where both parties benefit—humans improve, and AI gets better—or it can also be parasitic, where one party benefits at the detriment of the other, where AI pulls humanity down. Currently the world is tending to treat AI as if it is human, forgetting that it is a machine, simply a huge dataset with a dead kind of ice-cold brilliance. It can seem evil. Rudolf Steiner often wrote that what seems evil can in the long run also serve the good, if one can transform it into helpful activity. My work now is to bring questions of what ways AI can be of service to the ideals of humanity into the conversations about AI and avoiding its downsides. How we choose to interact with the reality of AI will create the karma of our future as human beings.

3. Anthroposophy as Lifelong Learning

Gratitude for the Spiritual Science of Rudolf Steiner

Reflecting on my life, I think the 35 years before meeting anthroposophy were a karmic preparation, prepared in the spiritual world before incarnating into this life, to help me be ready to receive the foundational spiritual science of Rudolf Steiner and to work with it. Where I am now, at 75 years of age, I am in a new phase of life. I continue to struggle with the reality that the dragons around us in the world are within us and need to be tamed there before we can tame them in the world. Steiner was very clear that it is we ourselves who are creating the world we live in. The deep insights from anthroposophy continue to help me integrate many things in life, bringing me great energy and purpose in my work.

The ideas of karma and reincarnation have brought warmth and light to everything in my life, giving me guidance on how my actions can not only benefit me but also be of benefit to others and the world at large. For this I am deeply grateful to the work Rudolf Steiner did to research the spiritual world and document his findings. I am continuing to learn from his extensive body of work, bringing meaning for my life and the life of the world.

Developing Threefold Insights through Experience

Benjamin Bingham

It is hard to imagine my life without the influence of my father. Imagine him, a retired diplomat, after milking the family cow, straining the full pail of milk through a cheesecloth, putting on a worn tweed jacket and tie, and devoting the rest of his day to two things: studying, underlining, and creating page references in his large library of Rudolf Steiner's anthroposophical books, some of which he distributed to universities, and intermittently playing sports with some of us on the tail end of eleven children. Mostly we played in a miniature gym he had invented and built. That 12-by-24-by-10-foot-tall sport court with a rebound net he had fashioned taught me the value of efficient practice within a confined space. This has served me well in the practice of meditation since I was 21. I had always liked listening to my father's spiritual lectures as a child getting ready for school. He encouraged me to be a skeptic of the standard narratives I would hear. He also gave me confidence that my guardian angel would always protect me and that everyone I met in life I had probably met before in another lifetime. As I venture anywhere in the world, even now, I often experience extraordinary chance meetings on trains and planes because I had been taught to pay attention to the ones who sit next to me.

The following essay describes my trajectory as an adult into what may seem a random series of events looking back from age 75 after a full and varied life. It may also serve by including the threefold social ideals that stand as guides for me, even if only helping me make sense of my decisions after the fact. The ideals of the French Revolution, applied in a way that creates a threefold sense of order, rather than chaos in society, was one of my father's favorite themes. The backbone of this social threefolding was Rudolf Steiner's "Fundamental Social Law":

> The wellbeing of a community of people working together will be the greater, the less the individual claims for himself the proceeds of his work; that is, the more of these proceeds he makes over to his fellow workers, and the more his own needs are satisfied, not as the result of his own work but as the result of the work done by others.

This I experienced unconsciously already in my large family, where jobs were not assigned but everything got done because we took care of each other. Responsibility was taken, not given, and I was raised as much by my three sisters closest in age to me as I was by my mother.

Sent away to an elite boarding school because my father wanted us to be in positions of influence, I saw the fundamental law played out in team sports where I excelled not so much by my grace but by my outrageous willingness to suffer in order to win. Later, I realized that this law generally lives in those who place mission before self-interest, as in Camphill communities around the world.

Meeting Anthroposophy

Confused by the chaos at Yale in the spring of 1970, I told my father I was taking a leave-of-absence to venture out and explore the meaning of life. I felt uncomfortable, selfishly studying art and philosophy when my peers were either facing death in Vietnam or planning to blow up the law school in protest against the System. Instead of objecting, this conservative son of Hiram Bingham III—the American academic and explorer who discovered the lost Inca city of Machu Piccu, US senator, and, in the military, founder of the Air Service—gave no resistance. Rather, he took me out to lunch and handed me a brochure from Emerson College. Then he drove me to Spring Valley to meet the founder, Francis Edmunds. When I spoke about my fascination with light and darkness in photography, he listened and responded in a way I had never experienced before from a teacher. A month later he telegrammed me that he had found me a room with a family and that I should come.

The next day, I flew to England expecting to stay one semester. Instead, two years later I was trained in biodynamic agriculture, filled with inspiration about Rudolf Steiner's concept of the threefold social order, and at the start of a 50-year-plus marriage and family with Jenny!

As part of my studies in biodynamic soil science, Dr. Herbert H. Koepf (author of *Bio-Dynamic Agriculture*) had asked Michael Spence (author of *After Capitalism*) to teach me bookkeeping before I was to take over the family farm in Connecticut. I found this rather dull and instead we began studying all of Steiner's books on the threefold social order. We were joined by other students who were drawn to this approach. I learned to love the elegance of this way of understanding the dynamics of human society. I felt sure that a healthy world would ensue if we would simply wake up to the consequences of putting individual freedom (*liberté*) front of mind as the guiding principle in all creative work, equal rights (*égalité*) front of mind in the carrying out of all governance and differentiated human needs, and reciprocity (*fraternité*) front of mind to drive all commerce in the most efficient and profitable way. Understanding that these principles live and work in life has been a source of inspiration for me ever since.

Living in Communities Based on Threefolding

Jenny and I and our five children were surrounded by these ideals in *Camphill* communities for ten years. My Social Security records show 10 years without income as proof of the fact that we were freed from the enslavement of working for money. How freeing this was to work truly just to meet the needs of the community! Looking back, I recognize that living solely from the gifts, grants, and government funding to support the residents with special needs it was possible to lose touch with economic reality. We truly enjoyed a comfortable lifestyle with brand new shared cars and Waldorf education for our children. However, since this period of time we have never again worked 24/7 without breaks, always sharing our growing family with up to eight individuals who required special care. After our twins were born we had four children under four with one teenage helper. I left before breakfast to milk the cows, leaving Jenny with so much to juggle! And yet we never even thought about the lost financial opportunity cost. Like the sentiment expressed in the "Buddhist Economics" chapter in Schumacher's *Small is Beautiful,* nothing is more fulfilling than working to meet the needs of others. It is healing to realize that we live to work and, though it is the most common misunderstanding, it is illusory to think that we work to live.

Meanwhile, our children experienced a community consciously based on the aforementioned Fundamental Social Law: a functional law described by Rudolf Steiner in his collection of essays, *Anthroposophy and the Social Question,* which holds good for all social life with the absoluteness and necessity as any law of nature. They benefited as much or more by living with people of all kinds, learning, as we did, how unique each of us is, while at the same time how universal the sense of the human connection we can experience is, if we are open to it. Though we can reflect guiltily on the little time we had to focus on each of our children, we see how strong, independent, and open-hearted they have grown to be, creating their own healthy circles in meaning-filled lives.

Even bedtimes could be cut short, because there were meetings most nights to manage the community and to prepare each approaching festival with plays we performed with music and eurythmy. Spiritual life was strongly focused on these Christian festivals with services every Sunday alternating between the Consecration of the Human Being and the Offering Service which Steiner gave as a ritual for teachers or lay communities without priests, to practice lifting up our souls to the spirit. Organizationally, Jenny participated more in what were called middle sphere (otherwise known as the political or rights sphere) meetings to give space for deep listening to human karma, while I was drawn to the visioning work of the cultural sphere. In that context I was encouraged to design and construct a 9-by-9-foot monument to the four directions with the theme from Revelations of the lion, the bull, the eagle, and the angel, which today still stands at Camphill Copake 46 years later.

Learning the Skill of Fundraising

At that time, in my late twenties, I was asked to raise the funds to launch Camphill Triform Community in the Hudson River Valley where we wanted to develop a wooden-bed factory and a farm with meaningful work for individuals with intellectual disabilities but also a social desire to live in a campus-like setting. It was to be the first Camphill primarily focused on the third dimension, the "economic sphere": a commercial endeavor that would fund the needs of the community if successful. As Director of Planning and Development, I took a course in grantsmanship and was successful with writing for grants from foundations and government agencies. As the Lattoflex Bed business began to succeed out of the converted barn, we experienced directly the inevitable tension between social goals and economic costs.

Once we had reached our initial business success, I felt that the right thing to do would have been to make the business a for-profit with a pledge to dedicate a percentage of profits to the community. Money for a large factory to produce 100 beds per day would come from investors expecting a return. This was not an idea that was met with enthusiasm and my decision to stop fundraising caused pain. A seed was planted in me to heal this divide; somehow to bring the threefold ideals incubated in Camphill out into the widest possible context, inclusive of the economic realm.

Making a Life in the Wider Community

This opportunity came when it was decided that after seven years some of the founders should step back and make space for new initiatives at Triform. We exited with five children, no financial resources, and an old Jeep. Our priority was spiritual/cultural: to keep our children in Waldorf schools. This—for me—was achieved with five years of intermittent teaching, six years of part-time and full-time door to door sales, as well as delivering newspapers in the middle of the night, and as many years of waitressing, catering, and caring for women with special needs in our homes, for Jenny.

Happily, we found ourselves on the founding steering committee of Trauger Groh's initiative to bring the community supported agriculture (CSA) idea he had incubated in Germany to the Temple/Wilton Community Farm. Trauger helped so many people recognize that we all need a connection to the land itself, not just the fruits of the earth. That initial CSA set a standard that sadly has been mostly forgotten in CSA's that have blossomed all over this country.

Imagine us gathering in a circle in late winter with a clear vision for the year ahead and a budget from the farmers that would allow the plan to succeed. Then papers and pencils were passed around and each family would write down what they could afford to pay for this plan on a monthly basis. We were encouraged to be realistic and, if we could afford nothing, to write down zero! If, tallied up, there was not enough, we would go around until the budget was met! Then at harvest time, members were not "buying" food; they were sharing the harvest and only paid something for items like cheese or meat to cover processing costs. This model brought us all closer to the land, to each other, and to a sense of wholeness that tends to be lost when units of produce are conventionally paid for.

A New Socioeconomic Model Based on Mutuality (Fraternité)

Inspired by this economic model of mutual responsibility for healthy food production, Jenny became a leader of a support group that formed for struggling Waldorf parents: Friends of Waldorf Education. For one year this group met its goal to raise the money to pay full tuition for all of our children using bake sales, events, and the generosity of some of the members who freely chose to pay more each month if we fell short. However, with this success we realized that we had become a sub-culture of the school, and this felt unhealthy. As idealists we wanted the whole school to adopt our model or we would disband. The administrators turned down our proposal and the altruistic model of mutual support had to die for a time. Perhaps it will be picked up again; schools and farms may one day recognize that a fee for goods and services structure sacrifices creative social solutions that foster practical altruism, reciprocity, and community (*fraternité*). It is important to remember that self-sustaining agriculture is primarily a culture that spawns community and cultivates life in the soil. Whereas agri-business tends toward raping the earth and destroying the very resources we need for life.

Entrepreneurs for Impact... Lessons Learned

At 43, I began to use the fundraising skills I had learned at Triform to help launch socially relevant technology ventures. This was the start of many years of disappointed expectations. It seemed that the financing of economic endeavors based on the pure self-interest of investors, rather than fraternal altruism, inevitably led to poor outcomes for society.

For example, I learned that investors in healthcare generally liked the stopgap alleviation of symptoms rather than once-and-for-all cures. They wanted repeat business rather than long-term health outcomes. Similarly, I saw holistic approaches with broad health benefits passed over for targeted blockbuster drugs despite negative side effects. Repeatedly, in any industry, game changing technologies with broad beneficial applications would be licensed by competitors and shelved, never to make it to the market. All this was disheartening, but somehow later increased my motivation to enter deeper into that dark realm of finance and see what could be done.

Religious Renewal

At 50, I took a sabbatical year, leading 7 spiritual journeys to Peru. I developed connections there because my grandfather, Hiram

Bingham III, was credited for uncovering Machu Picchu. Exposure to sacred sites and the reverent ritual life of the Quechua people opened my mind to the possibility of priesthood. However, after three months at the Priest Seminary Stuttgart in Germany, life presented me with the idea that money itself had become the universal ritual that needed healing. If money in circulation is the blood of the community, and the higher self or I AM is carried by the blood, could money become the expression of our focused will to do the good?

Investing as a Spiritual Path

For the last 25 years I have been co-leading, with many others, a movement to change the way money works in the world. To do this, I became a professional wealth manager, a certified financial planner (CFP), and in 2011 launched a registered investment advisory (RIA) with my own team to work with investors who placed importance on the impact of their investments. Despite early successes, it has not been an easy, smooth sail for me, my team, or our clients. This is not a path for the faint of heart, when

- the most idealistic investors might be the angriest and most unreasonable in downturns;
- positive outcomes are often forgotten while failures are unforgivable;
- choosing partners is risky, as fear and greed around money can bring out the worst traits.

However, despite battle scars, about a third of our clients have been faithful for decades and my two close colleagues and I continue to find, foster, and fund effective investment strategies for a better world. Though some companies have failed, we are proud to have played a part in launching several game-changing initiatives each with their own dramatic story.

Our approach to investing was inspired in part by an intriguing graphic in a set of lectures by Rudolf Steiner (*Education as a Force for Social Change*), given around the founding of the first Waldorf school more than a hundred years ago. The diagram shows two concentric circles you might imagine with arrows going in two opposite directions. On one were the three aspects of the economy: capital, goods, and labor and, on the other, the three kinds of new thinking required for each.

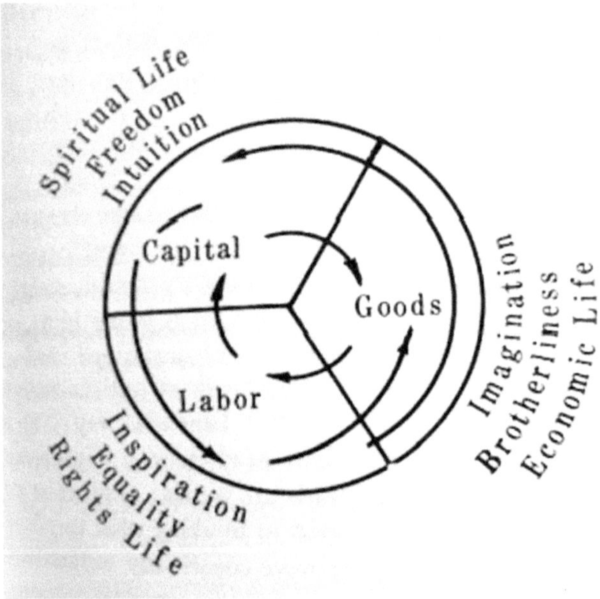

As I pondered these two concentric circles the image transformed in my mind into a lemniscate (figure eight) with Intuition at the head, transforming profits that had been redirected by the heart at the crossing point to become capital in the form of free gifts (liberty) and *future*-oriented investments for high impact; passing back through the heart I saw Inspiration drawing loan financing for infrastructure that addresses *current* social and/or environmental issues (equality); and around the base of the lemniscate I saw all the commercial cash transactions raying out into the world using Imagination to prioritize the sourcing of commodities without hurting the environment and services whose employees are known to have been treated well in the *past* (fraternity). This gives a future orientation to investment capital: "What will be most relevant in the future?" A present orientation to lending sparked by a current concern about the labor force or, in the widest sense, "What shall we lend support to for the common good now?" And, in buying commodities with exchange money, "What can we learn from the past if we bring imaginative pictures to mind, good or bad?"

Following Steiner's graphic above, here is one of many sketches I have made in pondering healthy money flow:

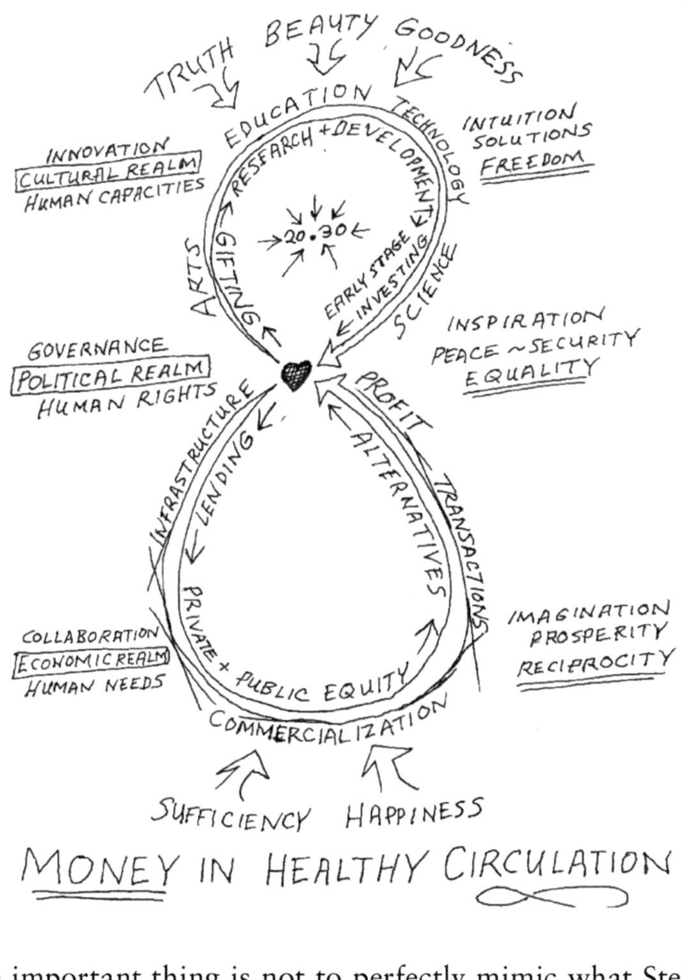

The important thing is not to perfectly mimic what Steiner put forward but to let the living thinking evolve out of life experience. You might wonder, for example, why the three forms of money don't all come under the economic ideal of fraternity. They do! And yet I have come to realize that each of the three spheres naturally embraces its own "threefoldness" within its greater purpose:

- Spiritual decisions about the future in any sphere can best be approached by giving freedom and responsibilities to individuals most capable;
- Current governance inspirations may be arrived at democratically; and
- Practical concerns may require imaginative research to see what approaches have had the best outcomes.

To summarize how we applied threefolding in our investment decisions:

- "Exchange money" (think cash/liquidity for spending) requires deep Imagination about sourcing;
- "Loan money" (direct private loans, bank loans, corporate or municipal bonds) requires a new level of Inspiration to be lifted up for current needs; and
- "Gift money" (pure philanthropy; or, if you will, money at risk in private or public equities) requires a new level of Intuition about the future.

Practical Examples

To pick three stories from my work at Scarab Funds, Ltd. (www.scarabfundsllc.com):

- Intuition about the future drove an equity investment we made as founders of this innovative technology (see Polymateria, Ltd., www.polymateria.com) that enables plastic to be recycled, but also when it inevitably hits the landfill or body of water, to decompose into carbon and water without breaking down into nano-particles.
- Inspiration led us to form the company Infinite Workflow (https://iworkflow.org) to coordinate the delivery of social services through a user-friendly app that empowers individuals and their families to choose and coordinate their pathway from homelessness and/or joblessness to real success.
- Imagination led us to two unique liquid solutions: 1) a partnership with Impact Deposits Corp. (impactdeposits.com),

which moves money from big banks to community banks that support local economies; and 2) a partnership with the California Cap-and-Trade Program, which gives us the right to invest up to $400M on behalf of investors in a way that can provide 2 to 4 percent more return than money markets, while pressuring utilities to reduce pollution <u>and</u> funding social and environmental programs in that state (see Cap-and-Trade Program (https://ww2.arb.ca.gov/our-work/programs/cap-and-trade-program).

This holistic way of thinking about investing is unique in the world of Socially Responsible Investing (SRI), or Environmental, Social, and Governance Standards (ESG). Perhaps it has had some influence in what some call triple bottom line (TBL) investing, which focuses on the threefold framework of people, planet, and profit.

Making a Difference through the Word

After publishing several articles on money in *New View*, I have written extensively for *Huffington Post* and *The Family Wealth Report*. Then ten years ago, my book *Making Money Matter: Impact Investing to Change the World* was published, which got me in front of significant audiences: pension fund trustees, family offices, financial planners, and MBA programs on sustainability. There seemed to be a consistent hope that I would bring the news that investment for the good would make more money. I knew that there will always be so many factors in the performance of investment portfolios, and that the only way this might become generally true would follow a cultural shift in which investors recognized their role in meeting the needs of others. In this way, as companies' missions become part of their recognized value, markets could become barometers for the good. Those companies that truly meet societal needs would be most highly valued. Investors would then be rewarded for funding the most beneficial initiatives. At our firm, 3Sisters Sustainable Management, LLC, we focus first on meeting human needs and then we do our best to avoid extraction, unnatural chemical formulations, pollution and exploitation of people. Because we did not invest in Big Oil, Big Pharma, or Tesla due to the deep dependence on extraction (e.g., copper and mineral sands), nor Facebook or Google because of the exploitation of personal data and censorship, the stock part of our portfolio trailed in public markets recently. In a nod to the needs of our investors I have decided this week to allow my trader to include Tesla, social media, and most technologies as long as we stay away from Big Oil and the Military-Medical-Industrial Complex.

Until a shift happens in the hearts of courageous investors who can afford risk, markets will only reflect financial value. This might require a general cultural shift to a world where science, art and religion are set free from government and business interests. I fear that too much effort (spiritual work void of intuition) has gone into standardization of non-financial values which become cumbersome and uninspiring metrics.

Rather, I hope that liberated research will give rise to many creative ways to transform the working of money in the world.

Secondly, in the realm of governance, a shift is needed so that the stewards of corporations represent the best interests of society, not just the investors.

And finally, the third key to a future healthy world as envisioned by Steiner is to foster the ideal of fraternity or taking responsibility for each other in the economic sphere.

What's Important Now

Reflecting back through this essay I realize that the threefold ideals have been living in me throughout my life and were particularly honed by living in an intentionally threefold community surrounded by wise elders. Now I carry the question of how to give back.

There is a deep and widespread desire for meaningful change to overcome the challenges of our time. The greatest challenge I feel as an individual is to stay awake and not slip into the comfort of consensus or groupthink. Even the concepts Steiner gave us can die when they are not continually renewed in life. I have watched

Camphill Communities and Waldorf schools, RSF Social Finance and Triodos Bank, among many other institutions in the anthroposophical movement, in my opinion, losing their foundational worldview based on spiritual experience and the threefold organizational structure that once served them so well.

For me, in the last few years, as a First Class holder, taking responsibility for the Esoteric School, the School of Michael at the core of anthroposophy, is both the greatest challenge and perhaps has the most potential. Choosing to do individual inner work in a space of solitude is a free deed that may be essential to the evolution of humanity toward creative freedom. I have been fortunate to have lived a life that allowed for and supported inner work and constant self-education, including exposure to disciplines like Spacial Dynamics®, Gestalt psychology, and, through Jenny, anthroposophical psychology. It is my goal now to find ways to bring people together to experience productive karmic meetings or "healing encounters." We are planning a second conference in Chapel Hill with this name, led by James Dyson, Jonah Evans, and Christina Beck in November 2025. There are many members of the Michael School who do not know their peers, and through such events polarities may be artistically resolved with michaelic courage.

As I grow older, perhaps poetry will become my best tool for change.

SECTION II

Biography and the Healing Conversation

Planting Seeds of Life

Joseph Rubano

I don't usually think of my work being for peace, justice, and social reform so it is interesting to think in these terms. I have called myself a counselor, so my work has been around having meaningful conversations with and coming to love many people. In thinking about it, I see that my engagement with peace, justice, and social reform has always been an inside job. The striving for peace started within myself and extended out into the life of relationships. I have learned that the presence of peace within influences the life of relationships, and the way we interact with others influences the experience of peace within.

I started on the road of becoming a counselor when I was in my early twenties. I was in Los Angeles. A friend had a book by Krishnamurti, *The First and Last Freedom*. I read it. I didn't understand much but it awakened something in me and pointed me in a direction. What does it mean to awaken? What is it to be free? How to shift one's perspective to get there?

At the same time as reading Krishnamurti, I was introduced to yoga and the idea and practice of meditation. I had the idea that going to graduate school to study psychology would help me to understand what Krishnamurti was talking about. So, I did a master's program in clinical psychology. It didn't really help me understand, but it was the first step both toward counseling and walking a spiritual path.

In one of my classes I met someone who had similar questions. We talked. Our conversations were enlivening. This was something new to me, special. I didn't think at the time about the power of conversation, but this guy made me think. And he was interested in my thoughts. This thinking and speaking about spiritual ideas and soul experiences was stimulating and enlivening and led to a deepening friendship. Our relationship initiated me in the exploration of inner soul realms and the realms of philosophical and spiritual ideas. They went together. This began the journey of becoming attentive to inner soul states, engaging in meditative practices, and devoting myself to conversations and relationships. Looking back, I think this was my first real friendship where there was a sharing of a deeper part of myself with another. I didn't know then that the creation of friendships with this kind of exploration and sharing would be at the foundation of my life. So here I am—I stumbled onto the road of peace—meditation, sharing deeply, being in a real relationship with another; these all bring a certain feeling of peace to the soul.

Years later, after encountering the writings and lectures of Rudolf Steiner, I read or heard: "The longing to be seen and heard in our full reality has arisen in every human being since the beginning of the [20th] century and will grow increasingly urgent." Also: "In the future...the meeting of one human being with another will be of the nature of a sacrament."

Steiner also says that the future doesn't just happen, it has to be prepared—the seeds of the future must be planted and tended now. Some of us are planting and tending. Yes, that is how it is. That has been my life. That's a pretty social thing to do and I guess one can say that it is a step in the direction of social reform or healing. Not just for me but for those I am in a relationship with. Another step on the road of peace came years later when I encountered biography work. I will get there in a bit, let me not get ahead of myself. First let me tell you how I met anthroposophy.

Anthroposophy entered my life in my late 20s when I married Patricia who already had a connection with Steiner through Waldorf education. Patricia and I met in Atlanta, Georgia when we were both in the Ananda Marga Yoga Society. An interesting side note here is that the leader of the international society, P. R.

Sarkar, known as Shrii Shrii Anandamurti, was in jail in India at the time for his social reform activity. Ananda Marga was about following an individual spiritual path and about social reform by supporting the arts and creating schools, children's homes, food distribution centers, disaster relief, medical centers, and community development projects. (Hmmm—justice and social reform were there all along!)

It took a while for anthroposophy to find its way into me but slowly, slowly I started reading a few books and joined a study group led by Gertrude Teutch in San Diego. We read *Theosophy* and then the *Philosophy of Freedom*. It became clear to me fairly early that anthroposophy is complex. Its picture of the human being and the path of development toward love and freedom was pretty profound—not easy to grasp but profound.

Out of my earlier readings and meditation practices from an Eastern point of view, I had the idea that the goal of this lifetime was to become enlightened or something like that. I was very relieved to hear from Steiner that this becoming-human-project was a many lifetimes project; that it wasn't about getting off the wheel of karma once and for all in this one lifetime. In fact it wasn't about trying not to come back again after this life on Earth was done. The picture of repeated Earth lives resonated with me and would become even more important when I started working with people as a counselor. But that was still a little way off.

I had to travel through the land of Taoist practices and the Jungian world as delivered by Robert Johnson, a direct student of Carl Jung. I had to live into Native American ceremonies, the sweat lodge and vision quest, and the profound practices of dyadic communication and techniques to help clear the mind as given by students of Charles Berner.

With all that as a foundation, life then took me to the Threefold Education Foundation in Spring Valley, New York, where my wife was to teach kindergarten and my children were to go to school. I was now right in the middle of the Steiner world.

I knew I wanted to keep walking a path of personal and spiritual development and I knew I wanted to help others by doing counseling work. I explored many ways but I couldn't say yes to any particular school of thought or way of working until I met biography work and biographical counseling. The first time I experienced a biography workshop with Chris and Signe Schaefer, I said to myself, *I can do this*. It was years before I did. Through Chris, I heard about an anthroposophic counseling training at the Centre for Social Development in England. I enrolled in it and 3 years later I was a certified biographical counselor. I had learned about developmental rhythms in life, about the laws and workings of karma and destiny, about temperaments, and about how the planets influence us. How old we are, where we are in the developmental phases of our life has meaning and matters. All these discoveries made a profound difference **in how to be with someone** and how to listen to the story they tell about this or that going on in them and their life.

I started a counseling practice in 1992. I also started to offer workshops and classes in biography work, as well as classes and workshops in the dyadic communication practice. I found that when you start bringing people together to do any kind of inner or spiritual work, a community forms that inspires and supports each to continue and deepen the work. I was already bringing people together by offering Native American inspired sweat lodge ceremonies in the heart of a Steiner community—pretty outrageous at the time, but I got away with it because people liked me and could recognize that I was serving the community.

The biography work was such a great way for people to meet each other in a deep and authentic way and to help each other to grow and develop. When you explore your life and share what you find with a small group of people doing the same it is healing in several ways. To have a number of people interested in you and listening attentively—your unique life somehow becomes more interesting and, in a way, special. You start to see your life from a wider perspective, in the eyes of others. And when you hear the stories of others, they become part of you and you become more. We get inspired by each other to become more this or that and come to accept and value our own way of being as an important part of the whole.

I mentioned earlier how biography work offered another step on the road toward peace. An important aspect of biography work is its deliberate and contemplative aspect. To look back into one's life in any fruitful way one has to decide to do so and then create a time to do it. This already is a start. Then you take the next step—review your life and experiences from a higher perspective, from the outside as if viewing another person. This practice frees us a bit from our usual self-centered egotistical perspective. But it is a practice. When we achieve even a piece of this, we notice that we are less churned up inside. We are more peaceful inside—in a way we are taking ourselves less personally. In *Social and Anti-social Forces in the Human Being* (Bern, 1918), Steiner says, "This objectifying of oneself, this freeing of oneself in the present from one's past, this shelling-out of the 'I' from its experiences, must be specially striven for in our present time. For the present has the tendency toward linking up the 'I' more and more with its experiences." This was a new idea to me. This is what I love about Steiner—he gives ideas that deepen, broaden, sometimes confuse, but often help me to understand other teachings or practices that I have worked with.

I could go on naming specific ideas that I have integrated or practices that I have taken up as a result of my relationship with Steiner's teachings—such as the idea that egotism and antisocial forces and what one might refer to as evil are all necessary obstacles and challenges for humanity on its path to developing love and freedom. Or that we "choose" with the help of various spiritual beings, the specific challenges in our life. I don't necessarily bring or work with this karmic perspective openly in a session but it is a lens or filter that helps in my seeing or questioning and wondering. Something more is going on here—the karmic ideas of recapitulation and compensation—the idea that we bring unintegrated aspects of our being from a previous life and what comes to us in this life is what is necessary for our growth and development. These ideas are helpful so as not to get caught in a blaming or victim consciousness. Helpful in order to be able to say Yes to life —Yes, this is my life, it all belongs to me.

I could also say how working with observation exercises of natural objects and phenomena in nature along with exercising the imagination have influenced my capacity to work with individuals and groups—and how practicing the six basic exercises is important for helping to navigate life in general—and this is all true. It is about standing in oneself and striving to see the world as it is. It is about opening to a reality beyond the ordinary senses and exercising choice.

But maybe just as important as any of the specific ideas and practices is the fact that the picture of the human being given by Steiner is so extensive and complex that I can't possibly say that I fully know or understand it all. This does two things—it gives me the feeling of being within a living system or reality that is much bigger than me, that I am part of and it is part of me. This living organism or Community of Being contains all the ideas and imaginations given and all the students of anthroposophy that I have either read or met. In this way there is a living substance that I am embraced by and that I am convinced helps me in my working in the world—counseling or leading workshops and retreats. I am not a separate lone individual; I am a living weaving of other individuals and ideas and a carrier of a worldview that is alive and never completely known. It matters what ideas we live with. They fill our being and subtly radiate out from us affecting the world and our interactions.

Secondly it keeps me humble and alive—there is no end to striving to understand, there is no end to life's challenges and to inner growth and development. This keeps me being a companion on the path and ever convinced that I do not know what is best for another. In my biographical counseling training it was often said that our work is to help the other to strengthen their own "I"; their connection to the essential core or center of their being. Each person can, and really must, tap into the knowing that lies within, must find the guide and trust in their own being.

This focus of strengthening the "I," experiencing the essential core of being, the true self, the higher "I," or inner Christ, has been and continues to be the core of my practice and work. Not only am I embraced by the anthroposophic worldview, I am also embraced by certain Native American teachings and ceremonies and by an international community of individuals connected to the Enlightenment Intensives (which grew out of the dyadic communication work) who are committed to awakening to their true essence as truth seekers and loving individuals. I have been fortunate to have found or been found by the sweat lodge and vision quest ceremonies and the Enlightenment Intensives in my mid-thirties. Both the vision quests and Enlightenment Intensives create a space for one to open to a spiritual seeing and knowing that is usually not possible with our normal everyday consciousness.

The vision quest, which I call the Desert Solo Experience, invites people to be alone for three days and nights with no tent and only water and open to the quiet and beauty of the natural world and come face to face with simply being with themselves. People often find themselves reviewing their life, touching the pain and blessings of being human and giving thanks for all their relations. The Enlightenment Intensives are structured to include both contemplation and communication. It is a three-day process whereby one is opening to the truth of oneself while connecting with others. Both retreats open people, allow masks to fall, revealing a more authentic being. I have participated in these experiences since the 1980s and have been guiding people in both of these retreat experiences since 2008. Needless to say each of these experiences unites the people who do it together—always a sense of connectedness and community feeling is created. And when people come year after year to the lodges, or desert solos, or Enlightenment Intensives, a kind of brother/sisterhood is formed; a community of striving individuals. It is a beautiful thing and a great gift.

Coming closer to the heart of anthroposophy is my work as a faculty member in the biography and social art training with Patricia. In this three-year training, an even deeper sense of community is created as people explore anthroposophic ideas about what it is to be a human being (connected to the earth, the elements, the cosmos, the planets, to their life and relationships), and engage in artistically exploring their lives in exercise after exercise in which they are asked to look at and share pieces of their life experiences with each other. From this exploration and interest in each other the people change, are transformed. Inner healings happen; new capacities are revealed or developed. They come to know themselves and each other more deeply than ever. It is a privilege to be in the energetic field that is created by meeting like this.

It is funny—whenever I lead or am around Enlightenment Intensive people, I wish they would spend some time with biography work and Steiner's teachings. And whenever I am around biography and Steiner people, I wish they would do an intensive. In my experience, they compliment each other beautifully in supporting individual growth and development and connection to life. Also, whenever I lead a sweat lodge around the solstices and equinoxes, I always bring ideas and imaginations from Steiner about the seasons and cycle of the year. And I offer Steiner quotes about relationship to the "I" and spiritual seeing in my EI retreats. I often say that I could never exist on a strict diet of only Steiner, but I am eternally grateful for its nourishment. It has grown to be the foundation on which I stand.

I have written poems during or after the experiences of the desert solo, the Enlightenment Intensive and the biography training. I would like to share one I wrote after one of the biography training weeks that I think somehow speaks to all of them. It is called "Standing in the Open":

It is a tender thing
a vulnerable thing
to be a person
to have a life
with real people and happenings
to touch again what was and is
to say "I" to another.

"I" is such a shy thing to say
"Look," "see" a quiet invitation
"Me" a wonder-filled mystery.

Life is tender and close to tears
Even the tip of our laughter
has a drop of water balanced
on the edge
ready to fall or shimmer
with color in morning light.

The attention of another:
a kind of light.

Whatever we say
is never quite it.
Whatever we say stirs into motion
underground streams
which set the base
of our being
vibrating
thinner and thinner
becoming more transparent
exposing sacred fault lines
that open a crack
revealing secret veins of the Precious
long stored out of view;

Which when they are spoken
may cause us to shy
or cause us to smile
as we stand awhile

in the open
in front of another
who opened a space
in the heart
of their heart
to let us walk in
to welcome us home.

And finally, I would like to give a few examples of how anthroposophic ideas have been beneficial to people I have worked with.

Early on, I was working with a woman whose father had recently passed. She was in mourning and at a loss for how to bear this pain. I spoke to her about accompanying someone across the threshold, about the benefit of reading to and thinking about one who has died. Just this simple practice lightened the burden tremendously—she could in fact do something to help and stay connected to her father. I have mentioned this practice of staying connected with one who has died to several other clients when a friend or family member passed. They were happy to know there was something they could do to accompany and help their relation.

In working with individuals, I often introduce the idea that we choose our parents and that the gifts or challenges of our relations with our parents and family is not deserving of blame but is part of our path of development. The questions I ask people are, "What are you being asked to develop because of this or that?" An additional question is, "What have you already developed?" The idea that we are continually formed by our relationships with others and the idea that modern life is a path of initiation is well received by those I speak to. These ideas change the picture and change the story. For me, no one needs to be "fixed." But, we all can use another way of perceiving. Maybe that is one of the big gifts of anthroposophy—it offers new ways of thinking about and perceiving our life.

I often work with couples in my counseling practice. And here is a rich field of karmic wondering. Sometimes an insight into past karmic connections happens spontaneously and sometimes we just wonder together. But just to wonder broadens the scope of what might contribute to the challenges in the relationship. Most of my work is with communication, learning to listen and striving to see and understand each other. Having each person write a brief biography and noting the course and challenges of each life is often helpful in understanding and accepting. But the ongoing work of developing the capacity to listen with the striving to understand is essential for any intimate relationship to survive and thrive.

I have been close to Waldorf schools now for over 40 years. I have worked with a number of schools helping with mediation and conflict resolution, and, along with Patricia, offering biography and communication workshops. Here we always bring the idea of social and antisocial forces—that in our time the antisocial forces are strong and growing stronger. We must do the hard work of bringing social forces to our interactions—interest, deep listening, speaking true. The hope in each case is to invite and support communication, interest and understanding in order to facilitate a healthier social life in the faculty and school community. "What is necessary and must be actively acquired is the interest of one person in the other.... This is indeed the backbone of all social life" (Rudolf Steiner, ibid.).

How do you want to live? Connected or isolated? In conscious relationship or unconscious separation? For me, anthroposophy is always asking this question and giving ideas and imaginations of how humanity came to be isolated and separate. It also gives ideas, imaginations, and practices of how individuals can enter into a conscious relationship with the world-all (the earth and cosmos), with oneself and with others. One key and very helpful idea that Steiner gives is that our present situation of contending with powerful forces leading to separation and isolation is not a mistake, it is a necessary step in humanity's evolution, it is exactly what is necessary in order to develop the inner strength to be able to be in conscious relationship, should one choose to.

Everyone says "I"—we each can say what do I choose? What does each "I" choose? That is the question that modern humanity is faced with. Nothing is given any more. We are each left to choose how we want to live. And you?

Seeds of Life
(winter in San Diego)

There are seeds of life
below the surface
All god's children are fields
gardens, empty lots,
dirt

It is January
and one rain,
each drop a kiss from
the lover of the deep,
is turning our brown world
wildly green

And I want to know
Who waters your seeds?
What kisses you awake?

Each of the intensive group processes I work in creates a palpable energetic field that forms a vessel of holding where people fairly quickly feel welcomed and at ease. They feel a part of an on-going community built up by the people who came before them and carried by the people in it now. I like to imagine that when someone has participated in the creation of a communal experience some aspect of what was created lives on in them as seed. They carry it back into their world where it can sprout—jump up and live again. And this does happen; people have told me how they have been able to enter into relationships differently, more harmoniously, more openheartedly. One tender shoot at a time.

Facing Karma: Anthroposophia, Me, Myself, and my "I"

Davina Muse

I have tried to wriggle out of this assignment. After months of avoiding, I realize that I owe so much to Steiner's work and to Anthroposophia as a being who radiates spiritual wisdom, from the heights to the innermost depths, that it would be ungrateful not to attempt this task and acknowledge the debt—however painful it may be to face my own self-judgment and fear of the judgment of others.

As a preparation for writing this article, I am asking: What has Anthroposophia done for me, and what have I done for Anthroposophia in the social realm and more generally? I have sought out what Steiner and others have said anthroposophy is "supposed" to do for us, humanity and the world.

Anthroposophy is "something that grows in our souls from mere knowledge and theory into immediate life...into an elixir of life...bringing strength, support and life-renewing energies....It offers a path toward self-knowledge and what may be called the pilgrimage toward becoming a good person" (Rudolf Steiner, *Facing Karma*, lecture Feb. 8, 1912 pp. 1–2). "For anthroposophy asserts that there is a spiritual experience that does not lose the world when thinking. One can also *live* in thought. Anthroposophy tells of an inward experience in which one does not lose the sense world when thinking, but gains the spirit world...in which the ego feels established" (Rudolf Steiner, July 13, 1924).

As a young woman rebelling against the hypocrisy of mainstream Christianity and the injustices of patriarchy, among other kinds of conditioning, I was drawn first to French Existentialism.

I was vaguely aware of an inner gesture of seeking, arising from dissatisfaction, and had no idea what I was longing for. I found the personal and the sociopolitical overlapping in the feminism of the 1970's and 80s. Then, seeking a more spiritual perspective, I found the Gnostic texts—glimpses of a Christianity "untouched by the church"—and the pre-Islamic Sufi path.

The social issues raised by the encounter with feminism became more and more interesting. At the same time my Quaker ancestry led me to support the peace movement in the UK (CND) and in the US (first opposing the Vietnam war and then the war in Iraq), and to question the covert nature of the arms industry as underpinning all economies, whether capitalist or communist. I am not really an activist, protester, or joiner of societies, but in my twenties, I briefly joined the women's protests against nuclear arms at Greenham Common in the UK, and marched with thousands of others in Britain, in support of peace in Vietnam, and later in Iraq.

I woke up to the issues and social questions arising around the ideas of gender equity when, as a thirteen-year-old, I visited my brother's school's "Open Day." I was flabbergasted by the difference between his school (founded in the 15th century) and mine. It was the art rooms (plural!) that really pricked my sense of injustice. The boys had opportunities in large studios to make and fire clay and bronze, work in oils, build sculptures...This was a far cry from the very basic sugar paper and charcoal art room at my own girl's boarding school, presided over by Miss Reis, who, I understand in hindsight, was a traumatized refugee from Germany. As one of the clever ones destined for university, I was not allowed to study art, but she kindly permitted me to go to this art room in my free time. Often, I would make posters for the various club events organized by the school girls. There was the beginning of another thread in my social biography: clear communication in community, and networking.

Many of the themes here—gender inequity, access to art in education, social and economic privilege, the psychological effects of boarding school experience—have guided me in my work as an educator, even as a textile conservator, where I felt I was honoring and preserving the anonymous work of women. These questions have been of abiding interest to me as a wife and the mother of a girl and a boy, and as a family therapist working with individuals, parents, and couples. My interest and understanding around these issues have deepened and broadened through my encounter with anthroposophy.

This first occurred when I was 31. I was living in London, working with ancient and antique textiles, in a doomed relationship with an Englishman who had recently completed the Foundation Course in Anthroposophy, which I knew nothing about and could not pronounce. When he took me to see a mystery drama at Emerson College, I left at the intermission! For reasons no longer entirely clear we found ourselves floundering in New York City. We did a fate bet: if we could get a really fun car for a drive-away service (remember the days of "drive-aways"?) we would drive across the US to Los Angeles. Well, we were assigned a gold Cadillac and took 10 days to get there, the relationship disintegrating as we went. A highlight of that epic journey was peering over the edge of the Grand Canyon, and astounding sunsets at gas stations en route. One of my brothers had recently graduated from the aforementioned school and, with some other young Adonises, had founded the Old School Butler company in LA. They were enjoying great success as butlers to the stars in Hollywood, and one of them, again for reasons not clear, had access to a completely empty house in Venice Beach. Here we stayed, and since I had nothing to read, no solace, the no-longer boyfriend loaned me his copy of *Occult Science*. I still wonder at all the haps and mishaps that had to weave themselves together for me to find myself with that book—and no distractions—on the border of the Pacific at the crumbling edge of North America. I read it on the beach, on the boardwalk with the rollerbladers whizzing past, by the canals, leaning against the walls of the furniture-free loaner house. Most of it went past me like a flock of sea birds... and yet something stayed, a new feeling of expandedness, of experiencing myself as having purpose in the vast scheme of cosmic, earth and human evolution. I realized that I mattered. For one who had been sent to a children's home for 2 years, from age 4 to 6 during a family crisis, that was a powerful message.

Then for 12 years that seed of anthroposophy went underground in my biography, until I had moved to America, started a family, and my children began attending the tiny two-year-old Enchanted Desert Waldorf Kindergarten in Tucson, Arizona. There I was offered as a parent two things mostly missing in my own education—"singing and making things" and adult/parent education workshops with introductions to clay work, biography work, Waldorf education, and anthroposophy. I was inspired to begin reading Steiner, to join the school's board, and to help with fundraising. Such a young school wasn't ready to begin a first grade at the end of kindergarten, so a group of us parents, with the express disapproval of AWSNA, started The Meanwhile School initiative to bridge the gap between kindergarten and grade 3. This was a truly pioneer initiative with all the exhilaration and relational possibilities that entails. Many of us are close friends to this day, parents, and children.

At the end of the three years, the "meanwhile" came to an end, proudly in the black on the account sheet, as the school's board took on opening the grades. Although at the time there was considerable self-interest in this venture, now I see that it was guided by Anthroposophia. I guess she can turn human self-interest to her own ends when the time is right.

Our family then moved to Santa Fe, which boasted a well-established Waldorf school in a magnificent Southwestern setting, and here again as our children went through the grades, I was able to serve the school and the education in several capacities, as a board member and through leading volunteer efforts and fundraising. Here, my daughter learned about biodynamic farming, for which she is now a passionate advocate and activist. I learned so much from parent-teacher evenings, from the visiting lecturers (thank you,

Douglas Gerwin!) and workshops, and from the teachers and the administration, all of whom seemed to be living and thinking in anthroposophical—or at least different and inspiring—ways that deeply impressed me. I continued to read Steiner's lectures, and for years attended painting classes in the Gerard Wagner approach. Working—collaborating—with color changed me in ways I still don't understand. My relationship with color had already acquired depth and nuance from working with some of the Near and Middle East's finest textiles, especially plant-dyed 14th- to 18th-century carpets. As a textile conservator specializing in mounting carpet fragments, I often had to dye backing fabrics myself that would harmonize the missing sections with the remnants of the original carpet. Perhaps this was a preparation for the collaboration with color required by the Wagner processes and Steiner's indications for painting, which gradually brought a new level of awareness, in particular of the processes of emergence.

In Santa Fe, I read an article about Archangel Michael and the Michael School. I realized that my role in this lifetime might be to be a bridge person between mainstream thinking and anthroposophy. In spite of not being a joiner or card-carrier, I did join the Society, and later the First Class.

As the demands of mothering eased, I looked for a new career with a more social gesture, and achieved a master's degree in family counseling, firmly centered on systems thinking. At the same time my relationship to the Sophia deepened; now I see that systems-thinking is Sophianic in perspective and practice. I was fortunate enough to be in the cohort that could take the three-year Waldorf Collaborative Counselling course at Antioch University, led by Kim John Payne, with Torin Finzer, William Bento, Margli Matthews, and others. This was a veritable feast of anthroposophical knowledge, which I am still digesting.

These two educational experiences, in my early fifties, laid the foundation for my work as a family therapist. I felt strongly that there must be a way to offer some of the riches of Waldorf education and the anthroposophical perspective on childhood to a wider audience than inside the schools. I was blessed to work for many years with Kim John Payne, offering an initiative training for group leaders to work with parents, based on Payne's *Simplicity Parenting* books, which are in turn deeply influenced by Steiner's indications regarding child development. We trained more than a thousand lay people and professional caretakers and educators to lead parent groups. It was another exhilarating time to be co-creating ways to build parent community, support, and learning. As the work became increasingly digitized, throughout the Covid virus years, I began to think about how to create a living community experience through online training and connections. My experiences with online workshops, seminars and webinars show that while there are disadvantages, much can be achieved in this realm to foster learning and relationship, even love, overcoming distances, and perhaps redeeming the internet. This was especially true of the years I was a member of an online group studying the threefold nature of the social organism. At the time I was living in a community land trust, and really appreciating the feeling of stewardship in community, without land ownership; and the rightness of taking land values out of the mainstream economy in trust for the future.

As I began to grasp the immensity of Steiner's thinking about many realms of human and cosmic activity, I also looked at his indications for personal development in *Guidance in Esoteric Training*. This work has brought deep joy, a kind of trust and self-security—the "established ego"—that replaces fearfulness; and of course, it has gifted me with much frustration with myself. The six "basic exercises" are a case in point. For seven cycles of six months—three-and-a-half years—a small group of friends "met" monthly by phone to bewail our failures and celebrate small successes. I highly recommend setting up this level of accountability in a group: it makes the inner work involved more supported and more transformative.

Exercise one, especially, helped to develop that sense of connectedness with the whole world that is a prerequisite for healthy social activity. Now, more than 20 years later, I am beginning to find in myself the inner harmony that comes from building self-mastery and consciousness in the other five realms. I write this with humility. Inner development is a long, exasperating, and humbling process.

Surrounding this intimate work has been a growing understanding of the intricacies of karma and reincarnation, as a backdrop to my own development and to social and world events.

The idea that we incarnate in groups is especially impressive when I come to look at myself as a social being in this lifetime.

My education hard-baked into me the "either/or" paradigm of separation, of disconnection. Doing the six exercises led me to find a place of comfort with not knowing, with the shocking possibility I might be wrong, there might be other perspectives than my own, equally valid. A comfort with the sometimes-unbearable experience that I am intimately connected with all that is. Increasingly, I can experience the truth of "both/and," that everything is everything, and everything is reciprocal, not as a mindless mantra but as an unfolding living possibility—the hallmark of the birthing consciousness soul.

Many years attending The Christian Community in Hillsdale, New York, deepened my experience of both the Christ and Sophia. I had a vision in Santa Fe, set in the bright clear light of the mountains, under a blue sky. In this vision, the light was like the light we see when flying above clouds; a particular kind of luminosity. First, I saw a flock of birds carrying a heavy log through the air. All the birds were the same kind of bird, elegantly white and beautiful, and they carried the log easily. Then I saw a flock of all different birds—sparrows, owls, crows, a swan—also carrying a heavy log through the air, very clumsily and incompetently. Often it seemed the log would fall. As I looked at these images, I knew with all my intuition that we must follow the second way of community, which is challenging, clumsy, inclusive, and requires constant collaboration and communication. That effort is so transformative that perhaps in the end we can become like the white birds who carry the log with ease.

I have shared this vision with very few people. Perhaps the time is right now for it to go out into the world bearing its cargo of meanings.

In my personal work and in my work as a therapist, I have found the image below offers reassuring and helpful guidance. (Thank you to Katharine Payne for the beautiful drawing, reproduced with permission.) It's a visual reminder that there is always a middle way between too much or too little, between too harsh or too soft, between ahrimanic and luciferic energetic forces—the middle way, the place of healthy weaving between one pole and the other, the path of the conscious heart.

The heart is an organ of perception
The heart is an organ for finding the creating center
Love is an activity

Anthroposophia has taken me on a long journey, still continuing. Here I must express my gratitude to the many older, more experienced anthroposophers who have helped me on the way by listening, sharing, and suggesting. Let's remember, if we are elders we may have a lot to offer as mentors and co-pilgrims on "the way to becoming a good person."

The journey has involved a gradual movement from living entirely in the small closed world of matter and materialism, to an understanding of process, development, and then—beginning now in my mid-seventies!—to a lived experience of the beingness, the ensouled-ness, of all things, processes, events, and experiences. The most transformative change Anthroposophia has wrought in me is in my thinking, and in my consciousness as a thinker. Engaging consciously and trustingly—"trusting in the ever-present help of the spiritual world"—with imagination, inspiration and intuition has expanded my possibility for creativity in the personal and the social realm. My ever-growing trust in her is based on a lived experience of the coherence and integrity inherent in anthroposophy, the vessel for spiritual wisdom to pour into the world. Each time I can add a new perspective, insight, or experience, this coherence deepens and grows. For this I am wholeheartedly grateful.

As I age, of course, I am becoming more aware of and interested in mortality. I've felt truly honored to work closely with elders and to accompany several to the threshold. As a young person, I was deeply critical of the industrialization of medicine and education; now I see the spiritual danger in the industrialization and materialism of Western approaches to death and dying. So now I begin my, I think, fifth "career" (counting motherhood): training as a *myrrhophore*—one who carries the ancient and sacred oral traditions of working with oils for anointing during transitions. Here the archetype is Mary Magdalene, and studying the fragmentary text of the Gospel of Mary Magdalene has connected with my long-ago interest in the Gnostic gospels. I am very curious where this work will take me as I plant a medicinal-herb garden and prepare to make essential oils.

Looking back at the intention and purpose of anthroposophy, as stated by Steiner and others, I see that, for me, it has "done what it said on the box"—it brought about a continuing transformation in consciousness. I'm not sure I can ever repay the debt I owe, by service to the world: I can keep trying. And as a Waldorf kindergarten teacher said to me once, "That is what the angels see, our striving."

As I look to the future and consider Steiner's predictions about the beginning of the 21st century, I feel the urgency of the need for the spiritualization of human beings, for the three-membered restructuring of society, for the Christening of the world and her creatures through human consciousness.

What as an elder can I bring or develop in myself, to help that come about?

Finding My Way with Anthroposophia

Signe Eklund Schaefer

I am beginning this essay on January 20, 2025, the inauguration day of Donald Trump as president of the United States. It is impossible for me not to note that the only two women to seriously run for president in the history of the country were both defeated by Trump. From one point of view this is an obvious, even banal, observation but it warrants a second look. Both Hillary Clinton and Kamala Harris are women influenced by the women's movement that began in the 1960s. Both are trained lawyers and were already familiar with the challenges and the hopes of stepping forward as women into positions of national leadership.

In both elections (2016 and 2024) it would have been possible for their opponent to have been a man touched in some way by the recent decades of feminist attention. He could even have been attentive to a need for greater balance between masculine and feminine forces at work in society, in individuals, or even in himself. But instead, each time the opposing candidate was Donald Trump.

Thinking about this I suddenly saw Trump as a clear example of a retrogressive shadow image of lingering patriarchal influence, even as our global culture is inching toward a new step in the evolution of human consciousness. For thousands of years the patriarchy served the development of separation, hierarchy, domination, and power, and also the emergence of the individual. Our times now call for a new story—built by conscious individuals on mutual self-responsibility and an evolving understanding of our human interconnectivity with nature, the spiritual world, and each other.

Like the Amazons of Greek mythology, who clung fiercely to a bygone era of maternal influence, resisting the emerging heroes and the future human and social development they were heralding, Trump now seems to be clinging to ever more outdated images of being a "man," as well as of what leadership is. New ideas of wholeness, balance, and collaboration at all levels of social interaction, governance, and also self-awareness, do not seem to have awoken in him. In its time the patriarchy brought much that was good to our evolving human story, but where it lingers on now, it has become too one-sided with its worn-out images of ongoing separation, conflict, and the power of a "strongman." It is time for humanity to move on, to find our way through the ever more destructive shadows of a former way of being, to discover new relationships to the wholeness of our living, multicultural, multiethnic, multi-gendered reality.

Questions of wholeness and balance have been with me since childhood. For example, it never occurred to me that boys were superior or should have more rights than I could have. My parents supported my rather quirky confidence and my independent spirit. My father was a polar explorer, and a mood of ongoing discovery, experimentation, learning, and personal responsibility permeated our family life.

What was not there in my family life was any real conception of the spirit. Ethical behavior was modeled and expected, but my parents made it clear that religion was not the inspiration for their behavior. Within myself, however, I remember knowing since early childhood that there was an "other" world beyond the one I experienced with my senses, and also that we surely lived more than one life.

When I was twenty, Chris—whom I would later marry, but this was only our second date—told me about the Waldorf schools he had attended, where his teachers were on a path of spiritual development, and that reincarnation was part of the ideas of something called *anthroposophy* which underlay the education. He said that all this had been introduced by someone named Rudolf Steiner. My whole world opened up, and I wanted to know where those schools were, and who was Rudolf Steiner, and what was anthroposophy, and also, who was the Sophia implied in the word? I recognized at that moment that I was hearing about something which I was born to encounter. Gradually, as I began to read Steiner, I discovered there were words and concepts for previously unnamed experiences I knew inside myself.

A few years later, after we were married, I was shocked to realize that anyone could now define me as just Chris's "wife." Thankfully, this was not from him, but it was too common for my liking. Our marriage was of great value to me, but that he was my husband and I his wife felt like characterizations that belonged to us, not really qualifiers relevant to others.

Once our two children were born, the apparent further diminishment of my former self as a student, a free-thinking young adult, and a capable woman was ongoingly shocking to me. I loved being a mother and knew that this was a central part of my life path and that my children were great teachers for me, stretching my heart and deepening my sense of what my "I" was doing as a woman in this lifetime. But often the world around me did not appear to look at motherhood that way, nor to welcome the many other interests and questions that also lived within me.

As I began my study of anthroposophy, I was equally drawn to the women's movement that was coming alive in the late 1960s and early 1970s. I soon felt that these two movements had much to say to each other—about civil rights and the meaning of individual freedom, of course, but also about the evolution of human consciousness—and I wanted to be part of that conversation.

In 1974, having moved as a family to England for study and work at Emerson College, a friend and I put up a notice at the college inviting any interested women to join us in forming a group to explore what parallels we might discover between Steiner's work and feminism as it was emerging around and within us. Seventeen women showed up to one of the most extraordinary gatherings I had ever experienced, and we continued to meet weekly for several months, discovering exciting parallels and many new questions.

Thus began years of encouraging such groups and engaging in deep study of spiritual science, mythology, history, psychology, and feminist scholarship. Eventually a core group of us, who met for seven years, named our work Ariadne after the maiden in Greek mythology who on Crete offered a helping thread to the hero Theseus so he could find his way out of the labyrinth and thus escape the Minotaur. Along the way we began to offer workshops, classes and conferences, created an international newsletter, and eventually published a book—*Ariadne's Awakening: Taking up the Threads of Consciousness*, with chapters by Margli Matthews, Betty Staley and me.

Our interest went beyond male and female as a polarity of genders, also beyond questions of rights and responsibilities. We felt there was a new call for balance in the evolution of human consciousness as the patriarchy, with its story of separation, was being challenged to open to more feminine forces of relatedness, collaboration and inclusion. We observed how feminine and masculine soul forces are at work in every individual regardless of gender, and also in relationships, and in society as well. We were inspired by the individual human potential for balance, and we sought to understand the eternal, nongendered "I" and the intentions toward wholeness that ongoing karma invites.

Of course, gender is only one aspect in a human biography, and I was also interested in the larger story of individual becoming. From the first time I heard a talk about Rudolf Steiner's picture of seven-year life phases, I knew this would also be part of my life's work. And I kept finding in Steiner ever more pieces of the puzzle of human development—temperaments, soul types, relationships, karma, and life between death and rebirth to name a few.

Anthroposophy helped me to appreciate the paradox of the "I" as an eternal self beyond differences like gender, temperament, ethnicity, family, and so on, who incarnates into a world of such distinctions for the learning, the gifts, and the challenges they offer the "I" on its long path of becoming ever more whole on earth. I wanted to awaken active appreciation for the wonder of difference without letting myself or others be diminished from our full human potential, or be boxed in by tradition or prejudice.

After eight years living in Europe, our family moved back to the States in 1981, first to Detroit to work with the Waldorf Institute, and then going with the institute to Spring Valley, New York, to develop Sunbridge College. For many years I directed Foundation Studies at the college. Working with colleagues to bring spiritual science alive for and with the students was a deep challenge and a great joy. We sought to create a spirit-filled learning environment, a place of peace, hard work, authenticity, discovery, creativity, and mutual support. This was not easy, of course, but it was a great gift of my destiny to be part of the effort. As the students sought to know more about anthroposophy, I wanted them to experience it not only as a body of knowledge, but more importantly, as a path of development that could serve their own awakening to their life tasks and to the spirit-filled realities that Rudolf Steiner described.

Every year I worked with groups reading *Intuitive Thinking as a Spiritual Path: A Philosophy of Freedom*. My guiding principle with this was something Rudolf Steiner wrote to his friend Rosa Mayreder when the book was first published. He described the book as: "a biographical account of how one human soul made the difficult ascent to freedom." I formulated biographical questions to accompany each chapter to keep our study from falling into an intellectual exercise. I wanted the students, and I myself year after year, to be attentive, in ever deepening ways, to our own unique journeys of awakening a deeper understanding and practice of ethical individualism, of moral imagination, inspiration and technique, and of the possibilities and responsibilities of human freedom.

For many years Chris and I co-taught a course called "The Individual in the 20th Century" (it had a revised name after 2000!). We were interested in the dynamic between community and self, nation and citizen, evolving world and striving individuals. The students presented projects relating their own experiences of some aspect of the general theme—questions of social reform, rights and responsibilities of the individual, how fear and prejudice work, climate challenges, spiritual life in a materialistic time, cultural disparities and exploitation, to name only a few. Always there was the challenge to see how working with anthroposophy—both on one's own inner path and in shared endeavors—could contribute to addressing the real needs of the times.

Another course I particularly enjoyed teaching was Human Development. Here I could share ideas and exercises about life phases, gender, and other dimensions of our destiny paths. Central to all my work has been the conviction that ideas come alive in conversation, and even more that we need each other to become our best selves. Of course, teachers need students and vice versa, but I mean something more than this. Rudolf Steiner speaks of how we become ourselves on earth through our interactions with the others of our life. While still in the spiritual world we inhabit between death and a new birth, as we begin to prepare for a new life, we gradually anticipate the conditions, challenges and opportunities we will need for this next earthly round. I imagine this is done through interaction between wise spiritual beings, our "higher I," and the others with whom our future biography will unfold.

Of course, everything is not "fated," but I have known since childhood that we come to life with the intention to meet particular challenges, opportunities, and people that will help our eternal "I" along its way. I think of the others in our lives as offering doors and windows to our becoming—sometimes consciously but oftentimes not—and of course we also do this for others. I am old enough now to look back and see the destiny appointments that appeared in my life. Sometimes I was ready to enter a yet unknown door, sometimes it took me a long time to come round to where I needed to be.

Along with my teaching, I also was involved in developing the Center for Life Studies, first at the Institute in Detroit and then later as part of Sunbridge College. Working with other colleagues who were also committed to finding ways to bring anthroposophical ideas alive in our contemporary world, we offered parent education, biography workshops, conferences on such themes as "Who is Raising our Daughters?" or "The Art of Working Together," as well as ongoing programs such as Side by Side, a service learning internship for young people (17–23).

Brochures about the Center for Life Studies often opened with these words of Rudolf Steiner's: "Spiritual science should bring strength, energy and open-mindedness to humanity so that people can meet what daily life and our times demand."

In the late 1990s, I was able to initiate a part-time training program at Sunbridge for people who were working with adults in many different helping professions—such as counselors, social workers, art therapists, nurses, parent educators, or those active in various kinds of community development projects. Meeting for three years—two weeks in the summer, and one week each in spring and fall—the program was initially called Biography and Adult Learning. After two cycles the name was changed to Biography and Social Art.

This professional development program was intense, experiential, and far-reaching in its intent to look at human development from many different perspectives, each illuminated by what anthroposophy could offer to a deepening understanding. Various themes for weekly blocks included: Biography and Destiny; Appreciating Difference (gender, temperament...); The Cycle of the Year; Planets, Trees and Soul Orientations; Life Phases; Working with Groups; The Twelve Senses; The Helping Conversation; The Evolution of Consciousness Through Art; and Thresholds. Every session included nature observation and practices in inner development. Working artistically (drawing, painting, clay, music, writing) and with movement (eurythmy and spatial dynamics) were integral parts of exploring the different themes. Story telling—fairy tales, myths, and personal narrative—were also instrumental in this hands-on learning.

I just used the past tense in describing the early development of the program, but the work continues and has evolved through the decades. After the fourth cycle of the training, with the encouragement of several graduates, Patricia Rubano (by then co-director) and I decided to create a new umbrella organization for the developing work. In 2010, the Center for Biography and Social Art was founded, although course work for the training program continues to take place on the Sunbridge campus.

In the years since its founding, the Center for Biography and Social Art has overseen the growing training, as well as organizing several professional development conferences for graduates and others involved in biography activities. There are also offerings for school faculties and parent groups, and monthly online public workshops on a host of biography related themes (Center for Biography and Social Art: www.biographysocialart.org).

In my early love for all aspects of human development, I knew that biography and social art activities would help people to better understand their own lives and destiny themes. And of course, this happens. But as the years have gone by, I have come to see another equally important result of this work. In the many small group sharings, including dyads, people are invited not only to speak their own truths, but also to really listen to others, to open their hearts to what another is sharing—without judging or trying to fix anything. In our ever more virtual world, where people often feel isolated from others and awkward in social interactions, biography exercises provide an opportunity to practice really listening and, in the process, to discover genuine interest in others. Both speaker and listener are offering something important into the space between. Brenda Ueland, the American journalist and writer, captures the importance of listening very succinctly: "When we are listened to, it creates us, makes us unfold and expand. Ideas actually begin to grow within us and come to life."

Since retiring from directing Foundation Studies in 2007, and then some years later also from the Biography and Social Art

Program, I have been able to write or edit four books: *Why on Earth? Biography and the Practice of Human Becoming; I Give You My Word: Women's Letters as Life Support, 1973–1987; She Was Always There: Sophia as a Story for Our Time;* and *Elder Flowering: Lived Experiences of Growing Older* (co-edited with Karen Gierlach). Making the time to let my years of working with these different themes find expression in written form has been deeply fulfilling.

In my work with anthroposophy over many decades I was often surprised that there has been so little interest in the being of Sophia. My own feeling, as expressed in the title of one of my books, has been that "she was always there." Already when I was young, I felt her as a presence knocking on my consciousness, at times from within my heart, and other times as if from all around the world. I understood from my readings in mythology and anthroposophy that Sophia was a name for the wisdom of the world. In this sense she has been with us from the beginning (as she herself says in Proverbs 8:23–31)—a Great Mother being from before any division into feminine and masculine, a mighty womb birthing the world into being. The sense of a knocking that I experience feels like a call to wake up, to take a new step in the evolution of our consciousness, in our understanding of the story of human becoming.

My studies in feminist literature helped me to grasp why her influence as a divine maternal being faded during patriarchal times. But now, as I suggested at the beginning of this chapter, unchecked patriarchal power would lead into ever greater separation, imbalance, and domination—into nowhere good. Now in this time of the consciousness soul, and after long ages of growing our individualities, we are challenged to freely, and with love, awaken to our interconnectedness—with each other, nature, and the spiritual world—and to our mutual responsibility. There can be no real peace or enduring social reform without this.

I observe that many people today are indeed responding to this wake-up call, whether they recognize it as coming from Sophia or not. More people begin to speak of a world of inter-being, scientists recognize that trees in a forest communicate with each other, the commitment to civil rights grows in spite of setbacks, there are growing efforts to bring indigenous wisdom and natural scientific knowledge together, ever more people are exploring new imaginations of life after death. I see all of these searches, and many more, as inspired by the wisdom of the world offering us new possibilities of knowing. They suggest our human movement toward a new story (post-patriarchal and also post-Kali Yuga) that can inspire us in our further becoming. We are being challenged to expand our consciousness, to practice mutual support, and to embrace the reality of paradox rather than staying behind in a dualistic, either/or, and so too often warring, world.

In 1923, at the re-founding of the Anthroposophical Society, Rudolf Steiner stated clearly that he was laying the Foundation Stone Meditation—which he referred to as a stone of love—into the hearts of human beings in order to build a home on earth for Anthroposophia, as an aspect of Divine Sophia. This was, and continues to be, a gift and a challenge to us as individuals and within the communities we would create.

I feel so grateful that my life and work have been so interwoven with Rudolf Steiner and anthroposophy. In my personal growth, with my family and friends, and in the many activities that have filled my working life, my intention with anthroposophy was that my studies and my inner work would open my heart to others and to the social needs around me, would serve a deeper understanding of the multi-leveled forces at work in the world, and would strengthen my courage to act with integrity, creativity, and compassion.

Engaging Socially with an Open Heart—Again and Again!

Karen Gierlach

> If, as anthroposophists, we set ourselves the task of extending our interests and widening our mental horizon, this will promote the universal sister and brotherhood of mankind. Progress is not gained by the mere preaching of universal love... but by interesting ourselves increasingly in souls with widely different characters, racial and national characteristics, and holding widely differing religious and philosophical views, and to approach them with understanding. Right interest, right understanding, call forth from the soul the right moral action.*

My biography naturally led me to address social questions and connected me to anthroposophy. Now that I am able to look back from the vantage point of my early eighties, I realize how many immersive experiences I have had that allowed me to see life from different perspectives. In this latest chapter, post age 63, using the valuable tool of biography and social art, I have been able to create bridging situations in which individuals from different world views can nonetheless meet as human beings and discover how much they have in common, despite assuming otherwise.

My father was a Waldorf school graduate from Michael Hall *in* Forest Row, England and it is through the school that he and my mother first met. I was born in wartime London and lived there until age 4. During some of that time V-2 long-range ballistic guided missiles, launched from Germany, rained down on nearby neighborhoods. Shortly after World War II ended, my parents moved to occupied Germany because my father, who spoke fluent German,

* Rudolf Steiner, *The Spiritual Foundation of Morality: Francis of Assisi and the Christ Impulse,* lecture 3, 1912.

was working there for the British. He had lived with a German family during high school as an exchange student at the Stuttgart Waldorf School. His postwar job was to help de-Nazify the country, so that eventually Germany could emerge from the horrors of the Nazi regime and once again become independent and democratic. These circumstances in my early years meant that I grew up with the "enemy." However, because my parents had many German friends—colleagues from work, as well as anthroposophists connected to the Waldorf schools or to The Christian Community—I was neither told nor led to think anything negative about the many German people who were part of my life during the 8 years I lived there. I interacted with neighbor children, with my Waldorf classmates and teachers, and as children do, I accepted this reality as quite normal. Evidence of the recent war was all around us: food was scarce and rationed, I could see acres and acres of buildings in ruins whenever I moved from one neighborhood to another, for instance on my tram trip to school in the morning. I knew these were "because of the war," but I was never told by my parents or teachers that the war had been between us English and "those Germans." Fortunately, that reality escaped me entirely.

Harder to ignore were the many tragic stories I overheard about people who had lost their lives and homes in those bombings and from others who had become refugees after fleeing from the advancing Russian troops as they entered Germany from the east. Many of those East German refugees lived in our midst, some even in our house. Flyers showing photos of missing children were posted in many public spaces, usually connected with lengthy ID numbers below the photo, requesting information about the child for which the parents were desperately searching. I remember looking at the children's happy faces in the photos and feeling so sad that they were lost. Clearly, war caused much human suffering and I felt grateful that it was over. Fortunately for me and for many of my generation, we have not had to be part of another war taking place in our own country through today.

Quite unconsciously, seeds were laid in me that made it possible to feel aware and concerned about the tragic consequences of war and at the same time feel comfortable in another culture, speaking a second language, and experiencing what war meant for those on "the other side." At age 12, we moved back to England when my father's job in Germany ended. The unexpected move made me both sad and angry because, for all my adolescent trying, I could not prevent it from happening. I felt living in Germany had become for me where I naturally belonged. Once back in rural England, I learned about prejudice and anti-German sentiment, which was still strong in England at that time. It impacted me directly when my sister and I were speaking German while out walking our dog. Suddenly, a passerby shouted at us and told us in no uncertain terms never to speak that horrible language again! We were very taken aback and, as a result, my sister and I never did speak German with each other again.

In middle and high school, I learned about the Holocaust and all the atrocities of Nazi Germany. When my peers reacted with great condemnation to all things German, I would also try to describe my many experiences of kindness and welcome that I had received in Germany, trying to balance out their understandably extreme reactions. I felt I needed to keep some middle ground of truth and to tell the other side of the story.

While still in high school I also had the great luck to visit my parents in Thailand where they had moved for 2 years. I was overwhelmed with wonder at the new climate, sights, smells, tastes, and sounds of that exotic country, satisfying all my wishes for experiencing "otherness." While my parents were in Thailand, I became a boarder at Michael Hall and discovered how much I enjoyed living in community with my peers. Later in my teens, my interest in other languages and cultures led to my spending time with a French family to perfect my French. Our senior trip was a history of art tour of Italy, opening up the many treasures as well as new kinds of foods (spaghetti was a wonder in those days!) to be found in that country as well. Instead of going directly to college, I chose to live and work in Spain for a year, thus adding Spanish to my clutch of languages. I also made new friends who were living unhappily under Francisco Franco's dictatorship and who reminisced about better, more liberal times in Spain, giving me some historical, political, and cultural lessons. While there, I also enjoyed the different aspects of myself that emerged while speaking another language, so in a sense they were a continuation of my early experiences living with and between different languages and cultures.

While working and studying in London, after returning from Spain, political activists, inspired by Bertrand Russell, frequently marched in London under the banner of "Ban the Bomb," strongly opposing the expansion of nuclear power. I, however, was more attracted to the bright colors of the daring Carnaby Street fashions, to the music of the Beatles and the Rolling Stones, and observed with interest the Flower Children movement, our English version of hippies, than to political involvement. I was charmed by a new flowering of color and art in England after the very drab and impoverished fifties when the lingering deprivations from the war were still much in evidence. Again, I was attracted to something new and different that had awoken in me, even if rather superficially while in my twenties.

Another opportunity for living in a community arose while I was still a college student. It is also related to the theme of World War II and its aftermath. Together with many other young people, I took a boat from Athens to Haifa to spend a month living and working on kibbutz Or Haner, near Gaza. It had no specific program for overseas volunteers, as could be found on other kibbutzim, but the second language that everyone spoke there was Spanish, the language the community members had grown up with in Mexico or Argentina before they moved to Israel. So, quite practically, I chose that place so that I could practice my Spanish at the same time!

Listening to the stories of these mostly young men on the kibbutz, I became inspired by how they had left behind all that they were used to, exchanging an urban life of comparative comfort and then moving to an agricultural, socialist community where the work was hard and safety was not guaranteed, to help build up this very new country of Israel. It was their answer to the great tragedy the Jewish people had suffered during the Holocaust and in pogroms in Europe and Russia for years and years before that. Here they would create a place where Jews could finally live safely without being persecuted as before. What a beautiful picture they held up for me! At that time, I heard nothing about their neighbors, the Palestinians, and I did not think to ask about them. The slogan I heard several times was "we found a land with no people for a people with no land." Another was, "we will never again go like lambs to the slaughter."

In the fateful year 1968, after the tragic assassinations of both Martin Luther King and Bobby Kennedy, I traveled out of curiosity to the United States. I lived first of all in Cambridge, Massachusetts, where I met my future husband Mike, who eventually became the father of our two children. Through Mike I quickly became educated and somewhat involved in the ongoing anti-war demonstrations there. Even though I strongly opposed the war, I found the often very angry and warlike statements, actions, and infighting among the leaders of the protesters, as well as the group chants, quite uncomfortable for me. I could somewhat sense the possibility of "becoming what you hate."

At that same time, I met Chris and Signe Schaefer, became involved for the first time with studying anthroposophy at their house, and joined a committee that was working to start a Waldorf kindergarten in Somerville, Massachusetts. This later became the Waldorf School of Lexington. At that time, I earned a living by teaching English to recent immigrants from Haiti, the Dominican Republic, and Cuba. The job opened my eyes to the very challenging lives of my students and the huge changes they had made to come to the US, often at great physical risk. I was happy to use my French and Spanish to communicate with them outside of English class and to hear more about their day-to-day experiences living in Boston, having left all that was familiar, but also often very difficult, behind them. It was another version of starting new lives in a new country that I had already witnessed on the kibbutz.

After our daughter was born, we eventually traveled to England to attend Emerson College for a year and my mother spent every morning looking after my two-year-old. There, my interest in anthroposophical studies was further awakened and then continued, focused particularly on education once I started working in Waldorf schools. Now, in my later years, living with and working out of anthroposophy has become ever more central to my life.

After returning from Emerson, my husband and I returned to Wilton, New Hampshire, my son was born and soon we enrolled our daughter at Pine Hill Waldorf School. There, I also picked up the thread of community living that had awakened in me at Michael Hall and again in Israel. I became one of the founding members of Hearthstone Community, a land trust-based living community of about ten households. I felt this community impulse, based on a sharing of financial resources to obtain the land and then to create a land trust, was a positive social impulse as well as a way to protect the land into the future. Interestingly and sadly, after spending many years being part of weekly planning meetings and even physically helping to clear brush after the big machinery had left the site, but before the building of our own house began, my husband and I divorced. I then moved away from Wilton to Detroit, so never actually lived in the community I had helped to bring to birth.

Busy years of raising two children on my own, while teaching in a Waldorf school, took all my time so my social involvement that began with the Hearthstone Community became more and more the work of trying to balance parenting with Waldorf teaching. After I retired from Waldorf work, I began to facilitate biography workshops for Waldorf teachers and parents. I had for some time already enjoyed and participated in anthroposophical biography workshops but had not taken up biography facilitation until then. I was eager to learn more about how seven-year life cycles underlie not only childhood development but also the adult years. Having almost come to the end of my biographical Saturn development years at age 60, when I began workshop facilitation, I had many life experiences to look back on and could observe how my own life had developed through those cycles and what threads were woven through the tapestry of my life. Those threads continue to weave in interesting ways to this day.

Once I was no longer working full-time and my children had left for college and beyond, I was also able to explore work outside of Waldorf education. After 9/11, I qualified as a hospice volunteer and began to visit patients, first in a hospital setting and eventually in private homes. This I continued doing when we moved to the Bay Area. Very soon after we arrived there, we were invited to join a group of monthly Social Science Section members who were joining the anti-Iraq war demonstrations in downtown San Francisco. On our way to the meeting, the BART train stopped in Berkeley and I expected to see many students board the train to join us. However, almost none appeared. Clearly the radical days of UC Berkeley and the Free Speech Movement activities on and off campus were very much a thing of the past and it was the older adults from the 1960s antiwar movement who made up a large part of the demonstrators that day!

After the massive demonstrations all over the world proved futile to stop the war in Iraq, we began to attend Social Science meetings in Berkeley at the home of Addie Bianchi and discussed many burning social questions, among them the war in Iraq and also the fate of Palestine. Addie had paid a visit to Israel and Palestine and was quite taken aback by the distressing situation in which she found the Palestinians.

Having always been concerned about refugees, I next volunteered to help recent arrivals in San Francisco through the International Rescue Committee. Through that work, I made a strong connection with a young woman from Iraq (I will call her Fatima), who in the end did not stay in the US because her father was not granted asylum to join her. Because Fatima was a fluent English speaker and therefore more employable, she felt financially responsible for both him and for her two older sisters, so she decided to give up her opportunity to be in the US and rejoin her family members in Amman. The three sisters and the father had initially fled there from Iraq after Fatima's life was threatened by fundamentalists who disapproved of her work as a translator for a British NGO. Having so opposed the Iraq War myself, I learned in great detail and with dismay about the consequences the war had visited upon this brave young woman and her family, which continue until this day.

Eventually Fatima and one sister crossed the Mediterranean in a rubber boat one December about 10 years ago, ending up in Austria before all the EU borders slammed shut against immigrants at the end of that year. She and her sister have remained in Austria since then. A few years ago, I helped raise funds to enable Fatima's second sister to also leave Jordan and join her siblings in Austria, so now finally they are all happily reunited and living a much safer life, though still employed below their actual abilities and qualifications. Although Fatima speaks such good English, she has had to learn German as well, a difficult language to start later in life.

In my late 60s, already far into my retirement years, a new or renewed chapter began, related to Israel. I was unexpectedly introduced to a remarkable woman from Los Angeles, Shepha Vainstein, a former Waldorf parent and a trauma therapist by profession. The NGO she had founded, reGeneration Education, was created to raise funds to support education for Arab and Jewish students in Israeli Waldorf schools (regenerationeducation.org). When I met her and eventually accompanied her to Israel, we visited Ein Bustan, a kindergarten in which Arab and Jewish children were jointly taught by Arab and Jewish teachers, speaking Arabic and Hebrew in the classroom and celebrating both the Muslim and the Jewish festivals with all the children. Shepha felt the calm Waldorf kindergarten approach was well suited to mitigate the high stress environment that the children inevitably felt in a country constantly in fear of attack from without. Getting to know "the other" in a shared and enjoyable environment would create a foundation for a positive relationship in the future. Naturally, the schools she told me about appealed to my interest in building bridges, a continuation of what I had done unconsciously as a child. Here again, at a young enough age, some children in Israel would have an opportunity to not grow up separated and feeling unfriendly toward children of a different faith and culture.

I was fortunately able to offer a biography workshop for the faculty and parents of both the Ein Bustan Arab Jewish kindergarten and adults from the Tamrat El Zeitoun Arab Waldorf School in nearby Shefa-Amr and a neighboring Jewish Waldorf School. Several participants commented on how they had never before had an opportunity to exchange stories from their daily lives with other Waldorf parents and teachers whose backgrounds were so different.

During this visit, I was also able to cross over into the West Bank and meet many Palestinians who were longing for a peaceful relationship between their people and the Israelis. Most of the teachers and parents we met offered us gracious Arab hospitality and open hearts, though none ever failed to mention how very hard it was to have lived under Israeli occupation for so many years, which affected everyday life for all of them in multiple ways. Many of their families had become displaced during the founding of Israel in 1948 and again when it expanded further after the Six-Day War. We were shown where previously farms and olive groves had provided for the village; these had now been cut off from their owners by the encroachment of the tall and menacing concrete separation wall between Israel and the West Bank. Again, I was being offered an opportunity to see the conflict from the other side and to have great sympathy for the citizens caught up in the effects of the less than conciliatory political policies on both sides.

In Israel life seemed easier and quite comfortable, certainly when compared to the way people had lived in uniform, modest, egalitarian apartments in the '60s during my first visit. However, even though this was not a time when attacks were happening in Israel like the bus bombings I had read about during the Second Intifada, nevertheless, there was a sense of anxiety that danger was always lurking. Once, when I went to catch a bus on a street corner in a leafy, quiet town in the Galilee, I came upon an unexpected swarm of police and soldiers. They had set in motion a small robot that was approaching a lone backpack sitting on the sidewalk at the bus stop. It turned out to be innocent, not packed with explosives as was feared, but had been left behind by someone accidentally. However, it opened my eyes to how fearfully people might go about their daily lives in Israel. When, in addition, the media stresses all the things that might and have become a real threat, then it was easy to build up a fear of Palestinians, even of those living within Israel. Tragically, the events of October 7th fulfilled all the fears that Israelis had carried for many years, and thereby has seriously set back hopes for reconciliation and peace.

I have not been able to return to Israel and the West Bank to continue bridging workshops like the one I held some years ago in Israel. I have, however, taken the initiative to create some workshops online in which I bring together Palestinian and Jewish peace activists, most of whom already know each other and have even worked together, to share with an audience from the US and Europe how they feel committed to building a more peaceful future, despite resistance of mainstream opinions and the politicians on both sides to any change in the status quo. By listening to each other, they have become strong allies in creating a new vision and at times a new reality in the region. They feel that only through meeting, hearing, and respecting each other's viewpoints—which are necessarily different—and freeing the Palestinians from Israeli occupation, will there ever be peace in the region.

During the last online workshop, I invited both audience and speakers to join a small breakout group and to share thoughts and feelings about working for peace and what is required of us as individuals in order to meet "the other" for such a task. Many of the participants expressed how valuable and moving it had been to hear the voices from both sides of the Israel/Palestine story and how it had changed them. Many friends here and in Europe have responded quite generously to periodic online fundraisers that I have organized to support a young woman in her family in Gaza even before this latest war. Those same friends eventually helped my young friend to leave Gaza for Egypt while that was still possible to do.

Bridging work in my backyard here in Sacramento has taken the form of teaching a six-week biography course at Sacramento State University adult education department for several years in a row. Called "Meeting Each Other through Sharing Life Stories," it is attended by lively older people with no background in anthroposophy and serves as an enjoyable life review for the students in the company of other classmates of a similar age. They love hearing each other's stories and comparing notes while observing the recurring themes threaded through their lives. They have also made comments to me, describing how very different this is from all the other courses they have attended at CSUS. At the end of this month, I have been invited to facilitate a workshop for Muslim and Jewish women through the Salaam Shalom Sisterhood organization in Sacramento. I look forward to yet another iteration of connecting two disparate groups with each other through the social art of biography.

Through anthroposophy, I know that my own inner work of recognizing and tamping down my prejudices and opinions in order to listen more fully and selflessly to others, as Rudolf Steiner so often encourages us to do, is one part. The other is to cultivate an interest in all people, regardless of their backgrounds and political beliefs, something that can over time serve as a small contribution toward transforming our Earth into a planet of love. Having the social art of biography as a tool is a great blessing, since it encourages us to listen to the other with as open a heart and mind as we can, and to meet with reverence and wonder the life experiences of another human being. I then feel connected with Michael, the guiding spirit of our time, whom I learned about through anthroposophy and with whom I formed a relationship already in the Waldorf school, and whose cosmopolitan, sun-like influence accompanies me in this work. And, when I see peace activists meet each other, inspired by Gandhi and by MLK and by their own spiritual practices, then I sense that the cosmic Christ is working in their midst, and I feel deep awe, admiration, and gratitude.

SECTION III

Waldorf Education and Community Life

Moments of Destiny

My Journey to Social Activism, Waldorf Education and Anthroposophy

Marti Stewart

I feel the essence of my being
So speaks an inward sense
Which in the sun-illumined world
Unites with flowing light.
For it would pour its warmth
Into thinking's clarity
And bind in one
The human being and the world.*

I brought three primary interests into this lifetime centered on matters of the spirit, social life, and artistic expression. These three threads found their origins and were nurtured within me, through my birth family and early experience, and have continued to draw me into the future. When I encountered Eastern philosophies and Western spiritual science (including anthroposophy) in my early 20s, I experienced a remembering. I felt an immediate and easy resonance, a "yes, of course," to the philosophy and teachings. Ideas regarding reincarnation and karma, and the purpose and meaning of human existence, provided a resonant backdrop and a comfortable framework into which these three central threads of my life are woven.

The picture of the individual soul on an evolutionary journey toward awakening and enlightenment is central to my

* Rudolf Steiner, *Calendar of the Soul,* week 4.

understanding of life, both reflecting back and looking forward. An essential part of this understanding includes our collective responsibility for one another and our interdependence. The concept of the Bodhisattva who delays their own liberation to help all sentient beings achieve enlightenment has always resonated with me. Steiner's articulation of the "fundamental social law" reflects a similar truth: that our lives are made meaningful or sacred through our work in service to others.

From a young age, I was very interested in nonviolent resistance and in the concept of doing no harm. This inclination was apparent in my early memories of being distressed when I accidentally stepped on a cricket in the kitchen at age 3, and caught my first fish off of a boat in Lake Michigan at age 5. Horrified, I insisted the fish be returned to the water. At this same tender age, I was taken to see "Gone with the Wind" and was stunned to see the death and destruction of war. I recognized early on that I had no appetite for killing things or bringing harm.

I recall being at home with my mother when she learned that John F. Kennedy was assassinated, and I deeply remember the assassination of Rev. Dr. Martin Luther King Jr. when I was 8 years old. These experiences have remained embedded in my memory due to the significant impact they had upon my mind and heart. The role of both violence and nonviolent resistance as political and social forces of change captured my attention. My strong resonance with the concept of *ahimsa,* which I encountered more formally later in childhood, always felt that it was carried forward from a past life.

I was born to parents who cared about social justice, and worked toward peace and social change within a faith community. My spiritual framework as a child was a progressive Christianity focused on loving your neighbor, standing with the oppressed, and doing good works in the world. My church was very active in social justice movements locally and nationally, including gay rights, women's rights, the causes of migrant workers and native peoples, and racial equality.

I had a meaningful relationship with God as a child, and I felt truly inspired by the stories about the life of Jesus and the teachings of Christianity. At the time of my 9-year change, I distinctly recall a night when I was overcome with an awareness that given the blessings and privileges of my birth, I was tremendously responsible to live my life in such a way that would benefit others. In 5th grade, I would often grieve "man's inhumanity to man" and felt that we were, as human beings, at a turning point. I completed a school project that I entitled "Which Way World?" which contrasted the forces of light and darkness at work in the world and the element of human choice.

Though I was raised in what I later deemed to be a cultural desert in Wichita, Kansas, my mother had a great appreciation of literature, theater, opera, history, and art. Whenever we traveled, we visited major art and history museums. When we visited the National Gallery in Washington, DC, when I was 10 years old, I had another revelatory experience. I was completely entranced by the paintings before me, and encountered the meaningful and transcendent power of art.

At age 11, I attended a week-long church camp, where I had a camp counselor, John Nelson, who was seeking his conscientious objector status during the Vietnam War. Meeting him and hearing him sing anti-war songs had a great impact on me, and moved me further along the path in my interest and compassion for the world, and all that was beyond my sheltered family life in the Midwestern city of Wichita, Kansas. The wider world began to open up before me.

I chose to write my sixth-grade book reports on books about the lives of Gandhi and Martin Luther King Jr.; I was enamored with the concept of satyagraha and nonviolent resistance. My mentor and "adopted" brother John sent me a copy of George Orwell's *1984* and the *Tao Te Ching,* providing two starkly opposing visions of our human capacity to shape social life. At 13, I visited New York City for the first time with my father. My outstanding memory was one of being shocked to see people living out of cardboard boxes. I was struck by the breadth and depth of human suffering. I was also captivated by the life of St. Francis as portrayed in the film *Brother Sun, Sister Moon,* and the Prayer of St. Francis became one of my favorite mantras.

During this time, I began identifying as an artist; I selected all the visual art classes available to me in my public junior high and high school. I took drawing and painting classes at the Wichita Center for the Arts where the smells of charcoal and paint in studio spaces were like an intoxicant.

I was first introduced to esoteric studies when one of my closest friends in seventh grade, who shared my interest in philosophy and religion, confided in me that she had joined the Rosicrucian order. (They were evidently unaware of her age!) She would quietly share with me some of the materials they sent to her over several years.

At the age of 16, I became a vegetarian after reading *Diet for a Small Planet.* When presented with the social and environmental consequences of eating meat, I easily arrived at this decision due to my natural aversion to meat and fish, and a natural affinity toward nonviolence. My interest in living a life guided by spiritual signposts and practices evolved. I had the opportunity to serve as a youth representative to the National Conference of Christians and Jews, and was the youngest delegate to the National Synod meeting of the United Church of Christ held in St. Paul, Minnesota.

The Weaving of Spirit, Art, and Social Action: Finding My Way in the World

I began my college career at Oberlin College, studying fine arts and political science, but decided to leave small-town Oberlin, Ohio, and move to California. From an artist's warehouse collective in San Francisco, I eventually found myself living downtown and working in a Jewish deli, and then at two businesses owned by East Indian families. But my time in California was short-lived. I hitchhiked up the West Coast with a friend and then took a Greyhound bus across the country to Madison, Wisconsin. I immediately found myself at home in Madison living in a large, historic, collectively run house, full of radicals and independent thinkers of all kinds and just blocks from the university. Within weeks I had joined an affinity group and was traveling to Portsmouth, New Hampshire, to be part of a large anti-nuclear demonstration, and later to Washington, DC, to camp out in front of the Nuclear Regulatory Commission and stage a die-in.

When we returned home, we formed the Madison Radioactivists. At age 19, I participated in an act of civil disobedience at a nuclear power plant in Waukegan, Illinois, and was arrested with 19 others from Madison and Chicago. My father, an attorney, who had business in Chicago, rented a car to come to the police station and witness our arraignment. A few months later, we returned to Waukegan for our trial. I represented myself in the courtroom and offered up several compelling arguments in our defense; we were acquitted on the basis of necessity.

Meanwhile, I enrolled at the University of Wisconsin, Madison, where I painted my way through college. My rich social life included other artists, seekers, and activists who were not a part of the mainstream university culture. I took courses in drawing and painting, history, Italian, and avant-garde film. It was here that I began to encounter both Eastern and esoteric philosophy. On a trip to the Black Hills in support of Lakota land rights, I met an acupuncturist who later introduced me to macrobiotics. My artistic work reflected my interest in the mysteries of the unseen world. I was drawn to the work of artists like Paul Klee, Wassily Kandinsky, Frida Kahlo, and Cy Twombly, along with Indian miniatures, tantric art, and mandalas. Before completing my degree in fine arts, I had developed a strong interest in esoteric studies, health and healing, natural foods, and the co-op movement.

My love of the arts took me to New York City where my first home was on East Broadway in Chinatown. Here, I began studying both Eastern and esoteric philosophies in earnest. I worked in a macrobiotic restaurant, began to study and practice Tai Chi, and studied Shiatsu at the Ohashi Institute. In 1981, the New Age movement was flourishing in New York City, and I was exposed to all manner of esoteric philosophies, divination, and healing practices. I discovered that I had both my natal Sun and the planet Mercury in the 12th house—the house of hidden things. This planetary configuration reflected my natural interest in esoteric studies, spiritual development, and the subtle world.

At age 24, I met two important mentors: Lea Ceria, a therapist and Italian immigrant who lived and practiced on the Upper West Side; and Carol Parish who had moved from Florida to Oklahoma to begin a spiritual community and seminary outside of Tahlequah.

Lea had an individual and group therapy practice but was also interested in the more esoteric side of healing; she took me under her wing and taught me long distance healing practices and redecision therapy. With a few of her other proteges, we began something we called "The Healing Foundation." We provided programs in New York City facilities like Riker's Island and "The Tombs," a Manhattan detention center. Lea regularly hosted gatherings to hear from individuals claiming to channel higher knowledge from the spiritual world, and invited me to attend healing circles to help the deceased, still attached to the physical world, move forward. One of my peers in this work was a woman named Jane who had attended the Garden City Waldorf School from kindergarten through grade 12. At that time, I made a mental note: If I ever have children, they will attend a Waldorf school.

Carol's work was more firmly planted in three areas of study: Esoteric Christianity, Agni Yoga, and the Kabbalah. As I engaged in study, I came across the work of Rudolf Steiner and purchased a copy of *Knowledge of the Higher Worlds*. As a young student of Western esoteric studies, I was familiar with concepts such as karma and reincarnation through theosophy and Eastern studies before I encountered anthroposophy.

Over the next several years, I was drawn to work in social services. At age 27, I began working for a nonprofit in Times Square that provided shelter and services to victims of domestic violence. I was in charge of opening a new safe house in Harlem, intaking new clients, and running support groups. My drive to spend my time in spiritual study and direct service to people in need took precedence over my identity as an artist. I had the opportunity to travel to Brazil to learn about traditional forms of healing, and to visit sacred sites in the western United States with a partner who was studying shamanism. I also traveled to Indonesia to experience Balinese culture and healing arts, and stayed in a Gandhian ashram.

Out of my work with Carol Parrish, I was ordained just before my 30th birthday. I continued to balance my own spiritual study with direct service work. When I moved to Minneapolis at age 30 in 1989, I first worked in a residential setting for troubled young girls, and later in a residential treatment center for young male offenders.

As I listened to the stories and family histories of these young people, the pattern of pain so often passed from one generation to another was starkly evident. These experiences highlighted questions I held about nature versus nurture and fate versus free will. How does one individual successfully access their soul forces to overcome or transform painful experiences to write their own story while others do not? How does a human being develop the consciousness and self-awareness to make real choices out of freedom? What intervention or support is helpful? These questions occupied my thinking as I sought to bridge what I understood as spiritual truths with the realities of human existence. I believed in karma and reincarnation and the power of the individual spirit—and viewed the experience of life as an opportunity for learning and growth. I also recognized that accessing our free will and transforming trauma are enormous tasks.

I took a break from the intense work in residential treatment programs to fulfill another lifelong passion for whole foods and natural food co-ops. I became the marketing and member services coordinator of a local co-op and worked there for several years, during which time I married a fellow tai chi practitioner, purchased a home, and had my first child, Maceo. These events brought an end to a period of frequent movement since the age of 18; I had lived in Kansas, Ohio, California, Wisconsin, New York, Oklahoma, Arkansas, and Minnesota.

Up until the age of 35, much of my early life seemed to be a careful recapitulation of past experiences. I had experienced meaningful connections and associations with a number of Eastern cultures including Japan, India, Indonesia, and China. My most meaningful relationships crossed cultures and included a Jewish man from New York who'd worked with Margaret Mead and studied in a Yeshiva in Israel, a Cuban born painter who'd also studied agriculture, a Chinese man from Hong Kong who was an architect and photographer turned shaman, a woman from Mississippi who was a freedom fighter, a hospital administrator, and a fellow seeker turned Christian contemplative. I was a student of ancient wisdom and Agni Yoga, and a tai chi practitioner, married to an African American man who was a bricklayer and shared my interest in the unseen world. During the course of our marriage, he joined the Freemasons and became a priest in the Liberal Catholic Church.

Three Destiny Meetings

After the birth of my second child, Maya, I found the local Waldorf school and began to renew my interest in Steiner's work and to discover the unique social mission of Waldorf education. On my 42nd birthday, I met with Frances Kane who was born into anthroposophy and was administrator of City of Lakes Waldorf School in Minneapolis. Upon meeting, we had an immediate sense of knowing one another. I recognized our meeting as a destiny moment; Frances stood at the threshold as a sure guidepost for me to know that I had arrived at the right place. A few weeks later, I was enrolled in an introductory biography course and introduced to Steiner's indications about the 7-year life cycles. I quickly involved myself in the local foundation studies program begun several years earlier by local students of anthroposophy and eager Waldorf school parents. I began taking classes and workshops, and applied to substitute teach at City of Lakes Waldorf School.

The school was in a long-range planning process led by consultant Christopher Schaefer. I attended one envisioning session led by a CLWS board member, a foreshadowing of my future involvement, but did not meet Chris at that time. This would wait until the summer of 2007 but was also clearly destined.

By fall 2002, I was hired by Frances Kane to serve as a part-time administrative assistant at City of Lakes Waldorf School. Simultaneously, I joined the board of foundation studies (subsequently renamed the Novalis Institute), and later served as the program administrator and board chair. I had the opportunity to work with Linda Bergh, an essential member of the Twin Cities Anthroposophical Circle and a biography facilitator, attending and assisting in biography classes. Linda's friendship and wisdom quickly became an anchor as I put down my roots in the Waldorf community. In July 2006, I accepted the position of administrative director—and the work that I had come here to do with all my heart began.

In 2007, I joined the 3-year program in Waldorf School Administration and Community Development at Sunbridge College. It was here, and through Chris, that the depth of Steiner's work and its applications in the world became alive for me. I recall being enthralled when Chris would speak; I relished the time at the end of the day where we would read a Steiner lecture and discuss inner development. Steiner's lectures "Brotherhood and the Struggle for Existence" and "The Social and Anti-social Forces in the Human Being" provided new depths of understanding with regard to the state of our world and our collective evolutionary journey. At last, I had found a profession that was a synthesis of my three primary interests and in complete alignment with my own spiritual path, weaving together my keen interest in social life and social questions, artistic expression, and inner development. My encounter with

Waldorf education was a culmination, a beginning, and an unparalleled gift; the three essential threads of my life were perfectly woven together in my work at the Waldorf school.

Years later, after establishing myself in my new role as a Waldorf school administrator, I had the privilege of working with Chris again as well as other colleagues in the redevelopment of the administrative course which led to the forming of Leading with Spirit. This work, along with serving as an Association of Waldorf Schools of North America (AWSNA) delegate and attending regional and continental conferences, served to strengthen my focus on the broader purpose of Waldorf education. I have worked over the past 20 years to assist others in experiencing the depth, breadth and purpose to be found in work within Waldorf schools in support of holistic human development and social renewal.

The Social Mission of Waldorf Education

Waldorf education was born out of a time of shock, grief, disruption and chaos following World War I—with the hope and intention that educating children in a new way would support social healing and renewal. As we enter the second 99-year period of Waldorf education, the relevance and potency of the pedagogy and its spiritual underpinnings only continues to grow.

Educating children to be whole people, and to breathe, work in collaboration with one another, and feel themselves as a part of a whole, are essential for our future. Young people today suffer from anxiety and mental health challenges, so much more than in 1919 when the first Waldorf school was founded, in part due to the increase of antisocial forces expressed through the rise of technology and social media. Children are often more isolated at home and in their neighborhoods. Parents and children spend substantial time on electronic devices and screens, undermining the ease and strength of social connections, and the child's relationship to nature. The slow Waldorf approach to academic instruction, lack of technology use in classrooms, emphasis on daily, weekly, and yearly rhythms aligned with planetary and cosmic cycles, integration of the arts, and commitment to play and time outdoors all serve to establish and maintain wellbeing, health, and balance within children.

The social environment in a Waldorf school is an intentional antidote to the antisocial forces at work within us, and within the world. Waldorf education supports individuation while also directly building the social capabilities of students, and consciously creating an awareness and appreciation for what it means to be in community. Students who travel as a class together from first through eighth grade form incredible bonds that help to inform their social experience throughout their lifetime. Close relationships to their class teacher and other faculty and staff instill in students a sense of their own intrinsic value; students move on to other experiences and educational environments with an assumption that they matter, and gain the capacity to connect with others across a wide spectrum of mutual interests.

The communal nature of an educational environment where "everybody does everything together" provides a rich body of shared experience, and promotes compassion, tolerance, and unity. Relationships with classmates provide a strong foundation for collaborative and connected social experiences through the countless opportunities they have to work and play together, solve problems, perform plays and concerts, share in successes, failures, joys, and sorrows.

For adults in the Waldorf community, the collaborative work is designed to cultivate connection, social capacities, and individual inner development. As a school administrator, daily tasks require self-examination and honest reflection, and promote the development of empathy, humility, resilience, and fortitude. Not unlike serving as a pastor of a church, the role demands true servant leadership, and a sustained and profound level of care and concern for a large group of people including children, coworkers, parents, and alumni families. In order to be worthy of imitation, and to meet each moment with equanimity, one must continually dig down to tap into one's deepest resources. As expressed in *Partnerships of*

Hope: Building Waldorf School Communities, a school community is a "social creation" and everything that happens takes place within a social context. Each Waldorf school is fertile ground for exploring what it means to be fully human.

Working in a Waldorf school, I've had the opportunity to learn about, experience, and promote the social mission of Waldorf schools. Participating in the three-year preparatory course on Waldorf Administration and Community Development at Sunbridge, and my work with Novalis Institute were essential to forming a deeper understanding of anthroposophy and of the goals of Waldorf education. This profound social mission captured my heart and imagination, and has inspired me to work tirelessly on behalf of the school and the educational movement over the past 22 years.

The questions of what it means to be human, and the trajectory over time of the development of the human soul are central to Waldorf education. The mission of Waldorf education, as articulated by Steiner is to: "*Receive the children in reverence, educate them in love, and send them forth in freedom.*" The methods and pedagogy are carefully designed to allow a child to fully develop all of their capacities in order to recognize and fulfill their individual destinies. Within the school, the task of working together in collaboration within a non-hierarchical structure, and the striving to always be worthy of imitation—are essential aspects of the Waldorf school mission to actively work toward the goal of social renewal.

Embracing the long view of this evolutionary journey and working with the rise of antisocial forces in the process of human individuation—are pursuits that have been central to my own vocational journey. I continue to explore the deep soul and social questions that have been a theme in my life from my childhood through study, human encounters, work, and artistic expression. I continue to struggle to comprehend why people are willing to cause harm or resort to violence in an effort to solve problems. I wonder at the persistent power of fear and ignorance to provide the basis for human cruelty and greed even in the face of disastrous results. I continue to look toward pathways to support myself and others in aligning with a higher purpose, centered in an understanding of, and harmony with, divine cosmic forces. Through observation, spiritual study, service, and life experience, I ponder the essential role of human relationships as a crucible in the developmental journey of the individual human soul.

> When out of world-wide spaces,
> The sun speaks to the human mind,
> And gladness from the depths of soul
> Becomes, in seeing, one with light
> Then rising from the sheath of self,
> Thoughts soar to distances of space
> And dimly bind
> The human being to the spirit's life.*

* Rudolf Steiner, *Calendar of the Soul,* week 1.

Understanding East and West: Anthropsophy and Social Reform

Chiaki Uchiyama

Born and raised in Yokohama, Japan—a vibrant port city just outside Tokyo—I was immersed in a predominantly monocultural and monolingual environment, where individuals were nurtured and educated to serve the collective: family, community, society, and country. In this culture, it was rare for people to be addressed by their first names; instead, they were often referred to by their family names or by their roles, such as "so-and-so's wife" or "so-and-so's mother." It was an unspoken expectation that the concept of "I" existed solely for the benefit of "we." A well-known Japanese adage, "The nail that sticks out will be hammered down," encapsulates this cultural ethos, where individuality was often equated with selfishness, and those who deviated from societal norms risked isolation.

Karma and reincarnation were not concepts I had to seek out—they were embedded in the worldview I grew up with. The understanding that every thought, feeling, and action inevitably returns to its source shaped our moral framework, emphasizing responsibility not just in this life but across lifetimes. Within this cultural fabric, morality was woven into the flow of existence itself, spanning many incarnations as well as the hereditary lineage of seven generations.

A life-altering event occurred when my third child, Kengo, died from sudden infant death syndrome at just two months old. This tragedy shattered everything I thought I understood about life, death, and destiny. Though I had grown up with the concept of karma, I struggled to find solace in it. Why had this happened? What meaning could there be in a life that lasted only two months? What was being asked of me in receiving and then losing this precious soul?

These questions extended beyond the conformity of Japanese society and its social norms. Because this experience was deeply personal, my search for answers became an intimate, solitary journey—one that no one else could fully comprehend. In my grief, spirituality became a path of individuality and self-actualization. Seeking clarity, I turned to Buddhist and Shinto traditions, meditation, prayers, and many other spiritual teachings, yearning for a deeper truth—one that could guide me in forging a direct connection to spiritual reality and the soul of my departed child.

In retrospect, I never fully grasped the depth of the imprint of Japanese culture on my being until I moved to the United States as a young mother of two children—then three and five years old—just a year after the profound loss of my third child. Uprooted from the familiar and immersed in a new cultural landscape, I found myself reflecting more deeply on the traditions, values, and ways of being that had shaped me.

Soon after my arrival, destiny led me to enroll my children in a Waldorf kindergarten. This decision, seemingly simple at the time, became a pivotal turning point. Two years later, I was invited to teach Japanese culture at a small Waldorf school, an opportunity that allowed me to share my heritage while simultaneously exploring new realms of education and human development.

As I delved deeper into teaching at the Waldorf school, I was drawn to anthroposophy not merely as a philosophy but as a lived experience—through eurythmy, Werbeck singing, astrosophy, lyre playing, and spatial dynamics. These practices gradually unveiled the intricate, living interconnectedness between nature, the cosmos, and human existence. What once seemed like separate domains converged into a profound journey of self-discovery and transformation.

Teaching Japanese to American students allowed me to see my own culture through a new lens. One particularly striking moment occurred while teaching brush calligraphy to a fourth-grade class. As I demonstrated how to write the character for "one," I painted a single, deliberate stroke at the center of the paper, leaving "living" space around it. To my surprise, the students instinctively filled the page with many more marks. While I had expected them to embrace the simplicity and spaciousness of the character, they seemed compelled to occupy every part of the paper. For them, these marks were personal expressions—statements of their presence, as if each stroke declared, "Here I am." In contrast, in Japanese tradition, writing is not merely a mark but an identifier, a gesture that initiates movement within the surrounding space. This contrast revealed a deeper cultural divergence in how we relate to figure, ground, personal identification, and self-expression.

Having spent nearly equal parts of my life in Japan and the United States, and speaking both languages daily, I have come to embody the intersection of these two cultural paradigms. Additionally, as my spiritual quest—guided by my intimate companion on the other side of the threshold—has unfolded over the same period, my consciousness has developed in three paradigms: Japanese, American, and the world of the dead.

In Japan, I experienced a culture where collective harmony takes precedence over individual desires, fostering a deep sense of respect and responsibility. This perspective is profoundly shaped by Shintoism, which teaches an intimate relationship with nature's deities—every tree, mountain, river, wind, stone, geographic location, and direction is seen as the embodiment of a god or goddess. Surrounded by these divine presences, humans are guided to live with reverence and gratitude.

Buddhism further shapes this worldview with its core principles of karma and reincarnation. Life is seen as an illusion (*maya*), and the purpose of incarnation is to detach from worldly attachments, and resolve karmic debts from past lives through following the Eightfold Path and the Middle Path. Through this practice, one strives to transcend negative emotions and attachments, ultimately aspiring to reach the stage of a Bodhisattva on the path to Nirvana.

What I appreciate about Japanese culture is its perception of selfless and kind moral actions as both aesthetic and noble. This sense of beauty, interwoven with daily life, permeates the social fabric. Working in harmony with others is a prerequisite for being a moral member of society; however, individuality is not only discouraged but sometimes viewed as an undesirable way of being. As a result, many people live according to expectations, responsibilities, and social ideals rather than personal freedom. This tension between obligation and self-expression leaves many struggling to find meaning in their lives.

In contrast to collectivist cultures that prioritize communal duty and social harmony, the perspective in the USA encourages individuals to seek fulfillment on their own terms, viewing organizations and society as resources rather than systems of control. Rooted in ideals of self-determination, the culture of the USA places great emphasis on individual agency, allowing people to define their own paths toward success, happiness, and meaning. Within this framework, individuals from diverse backgrounds actively navigate ways to coexist while asserting their own sense of justice, self-expression, and personal actualization.

The pursuit of freedom—whether in speech, religion, or lifestyle choices—is deeply embedded in the ethos of the United States, with democracy serving as both a guiding principle and a mechanism for resolving conflicts and striving for social harmony. Unlike cultures that emphasize collective duty, Americans are educated to question authority, challenge societal norms, and advocate for change based on personal convictions. This dynamic fosters innovation, social progress, and an ever-evolving understanding of human rights. The concept of the "American Dream" symbolizes the nation's enduring promise: that with determination and effort, individuals can achieve success and shape their own destinies.

While this self-determination fosters creativity, personal agency, and individuation, it can also lead to fragmentation. Individuals may become deeply invested in their own opinions and interests, sometimes at the expense of collective ideals and the common good. The challenge, then, lies in balancing the pursuit of personal fulfillment with a shared sense of responsibility—a task made even more complex by the nation's vast cultural, economic, and ideological diversity.

Spirituality in the United States is similarly diverse, with a wide spectrum of religious and philosophical traditions coexisting under the principle of religious freedom. However, this plurality can also lead to sectarianism, as communities seek to preserve their beliefs and traditions, sometimes at the cost of interfaith dialogue and broader societal cohesion. The tension between religious pluralism and exclusivity reflects the broader challenge of fostering unity while honoring individual and group identities.

Straddling these three worlds—Japanese (Far East), American (Far West), and Spiritual (Above)—I recognize the strengths, beauty, challenges, and suffering within each. Standing firmly on the Earth (Below) at the intersection of these where all humans can find a spiritual origin. Rudolf Steiner's worldview continues to give me hope for this possibility and has been the core motivation behind my study of anthroposophy since 1997. His vision of an ideal community as a "mirror of each human soul" represents a spiritual reality—one that remains distant from the current structures of both Japanese and American societies. Yet, it has become my inner goal and guiding aspiration in working with individuals, organizations, and the outer world.

Anthroposophy fully embraces reincarnation and karma, as well as an understanding of etheric formative forces, nature spirits, and elementals—all of which have provided me with a profound sense of comfort and a sense of belonging. It also introduced me to esoteric Christianity, the Mystery of Golgotha, and the Christ impulse—teachings that reveal true individual freedom not as the mere pursuit of personal desires but as the alignment of one's life with a higher spiritual purpose.

Steiner's statement in *The Philosophy of Freedom*, "A moral misunderstanding, a clash between men who are morally free, is out of the question," resonated deeply within me. This path calls for carrying one's own cross, undergoing the death of the earthly self, and experiencing resurrection into the wisdom of oneness with the Spirit—an understanding I had not encountered elsewhere.

Through anthroposophy, I have learned to stand at the center—between East and West, above and below—guided by an inner compass attuned to the origin of these forces. This awakening has illuminated my soul's higher destiny on Earth, offering both clarity and direction in my striving to serve the other. A true soul force, at the heart level, has awakened.

Yet, I must acknowledge that the vast, empty space in which I stand—between all things—can be a lonely place. This deep loneliness shatters dreams, expectations, material security, and earthly identities. It is a space unnoticed, even denied by contemporary people at any cost. And yet, it quietly awaits discovery.

Only after journeying through the inner trials of resistance—fear, hatred, anxiety, doubt, and envy—did I begin to confront that void. And in that silence, my baby Kengo started whispering his presence. He comforted me, grounding me in a place I had once feared. This discovery was nothing like what I had imagined the origin of the soul to be. In fact, it was the opposite—I had found my seat for the soul, a place where, detached from material lust, soul and spirit are most active—the place where everything begins to germinate.

Social Challenges of East and West

From this standpoint, all social challenges arise from a lack of knowledge—an unawareness of the other side of the void at the center: a lack of understanding of the East from the Western perspective, and an inability to perceive the spirit from the vantage point of the material.

Challenge in the Far East: Hollowed-out National Identities and Lost Spiritual Wisdom

In Japan, the concept of "we" takes precedence over the development of "I," fostering a profound sense of collective responsibility and social harmony. Conversely, the development of the astral body—often manifested as heightened self-interest, vanity, emotional turbulence, and a potential disconnect from the collective during adolescence—is seen as detrimental to the etheric harmony of society. As a result, it is consciously tempered and discouraged, in alignment with societal expectations. This intentional guidance ensures that etheric cohesion remains intact, and respect for the interconnected whole is upheld. Because of this strong etheric ambiance and the suppression of astral forces, individuals' souls often merge with societal expectations, making it difficult to distinguish between personal will and collective will.

The Meiji Restoration marked a pivotal moment in Japan's history, as the influx of Western culture, technology, and scientific consciousness reshaped the nation. The Japanese people assimilated these new impulses with curiosity and minimal resistance, as their astral sheath of national identity had historically been undermined.

After World War II, Japan embraced Western intellect—rooted in natural science, binary and hierarchical structures, and information-based education. Without a well-defined astral boundary to provide resistance and protection, Japan remained vulnerable—much like children absorbing external influences before their astral bodies fully developed. This openness left Japan susceptible to external forces, leading to the gradual erosion of its cultural identity, spirituality, and intrinsic self-worth. The deeply rooted Japanese wisdom, tied to spirituality and animism, was gradually overshadowed by Western intellectual materialism, often without full awareness of the consequences.

Today, Japan faces a profound crisis of meaning and spiritual disconnection. The leading cause of death among individuals aged 10 to 45 is suicide—an anomaly among G7 countries. The loss of purpose among younger and middle-aged individuals reflects a deeper societal issue. Despite material abundance and an improved standard of living, pervasive low self-esteem and fundamental self-doubt push children into an early intellectual education, a highly competitive academic system, and a culture of elitism. This relentless pressure leaves little room for self-fulfillment and the realization of one's inner calling.

Challenges in the West: The Lack of Inner Freedom and the Desire to Conquer the Other

Rudolf Steiner's concept of moral intuition and freedom suggests that a truly free individual does not impose their personal convictions on others but acts from an inner moral compass that recognizes and respects the sovereignty of others. However, in the Western world, moral freedom is often lacking—not because people lack opinions or ethical standards, but because they impose these standards upon others as absolute truths. This results in ideological conflicts, power struggles, and societal polarization.

The trajectory of Western history, especially from the Age of Exploration onward, has been marked by the conquest of the unknown—not just in a physical sense (territories, lands, resources) but also in intellectual, economic, and political spheres. The imposition of Western systems of thought, governance, and morality upon indigenous cultures, spiritual traditions, and social structures exemplifies this tendency. The belief that certain values or ways of thinking are universally "right" and must be applied to all has fueled colonialism, capitalism, and modern forms of cultural imperialism.

Astral Body, Sentient Soul, and Intellectual Soul Development and Social Fragmentation

In anthroposophy, the astral body is linked with sympathies and antipathies, the separation between self and other, and the capacity to follow one's instincts, impulses, and desires. In the Western world, the strong development of the astral body, in tandem with the sentient soul and intellectual soul, has contributed to a culture of individualism, personal ambition, and intellectual achievement. While these qualities have led to extraordinary advancements in science, philosophy, and the arts, they have also fostered a fragmented social fabric, where the sense of interconnectedness and communal wellbeing is often secondary to personal success.

This fragmentation, particularly in a country as diverse as the United States, exacerbates the challenge of cultivating a sense of collective responsibility. With a heightened emphasis on personal autonomy, it becomes harder to bridge the gaps between differing groups, ideologies, and backgrounds. The absence of shared values and common understanding leads to a growing alienation among individuals, hindering their ability to engage in compassionate dialogue. The strength of a society lies in its ability to weave together its many threads, but when these threads become too stretched apart by personal interests and ideological divides, it undermines the social fabric. To address this, there needs to be a concerted effort to cultivate the social aspects of the consciousness soul–empathy, mutual respect, self-reflection, and a greater sense of interconnectedness among people, regardless of their differences.

A Path Forward: Integrating Opposing Forces

Both Japanese and US tendencies present challenges and imbalances. While Japan's struggle lies in the suppression of the self within collective norms, the United States issue is an excess of individuation that fractures societal cohesion. The integration of these forces—recognizing the value of both individual autonomy and communal harmony—can serve as a path toward a more balanced and humane future.

The Underlying Influence of Materialism

The greatest impulse brought to the world by the fifth post-Atlantean (Western European) cultural epoch is a quest for individuality, freedom, and love, as well as the development of intellectual, scientific, and matter-centered worldviews. In *Ancient Myths and the New Isis Mystery*, Steiner contrasts this epoch with the Egyptian cultural epoch, stating: "The world picture of Copernicus,

Galileo, and Kepler is a luciferic construction." He elaborates that Lucifer seeks to sever morality—and all moral forces—from our understanding of reality, allowing only the laws of natural necessity to dominate our perception of the external world, reducing it to purely mechanical necessity (p. 172).

Steiner's caution aligns with the Japanese creation myth rooted in Shintoism. According to this myth, when primal Spirit and Matter unite to give birth to the deities of nature, Spirit must initiate the movement for Matter to create a harmonious and living world. However, if Matter initiates the movement, negative forces take hold, leading to the world's decline, chaos, and ultimate death.

In the modern scientific paradigm, spiritually rich cultures—once integral to nurturing both the Earth and humanity—have not only been dismissed and marginalized but also systematically undermined, destroyed, and replaced through proselytization.

This quote from Steiner beautifully emphasizes the spiritual task of our time: "Isis/Sophia was killed by Lucifer. The task of our age is to restore Imagination, Inspiration, and Intuition to human consciousness through an understanding of the Mystery of Golgotha." Steiner concludes that lecture by stating: "We should learn to say to ourselves: If we can manage to work together in love on the great tasks, then, and only then, do we understand Christ."

This principle is central to addressing the current challenges of social reformation.

Practical Application of Social Reform in Our Daily Lives: Social Renewal and the Path to Unity

True social renewal begins when each of us, as students of anthroposophy, takes even the smallest step toward fostering unity in human relationships by seeking to harmonize the material/spiritual, the individual/collective, past/future, and intellectual/kinesthetic, through cultivating our faculties of imagination, inspiration, and intuition (Isis/Sophia).

In Waldorf schools, tensions, misunderstandings, and gaps in collaboration among various operational roles—faculty and administration, faculty and board, faculty and parents, board and administration, and even among departments—are commonly known. These challenges often stem from mechanized, intellectualized (ahrimanic) assumptions that veil our ability to perceive the living whole, leading to alienation and dehumanization among colleagues.

When individuals become fixed in hierarchical ways of thinking, they may unconsciously elevate their own perspectives above others, creating division and eroding trust. This tendency—deeply ingrained in modern intellectual life—can lead to unnecessary conflict and pain within the community.

When disconnection occurs, it is essential to pause and reflect on how individuals may begin reacting from a "fight or flight" or "me vs. others" mindset, losing sight of the collective whole and reinforcing cycles of ideological division. This tendency may arise from an overreliance on Western intellectual frameworks, which often prioritize hierarchical structures and binary thinking.

The remedy lies in integrating Eastern harmony—fostering a sense of "we" under a shared aspiration that honors the hosting of Isis/Sophia within the space. This requires compassionate and selfless listening, releasing attachment to personal opinions, and creating a central vessel—a "third space"—within the binary, allowing the guiding spirit to enter and bring unity. It is also essential to examine the organization's structure to ensure it fosters collaboration and provides space for the spirit to nurture the process.

Transformational Leadership and Collaboration

At the heart of my daily work as a school director in a Waldorf school in the United States lies the ongoing effort to dissolve moral, ideological, cultural, and relational tensions, fostering collaboration across all levels of the school's operations. Leadership, in this sense, is not about enforcing authority or managing people from a hierarchical position but about creating an environment where individuals feel seen, valued, and empowered to contribute meaningfully, regardless of their origin or background.

This collaborative culture is not built overnight; it requires an ongoing commitment to mutual understanding and trust. Such trust is not merely an abstract ideal but is actively cultivated through shared experiences, transparent decision-making, and the continuous alignment of our actions with the school's mission and values. It emerges when individuals recognize that they are working toward a common purpose, one that transcends personal differences and unites us in service to the wellbeing of the students, faculty, and broader school community.

Effective communication is at the core of this work. Creating a culture of inclusive dialogue—where every voice is invited to speak and is genuinely heard—allows tensions to be addressed with openness and care. Thoughtful, intentional exchanges rooted in shared purpose ensure that collaboration is not merely procedural but a lived experience. This approach fosters a deep sense of responsibility and accountability, where each individual understands their role and feels a true connection to the larger whole, recognizing how their contributions shape and sustain the community.

Beyond its practical implications, this work has a deeper dimension. When individuals engage in meaningful collaboration, they are not just performing tasks; they are on a path of inner development. In striving toward harmonious cooperation, each person finds opportunities for personal growth, self-awareness, and even spiritual nourishment. When leadership is exercised with this awareness, it transforms the workplace into a living organism, where relationships are not merely functional but infused with purpose and a sense of belonging.

By embracing this vision of leadership, the school becomes more than an institution—it becomes a space where human potential is nurtured, where both students and adults are engaged in a process of becoming. It ensures that our collective purpose is not just upheld in principle but actively embodied in our daily interactions, sustaining a school culture that is both vibrant and deeply fulfilling for all involved.

Lifting the Veil of Anthroposophia

Anthroposophy is not a doctrine to be intellectually preached by those in positions of authority, nor should it be confined to abstract discourse. Rather, it is a living path of inner development—one that must be discovered and cultivated within each human soul on earth. True anthroposophy arises through an individual's striving for self-knowledge, ethical action, and spiritual insight—gained not in isolation, but *through working together.* It is an awakening of will that emerges from within, rather than being imposed from the outside.

Anthroposophy does not belong to any single culture, geography, or tradition. While its modern expression took shape in the West, its essence transcends cultural boundaries, drawing from the universal human experience. The wisdom of the East, with its profound understanding of interconnectedness, altruism, karma, and reincarnation, harmonizes with the Western impulse for individuality and intellectual clarity. Through this synthesis—where the "I" and the "We" are held in balance, and love and freedom emerge—the deeper mission of anthroposophy can truly unfold.

For this reason, anthroposophical organizations must strive toward unity—not through rigid conformity, but through a shared commitment to the spiritual ideals at their foundation. This applies to all anthroposophical institutions, including but not limited to the Anthroposophical Society, the School of Spiritual Science, and Waldorf schools. When these institutions become fragmented—whether through ideological division, moral misunderstanding, or personal attachment to power—they risk falling into luciferic temptation, weakening the very soul forces that sustain their true mission. Conversely, when anthroposophical organizations uphold this task, their collective harmony can pulsate as a heart center, radiating its influence into the world.

Now is the time to pause, step beyond the confines of our habitual perspectives, and to see our organizations, communities, and initiatives not as isolated entities but as interconnected expressions of a greater whole. By shifting our gaze in all directions—across disciplines, cultures, and spiritual traditions—we may find the path forward illuminated not by individual ambition but by higher wisdom seeking to manifest through us, through which Steiner's vision of an ideal community as a "mirror of each human soul" can be achieved.

> Love is higher than opinion. If people love one another the most varied opinions can be reconciled—thus one of the most important tasks for humankind today and in the future is that we should learn to live together and understand one another. If this human fellowship is not achieved, all talk of development is empty. (Rudolf Steiner, *Founding a Science of the Spirit*, Sept. 1, 1906)

Waldorf High School Education and Social Health

Paul Gierlach

PART I

There are many ways to understand and teach history. I was a humanities and class teacher in Waldorf schools for over forty years and therefore have been engaged with social issues for at least that long. Yet, I was not an activist, as the word is usually understood. One of my many goals as a teacher was to socialize the students, in the best sense of course: that is, to prepare each one to be an active and informed individual in a community of other individuals.

I had to identify and respond to the students' readiness to take up their destinies. This implies that we teachers ready ourselves, and that we identify the many levels of readiness that exist in the students who are in front of us. This short essay attempts to show how this can be done.

I wrote the first part of this article in outline form so as to draw attention to these relationships in an overt way. Every entry could be the starting point of a more comprehensive treatment because each is, in fact, a distillation of four decades of classroom activity. I make no attempt to prove the statements; there is, rather, an attempt to treat both the individual and the society as two threads that weave their way daily through four years of high school activity. Every comment has a timely, phenomenological foundation.

Every comment echoes the wisdom of Shakespeare's advice, through Hamlet, that questions of destiny *are* difficult to resolve, but one certainty does exist: "the readiness is all" (*Hamlet* V, ii).

Cosmic Rhythm

- *Human activity in an earthly world is the domain of history teaching.* In that, Waldorf pedagogy is conventional.
- We do have a specific view of the nature of the human being which differs from that of most contemporary historians.
- A human being is a spiritual being who has taken up the task and joy of being a human being on Earth, with the goal of returning to the spiritual source, the heavens if you like, as quite different from other spiritual beings who have not had the experiences of incarnation.
- Whereas conventional history considers the tool-making capacity of early humans as primary to its evolution, Waldorf exploration of history more broadly sees that this created tool is, for the present and to assure a future, the human being! (*An Outline of Esoteric Science,* p. 29)
- Individuals create social forms on Earth out of their spiritual and earthy heritage.
- The task is to be free—other spiritual beings are not; the goal is to incarnate love into the self, the species, the destiny events that are otherwise called history. The Earth itself has a destiny: to be the cosmos of love that is grown from the cosmos of wisdom (*An Outline of Esoteric Science*, p. 397.)

Such tasks and goals are lifelong; education, at its heart, helps us ready ourselves to take up our destinies.

Waldorf Pedagogy as a Model of Readiness

We can only engage with something we know or have a deeper relationship with, otherwise it passes us by.

- Readiness is implied in the word *capacity.* And it is well known that Waldorf curriculum and pedagogy (way of teaching the curriculum) are, at heart, meant to lead students to uncover and develop capacities. This "age-appropriate" education is a foundational concept.
- In effect, *age-appropriate education* allows the spirit, the individuality of a being, to incarnate into its physical vessels: the physical body, etheric body, astral body, and ego.

- These bodies are born rhythmically in the human being: physical body, birth—7; etheric body, 7—14; astral body, 14—21; ego (organization) 21—beyond.
- In the first birth, we recognize the child; in the second, youth; in the third, adolescence; in the fourth and beyond, the adult.

We can see that the spirit proceeds persistently; the soul accepts the spirit rhythmically. We must look more deeply into the "nature" of this spirit incarnation in a phenomenological way: *Incarnation and the 7-year rhythm:*

- All newborns who are healthy incarnate with the same rhythm:
    - Birth–age 1: stand upright and walk; defy gravity of Earth
    - Birth–age 2: sounds are formed into words and sentences
    - Birth–age 3: the child says "I"
- This 3-year change is the first noticeable incision into life; it is followed by
- the 5-year change, in which the child actually begins to explore the world.

We can see that the 7-year soul rhythm is divided into three periods, or thirds. This rhythm of thirds is repeated in the second 7-year rhythm, youth:

- The 9-year change finds the child bereft of its feeling of a spiritual home.
- The 12-year change again sees the child reaching out to know the world.

This rhythm of thirds is repeatable in the adolescent world:

- The 16-year change is an opportunity to see one's own self.
- The 18-year change is a reaching out: graduation from high school.

And so:

- We can say: first third, spirit approaches the human being from outside: Willing
- We can say: second third, spirit weaves in the soul: Feeling
- We can see: third third, spirit leads human being into the world: Thinking

We recognize this active spirit as the individuality forming the different bodies. Birth of the different bodies in the seven-year rhythm is not a metaphor but an observable fact, as every teacher and parent knows.

The rhythm of thirds puts us in mind of our own threefold nature: body, soul, spirit *and its reflection in* the soul: thinking, feeling, willing *and its residence in* our human bodies as the nerve-sense system, heart-lung system, metabolic-limb system. Every human being manifests in this threefoldness. Capacities are discovered and then nurtured in these manifestations when we teach in an age-appropriate way.

Grade School

In the grade school, the newly birthed etheric body is our workspace:

- For the first three grades or so (9-year change), we teachers rein in the wills of the children and regale them with fairy tales from around the globe, animal tales, and tales from the Old Testament.
- In the second third, up to grade 6, we encourage a feeling of connection with the many peoples of the world who built individual and family dwellings out of the earth's materials; we include the history teaching as well, especially of the ancient and Greek civilizations in the old and new world.
- In the third third, the discoveries that lead to our modern times—be they geographical, cultural, political, economic—are introduced. We bring the students closer to the time in which they live because their own astral body has forsaken its quiet gestation and in this last third makes itself felt.

High School

Students need to leave the protection of the grade school and encounter the disciplines of the high school. Usually, they roar into the high school. The *astral body's* birth, growth, and nurturing constitute the workplace of the high school curriculum and teachers.

Different structures in the high school support the forming of this newly born astrality.

There are many consequent differences between the grade school teaching and that done in the high school. I will mention those that are particularly important for the creation of a healthy relationship between the nature of individuals and the society created by and for them. Being a history teacher, I will confine my pedagogical comments to that sphere.

Fourfold Environment

High school teachers rely on their understanding of the fourfold human being. The comprehension of the human being as body, soul, and spirit is more aptly and precisely seen as fourfold: *body* is parsed into the physical body and the etheric body; *soul* is discoverable in its astrality; and *spirit* is still mysteriously spirit in these years.

> Each high-school year *approximately accommodates* two grade-school years:
>
> 9: grades 1 and 2
> 10: grades 3 and 4
> 11: grades 5 and 6
> 12: grades 7 and 8.

When we look at the fourfold human being, we see the incarnation of the individuality and its manifestation in the personality of the adolescent. Each of the four years supports this incarnation:

> Grade 9, the physical body
> Grade 10, the etheric
> Grade 11, the astral
> Grade 12, the ego.

Essentially, we history teachers tell the tale of the relationship of the individual and society within the wide world of this paradigm. It is not possible to overvalue the importance of this approach, both as a concept and in its practical expression. Throughout our time on earth, we human beings create out of this fourfold incarnation. History allows us to mimic in our thoughts the deeds we have done.

High School Curriculum

We will look first at the presentation of "society" in high school. Grade 9 history curriculum is a repetition of grade 8. Why?

- Grade-school students were taught to create pictures in their minds (and notebooks) of the historical events and characters of the hundreds of stories that were told; they were expected to create these pictures out of their feelings.
- In grade 9, we teach the students to think *about* those pictures!
- We also help them learn to think *through* the pictures.
- For example, the grade 8 students can see the American Revolution as epochal and understand certain broad reasons that explain it; the grade 9 student will see more clearly what epochal means and what a revolution is.

In this way, grade 9 readies the students to move into the more conscious attempt to understand themselves and their worlds.

- They are readied in the early grades to begin to meet their deeper (astral) selves in the high school. *They think about their own pictures.* We can work with the thinking facility of the students, which is our given task as high-school teachers, when preparation is made and capacities are recognizable.
- As the students look more deeply into revolutions, they can be led beyond the few that were covered in grade 8—usually the French and Russian—and begin to make distinctions that characterize those in Haiti, Cuba, China, and many others.
- All history blocks in grade 9 lead students into their own thinking.

Thus, we can see that grade 9 is the world of the physical body.

The grade-10 curriculum offers its own particular challenge and opportunities.

- We begin our march to the present (modern times) by moving from East to West, in ancient India and Persia, historical Mesopotamia and Egypt, up to the Greeks and all they signify for the West.
- Changes of consciousness are supported by the ways people arrange themselves. Family is the smallest social unit: it expands into extended families, clans, tribes, nations that take up expanding residences in villages, towns, cities, city-states that are then gathered into empires.
- A consciousness that is more aligned with the spiritual-soul aspect of a human being than its more earthy part, that is, an awareness of spirit in nature and in the self is noted. Owen Barfield calls it "participatory" because our thinking is not quite "ours" yet.
- It merges with the phenomenon; it receives its thoughts from the gods.
- It becomes, over time and with the early Greeks, an awareness that questions the presence of the gods, as Odysseus questions the advice of Athena.
- Grade 10 offers us all a picture of the Sentient Soul epoch.

Thus, we can see that grade 10 is the world of the ether body.

The grade-11 curriculum pictures the world of the astral body.

- Historical manifestation of this lies in the emergence of the Romans on the scene and their unlimited contributions to the civilization we recognize as ours. A self-aware individual, a citizen, is transplanted into the Western world. Law is devised by conflict of diverse human needs. Engineering re-faces nature. Civilizations rise; they fall; in the East, they last an additional 1,000 years!
- Peoples with widely different customs migrate or conquer—they mingle and struggle with new peoples and occupy large tracts of lands that they will eventually govern as duchies, nations, and empires.

- Peoples continue—or they don't.
- Not only in Europe but also in the East and Far East they struggle with each other and with different modes of understanding.
- Different religions arise and vie for dominance and spatial expansion.

Where do we end our history rendering in grade 11 is an important question: can we speak of the

- Reformation with its remodeling of Christianity?
- Renaissance with its recognition of an awakening Individual presence in himself and in society?
- Enlightenment whose name carries its message?
- Age of Reason, which, like the Ring of Sauron, controls all rings? Even into the East?

There is no end to questions for grade 11 as it is the world of the astral body.

The grade-12 curriculum is the domain of the ego.

- The full force of issues of our times, expressed in concepts and personal experiences—often traumas—of race, gender, colonialization of thought and nationalisms, patriarchy of vision and power, all the other social and economic isms, and much more, come to the fore.
- For we reach modern times in our narrative. That is, we continue the narrative that was begun in grade 11. This is no surprise, for the ego is very much attached to the astral body in our times.
- The individual has arrived in the constructed world of ideas, boundaries, and massive inequities of our present age.
- If we teachers are successful, the student is no longer prone to see the world outside themselves as something so different from their selves that there is no connection.
- There is hope that the students can operate in the societal forms they are graduating into; the world lives inside them.

I am not sure that any history teacher actually ever finishes teaching grade 12. Just like no parent actually finishes a relationship with their children. That being said, we do send them out into the world:

- They are 18—of course they go out into the world. So says the cosmic rule of thirds. They are nearing the birth of the ego. (This is not the domain of high-school teachers as faculty members of a school; at the same time, it is rewarding when a student or two returns from wherever they have gone after graduation and wants to share what they have done.)
- They are enthusiastic, for they are, more or less, ready.
- They are still interested in the world around them, if we teachers and parents have done our job. This world, after all, is also inside them.
- We can also feel, with justification, that history is alive to and in them: *Conscience has a voice in the narrative because the students have not been allowed to see history as something outside themselves.*

Postures of the Soul

An astute reader will question the previous short section, an outline you will remember that really deserves a book—and rightly so. We are not ready for the conclusion. We must first weave the students as individuals into the social construct of the curriculum's four-year progress. Granted, these days, so many *individuals* show up at our grade 9 threshold. Each student is an individual (these days), yet each will go through a similar pattern of self-recognition sometime in their lives.

One powerful way to relate the students to the spirit is to mimic their very own incarnation! We can (and should) teach every main lesson in a certain rhythm:

- Morning verse, which connects us to something greater than ourselves
- Artistic activity, which leads to the entire class breathing together

- Review of previous lessons, which through memory connects the past with the present.
- The lesson, which moves the very awake high-school student to the new material.
- Written work, which brings the will into play.

Every time we enact this pattern, we connect each student with their social group in a way that does not create automatons but, eventually, thoughtful individuals.

One significant way to relate the students to their own soul qualities is to meet them in the right way. Each year we meet them as someone different! For they are. Or should be.

- Grade 9: they *assert* their position or thought. No need for discussion.
- Grade 10: they *argue,* which is an advance of sorts since arguing implies more than one point of view

Grade 10 signals the first of the "adolescent thirds." The student experiences in their astral body the same "awakening" that the 3-year-old experienced by growing into their physical body and the 9-year-old experienced in their etheric body. They have the opportunity to look at themselves and see something "new," something that comes from without.

- The 3-year-old has no choice but accepts the awareness and says "I"
- The 9-year-old has no choice, though the acceptance might extend for a year or more.
- The 16-year-old has a choice and does not have to accept the challenge to look at the self and change. By living in the astral, a 16-year-old has the birthright of choice among many options.
- Our social world in the United States is littered with 10th-graders, who are resolutely and adamantly certain of their own thoughts and feelings. This phenomenon is the bane of any society's existence if the goal of that society is to create free individuals who are resolutely responsible for change and

for each other. (We will return to this phenomenon in the second part of this article.) That's why we teachers pay close attention to what follows grade 10:

- Grade 11: We offer *debate*, formally or in the lessons, so that students hear, consider, and honestly contend with the ideas of others, so that:
- Grade 12: the students can have *conversations* with their classmates, not as they did in the early grades or grade 8, but as those who are about to embark on the final third of their astral development as they go out into the world.

There is yet one more way to weave the students' inner lives with their own maturation through time (four years) and the narrative of our history lessons (circa 5,000 years and counting).

Four Questions

There are four questions that the teacher can use to weave the students into the curriculum, and vice versa. The very notion of a question suggests the intellect, the astral, which is so. But when we look at these questions as more than food for the mind, if we see them as medicaments, we can glimpse the healthy foundations of Waldorf pedagogy.

- In grade 9: I emphasize the physical and the structural element with the question: "What?"
- In grade 10: to catch the weaving, living element of the etheric, I add the question: "How?"
- In grade 11: I add the astral body's favorite question: "Why?"
- In grade 12: I meet the nature of conversations with the impulse of the mysterious: "Who?"

Now that we have found four words that capture all the teacherly activity in the high school, we can end this narrative with the feeling that we teachers—and parents—have finished our responsibility of helping the students to incarnate properly and can, therefore, send them off into the world as graduates.

We can feel that the seeds for a healthy relationship of unique individuals with other unique individuals could be the rightful foundation of social forms that are fit for our times. I truly believed that narrative. The students are ready.

PART II

I still do. But our times in the United States have changed so radically in the last dozen or so years that one wonders: Are any of us ready? A question that I hear every day from lips other than my own is: "What can I do?" I would like to speak to that question. I offer no narrative as I did in the first part, because there is no fixed narrative. Since I don't really know what form to use to express these thoughts, I will simply state them.

As the civilization I know in the United States slowly disintegrates into uncivil, primitive instinctual behavior—especially in the legal sphere out of which the United States birthed itself and in which it is dramatically, tragically dying—I realized that Hamlet's comment to Horatio, "the readiness is all," is insufficient if isolated; that actually, another comment by the initiate Shakespeare is equally operative in our consciousness soul times: "There are more things in Heaven and earth, Horatio, than are dreamt of in your philosophy" (I, 5).

This admonition is a paraphrase of the essential nature of our consciousness soul existence, for it is during this time when, once again, the spirit will make itself present as a force in our soul lives. It is our spiritual reality which seems foreign to our thinking only because our thinking in this materialistic and secular age does not readily recognize the spirit! We have as citizens created a very unhealthy society.

We have seen this incursion of the spirit when looking at the 3-, 9-, and 16-year changes: it always brought the necessary spirit into our consciousness which, according to the rhythms in the cosmos, we find again in our consciousness soul epoch. One third of the 2,100-year-time period for this epoch is 700 years. In the year

2025, we are more than 600 years into its time frame! 600 of 700. We are nearly one-third of the way into the experience of waking up again! Of saying "I" in a new way (3-year change), of feeling separated from ourselves (9-year change). Of having to make the 16-year choice to be content with one's self or be open to the worlds of others.

No wonder our times are so inexorable, so unsettling, so demanding. No wonder we cannot seem to get a rational handle on it. Our times respond to the exigencies of the spirit, and we can but recognize that to find our way to the spirit becomes a necessity. The fact that every walk of life is undergoing significant challenges is the expression of this ongoing fundamental change within which we progress to selfhood, or we don't.

It is no longer enough to be responsive to soul needs—we need to allow the spirit to enter our lives as a guide, a prod, a sense of reckoning—whatever is needed. This powerful concept of human spirituality is a force that, by definition, changes one's view of every aspect of living and dying, as well as returning for a number of lives on Earth; spirit does not die. *We need to look at our time on Earth from the point of view of the spiritual.* Thus, there is a call for a "new history." We can change our history only by changing ourselves. Are we ready for that? Really, the question is: "What can I as an individual do?"

Since it was the question that I as a teacher asked myself, every time I met a student or a colleague, it is not unfamiliar. As a Waldorf teacher my tendency is to continue to create environments in which "students" find a way to recognize the meaning in our striving.

I would like to suggest a way to inculcate the spirit into our selves and, therefore, our times. The relationship of the individual to societies is still the topic of our discourse. Our times demand that we take action in the domain of our ideas and ideals.

Analogs

I must meet my own self in whatever I do. That is a given. An analog is a rather simple yet very powerful way for us to look beneath the surface of events to see something that impels them. Just as an analogy is a sophisticated indicator of a relationship, so also are analogs reliable, yet often subtle, indications of a *force or power that causes relationships.*

When we successfully engage our thinking in an analogous manner, we find an honest way to ease the grasp of repetitive and/or fixated thinking. We meet our own intolerance. Our goal is to discover new thoughts that are as reliable as those we already use.

In the first part, we recognized ourselves as fourfold. When we explored the Waldorf history curriculum, we referred to the four high school grades that replicate the eight grade school grades; we noted the important soul moods of the students that change over the four years and the questions that encourage the students to link their own ideas and levels of consciousness—developmental stages—with the account of human activity on earth, called history. We think of child development as fourfold. It manifests in 7-year rhythms. Let us write all these categories so we can see them. We naturally write them on the horizontal and make a list.

Human Being:	Physical	Etheric	Astral	Ego
High-school grades:	9	10	11	12
Grade-school grades:	1–2	3–4	5–6	7–8
Soul moods:	assert	argue	debate	conversation
Questions:	what	how	why	who
Developmental stages:	child	youth	adolescent	adult
7-year rhythm:	birth–7	7–14	14–21	21–up

There is no end to the examples of a fourfold nature of ourselves and our world. For instance, let's add something as comprehensive as the curriculum: the world of nature.

NATURE KINGDOMS:	mineral	plant	animal	human

We can as students of anthroposophy expand this observed world to the world seen by the initiate Rudolf Steiner when he talks about cosmic evolution:

PLANETARY EVOLUTION				
PAST:	Saturn	Sun	Moon	Earth
FUTURE:	Earth	Jupiter	Venus	Vulcan

And life becomes more interesting, not solely because of the topic but also the apparent paradox that "Earth" appears in two renderings...and we sense a creative complication of the first order.

Speaking of Rudolf Steiner, and in relation to creative complication, let's add the four modes of thinking he enumerates for our cognitive advances in and beyond the material world.

COGNITION:	sensory	imagination	inspiration	intuitive

There is no benefit to simply adding more categories if we do not make something of them. That's the nature of a spirit-human whom, in the first part, we called the tool maker. Rather than tease you with a lot of questions—as I used to enjoy doing with students—let me simply assert the obvious: When we want to know something factual, we think within these "worlds" of facts. Each horizontal line can be understood as its own "world of facts."

As individuals it is very easy to be more interested in one horizontal line's world than another. For example, I was born to read and need to add the novel to the list:

Novel (fiction):	story	plot	ideas, character	author (style)

We read on the horizontal to know what we know. At the same time, we feel this fourfoldness as having its own meaning. We know these disparate categories belong together, somehow.

When we want to understand *how such a fourfoldness can exist* we must free ourselves from the literal and look at it differently. We must see our thoughts differently. There are also four columns that we can read on the vertical. So as not to interfere with your own righteous thinking, I will point out as an example that the first vertical column has a "foundational quality" to it which does not exist in the other three. What does unite them? This you can live into, using that which so characterizes our times: the free use of our own intellect.

In reading the vertical, we can make a wholeness of ourselves and our many physical, psychic, and spiritual environments. We can realize that we live in a world that is more than the literal, materialistic world of facts, figures, and conceptions based on brain-bound perceptions—that is, the horizontal.

We can, over time, become more tolerant of others who according to their destinies gravitate to other horizontal worlds than our own.

We can perhaps get a real feeling for what Rudolf Steiner calls the etheric realm, for that is the world we enter on the vertical.

Conclusion: An Image

To add even more examples of our fourfolded world would be to court a kind of redundancy, given that the point has been made. (And god knows I don't want to support the unspoken goal of AI's task which is obviously to make our very selves redundant as we are charged to lead the lives we lead.)

I want, rather, to conclude with an image and a thought. The image is artistic and reminds us of the core of Waldorf education: the arts as a formative experience.

The grid of vertical and horizontal lines did not just arise; it has a heritage that goes back to grade 4! I asked the students to make a picture of the times-tables, 2–13. We did. I expected it to be factually correct, but didn't really worry if it wasn't because, more importantly, every times-table had been walked and run and jumped numerous times. I did demand that it be *beautiful.*

In grade 10, I helped the students organize the temporal existences of seven or eight early cultures by making a timeline. They put the time frame at the top of the page, or the sides; they put the individual cultures/civilizations at the top of the page, or the sides. Too many words made the timelines very unattractive; pictures that characterized, symbolized, the different cultures were very useful. I expected the students to make beautiful timelines; I demanded that they be accurate. That is to say, *true t*o the best of their knowledge (and mine).

The picture and the timeline prepared me to see the grid in my 60s! This third iteration of such a form suggests two things to me: the sequence leads from the beautiful and the true to the third soul attribute: the *good. And I conclude on no other evidence that goodness, even in our times, will arise from this cognitive activity.*

It appears that Shakespeare does indeed speak for our age, our times, and ourselves.

As a history teacher, I entertain a premonition that arises from the form. It reminds me of the warp and woof of weaving. I think of the essential nature of the etheric as a weaving activity. I see the future as coming to us, and I expect it to be woven. Not obeyed. I am hopeful that the first half of our sojourn on Earth as spiritual beings—explained in historical narratives as Iron Age et al. and hallmarked with the mastery of the elements of the Earth—will be supplanted with the kinder and no less powerful art of weaving.

Penelope's cunning will no longer be secondary to that of Odysseus. After all, she is the reason he had a home to return to, if eventually.

Attempting a Whole-Cloth Life

Lisa Mahar

Truth in the Unseen

I was ten years old and sitting through mass on a sweltering summer Sunday, willing the huge floor fans around the altar to move some air in our direction. My gaze was fixed on one fan. I had a sudden insight, a new thought, unbidden and arresting: I knew the fan had huge blades whirring fast in this summer heat, yet I could not see them. The blades were there but spinning so fast that I could see right through them. I understood at that moment that my world was made up of things that existed but could not be seen with my human eyes. This was a child's lesson in the truth of the unseen.

Practical Deeds

In the church of my youth, I heard the Sermon on the Mount and met the corporal works of mercy—feeding the hungry, caring for the sick, visiting the imprisoned, sheltering the homeless, burying the dead. I met the Carmelite nun Saint Teresa of Avila who told us "Christ has no body but yours. No hands, no feet on Earth but yours. Yours are the eyes with which he looks with compassion on this world. Yours are the feet with which he walks to do good. Yours are the hands with which he blesses all the world." This was a young person's lesson in faith in action.

As a teenager, I learned about Dorothy Day—journalist, Catholic, pacifist, social activist—who refused to participate in New York City's mandatory civil defense drills in 1955 and instead stood with 25 others in Washington Square Park with signs that read: "End war! The *only* defense against atomic weapons." They were arrested and jailed. This was a young person's lesson in civil disobedience as spiritual obedience.

As a child at our family dinner table, I listened to my father talk about a visitor from South Africa who had spoken to his Rotary Club at lunch that day. The speaker described a sweeping and brutal government-sanctioned policy—known by its Afrikaans name, *apartheid*—that denied rights to Black South Africans and forced them to live in brutally impoverished conditions, separated from white South Africans. I could not believe what I was hearing. I had no idea that governments could treat people this way. This was a young person's lesson in Martin Luther King's compelling admonition: "No one is free until we are all free."

These early experiences flowed into my adulthood and gave me a foundation: Have faith in an unseen guidance, full of wisdom. Faith without action is a squandered faith. When we take action we take on the consequences of those actions. We must strive to live out of the spiritual truth that we are not separate from one another but that we are one interwoven tapestry.

Whole-Cloth Striving

That interwoven tapestry made me long for a whole-cloth life, one where my beliefs and my actions are seamlessly woven together. What I have achieved is a whole-cloth striving with a bumpy pattern of dropped stitches, broken threads, and knotted tufts. In the wisdom of Ammon Hennacy—pacifist, activist, Catholic Worker and friend to Dorothy Day—who, when asked about the futility of trying to change the world, replied, "I'm not trying to change the world. I'm trying to keep the world from changing me."

I have been blessed to have found my way to a group of spiritually striving activist friends. These relationships—full of searching, humor, challenge, urgency, analysis, creativity, support, courage, resourcefulness, and sometimes strife—have guided my path and helped me put faith into action. I have been drawn to community life and to the challenges and gifts of living day-to-day with a larger group of people with whom I share belief and a bias toward action and who are nonetheless human beings with all our frailties and faults. Community life has given me firsthand knowledge of the challenge of people living together and the brilliance of committing deeply to a group of people who somehow—even after they've gotten to know you—love you in spite of yourself!

Noonday Farm

Way back in the 1900s, this dynamic collection of friends and peace colleagues came together to establish a farm in central Massachusetts on which we would grow food for soup kitchens and food pantries, hold our income in common, consciously steward the land, resist war taxes, support and participate in radical social justice activities, and provide hospitality to those in need. Our attempt at whole cloth living.

We provided logistical support to those on trial for civil disobedience, especially those engaged in what became known as Plowshares actions. We demonstrated against nuclear weapons, occupying AVCO and Draper Labs where nuclear weapons guidance systems were being developed and manufactured. We marched in Washington against apartheid—sitting down in front of the White House and getting arrested. We had our wages garnished for not paying the part of our income tax that would go to the military effort. We sent community members to participate in Witness for Peace—US citizens standing with the campesinos in Nicaragua to draw attention to the fight for freedom. We raised vegetables and flowers and tended laying hens, delivering food and flowers—bread and roses—to soup kitchens and food pantries in Boston. We hosted men and women from those soup kitchens for respite in our home. We studied and worshipped together—a ragtag group of Buddhists, Jews, Christians, and agnostics. We welcomed refugees from Central America on their way to permanent homes in Canada while their cases made their way through the US courts. We were attempting to live a whole-cloth life.

Meeting Rudolf Steiner

Though I had been aware of the work of Rudolf Steiner as a teenager, it was mostly a secondhand exposure to theosophy and the esotericism of Annie Besant, Madame Blavatsky, and Krishnamurti. When I think back on those times, I admit to a strong negative reaction. This esotericism didn't pass the insight-leads-to-action test. I observed there were lots of intellectual conversations, so many books, lots of journaling, lots of study groups—but it left me with questions: How do these intellectual pursuits help the world? Are people better fed, housed, and clothed as a result? Is suffering diminished? Justice served?

Later, as an education major at my college, we had an opportunity to visit a Waldorf school. It was a little preschool/kindergarten, and I found it confusing. Why was Raphael's *Madonna and Child* hung prominently in the classroom? Where were the specialized educational "materials" being encouraged in my college studies? Where were the bright primary colors and shelves of books common to classrooms I was familiar with? Where was the core instructional time? The directed leadership of the teacher? But I was also intrigued by the mood of joyful engagement. I could feel a kind of respect for childhood that I didn't yet understand.

Searching for Whole-Cloth Education

All the while in community, we were also raising our families, and we were actively trying to imagine a whole-cloth approach to our children's schooling. When we began our search for schooling that was in concert with our values, we started with our local public school. But we had a formative and jarring experience with our oldest child—an indigenous Havasupai who came to our family when she was eight years old. In the spring of grade five there was a competition at school for the best essay on the topic "What Memorial Day means to me." The winner would have the honor of raising the flag up the flagpole for the Memorial Day celebrations.

She wrote an essay that included thoughts like "Memorial Day is the day when we honor all the brave men who sacrificed their lives in war so we can enjoy our full rights and freedoms." When we gently asked, "Is this what Memorial Day means to you?" she answered "No." When we asked why she had written it this way, she answered, "Because I want to win the contest." The next question was one we asked ourselves, "Where do we even begin . . . ?"

We continued our search for an approach to schooling that was in concert with our values and that led us to visit the Waldorf school in our area. As part of our inquiry process, we sat in the back of the school assembly room for a Friday afternoon whole-school assembly. To start, I was surprised at how attentive the students were as one student from each class came up to the front to add a flower to a vase, slowly building a beautiful bouquet. The students listened whole-heartedly and laughed uproariously at a long and complex story told by one of the teachers who consulted not a single note. The audience of students seemed to lean forward in silent support as each of several classes came forward to offer something from their week's studies: a gesture and rhythm filled rhyme from the first graders, a little French market play from the third graders, a complicated multiplication circle from the fourth graders, and a masterful four-part choral piece from the middle-schoolers. The student presenters were poised and enthusiastic. Each offering was followed by warm applause. I was moved and intrigued and knew I had to find out more.

Waldorf School Parent, Administrator, Adviser

We soon knew we had found a school that resonated with our values, a kind of whole-cloth education. All three of our children attended that Waldorf school for many years. Forty years later they are grown with children of their own and are Waldorf parents themselves. We found in that first visit an educational approach that married spiritual insight with practical action.

Over these 40 years, I have been lucky enough to have had a deeply formative and nourishing professional life within Waldorf education as the administrative leader of our school. I've been blessed with a whole-cloth kind of professional life. I long ago moved away from the Catholic Church, where I experienced so much early formation. Examples of faith in action permeated my young life, and I met their echo again in Rudolf Steiner's guidance that spirit is never without matter, matter never without spirit. My work in Waldorf education is an expression of the spiritual works of mercy: counsel the doubtful, educate the uneducated, encourage repentance, bear wrongs patiently, forgive, comfort the afflicted (and afflict the comfortable!), and pray for the living and the dead.

Waldorf education, and the spiritual insights that stand behind it, have provided me with guidance and support for this human journey. The work with the students, collegial work, and the gift of work in the College of Teachers provide daily opportunities to put insight into actions.

Explorations of karma, destiny, and reincarnation have given me the framework to know that there is so much more to our human relationships than our simple day-to-day encounters. These spiritual truths provide meaning, offer comfort, and encourage me to take up my challenges. I learned the presence of the unseen all those summers ago sitting in a sweltering church, and insight echoed again when I met anthroposophy.

Community as a Crucible

I have always been interested in how groups of human beings work together. Healthy social forms based on conscious awareness, mutual agreement, loving engagement, resolute action, and exacting reflection build substance that contributes to the wellbeing of our world. I learned this in an intentional community, and I experienced it every day in the Waldorf school.

Rudolf Steiner's insight into our work in groups has been deeply meaningful to me. When we gather together, we can imagine our angel standing behind each of us, laying hands on us. We can imagine the archangels sweeping around our heads, bringing strength from one to the other. This spiritual circulating creates a kind of spiritual chalice into which a drop of light can fall, a drop of light offered from the archai. This drop of light enables the group to work together, making space for inspiration, intuition, and imagination. We can infer from this image that this is not work we can do alone; these particular spiritual gifts can only come when we gather together. There is a special spiritual help that is only available to us in a group.

Good Work to Do Today

There were so many mornings during my long tenure in my school when I woke to a world that seemed to be falling apart—the war we marched against broke out anyway, and innocents were dying; the government made a wrong turn around health care, and people were suffering; living life was getting more unsafe for young Black men; women's rights to bodily self-determination were being ignored and undermined; another huge piece of the Arctic ice cap fell into the sea. On these mornings I was especially grateful—joyful even—to have good work to do today. I was blessed to have an opportunity to contribute to the long-term wellbeing of the world. I got to greet the lively enthusiastic students and join with colleagues I respected to support the health and wellbeing of the children in our educational care, contributing to their ability to take up the tasks of life with courage, compassion, and conviction. Their own whole-cloth living.

I've come to see my social activism as the on-the-ground situational actions required by the events of the moment and to see my work in Waldorf education as the long-term work that serves the unknown future. Both are absolutely necessary and when taken together contribute to the whole-cloth approach to living.

Cloud of Witnesses

I have my cloud of witnesses—Dorothy Day, Martin Luther King, Teresa of Avila, Ammon Hennacy, Nelson Mandela, Bishop Desmond Tutu, Rudolf Steiner, Eleanor Roosevelt, Thich Nhat Hanh, Mohandas Gandhi, Simone Weil, Dietrich Bonhoeffer, Wangari Maathai, Dolores Chavez, Jane Addams—the faith-with-works crew—to inspire and guide me to action. And I have Waldorf education and anthroposophy to plumb the depths and set the daily tasks for the long road to the better world ahead.

SECTION IV

People, Land, and Society: Initiatives for a Better World

Working with Inner-City Young People in Detroit

Bart Eddy

My interest in social ideals and anthroposophy evolved side-by-side and only began to come together in 1982 which is where I have picked up the thread of this essay. Prior to that time, I had worked in the New York City Department of Social Services where I was assigned to be an employment counselor stationed in Harlem. This was in 1966/67 during the Vietnam War and the Civil Rights Movement, and I was shocked and in despair over the lack of meaningful vocational possibilities for the young black men and women of Harlem. By the late spring of 1968, after the assassination of Martin Luther King Jr. and prior to the assassination of Robert F. Kennedy, I left New York City and headed to the western slope of Colorado, where I participated in a small "back-to-the-land" community in the town of Paonia. It was there that I picked up the study of theosophy as given by Madame Blavatsky and was also introduced to biodynamic agriculture and Rudolf Steiner. By the fall of 1979, I had entered the Waldorf Institute in Detroit for their orientation program and the following year the Curative Education program with Janet McGavin. I will conclude this introduction with a brief timeline as an orientation to the content of this essay.

During the 1981–82 year, I was a student at the Centre for Social Development in Forest Row, UK. From there I returned to Detroit to work with the Center for Life Studies while creating a hands-on program for employment called Good Works. In 1983, a group of us established the Barnabas Project for youth employment, and I was directly connected with this initiative until 1988, after which I taught grades one through eight at the Detroit Waldorf School (DWS). In the fall of 1997, Candyce Sweda and I opened Detroit Community High School and Kindergarten as a public charter school. We are now a K-12 public school academy with a slight name change to Detroit Community Schools. Along the way we created two non-profits, Community for the Renewal of Education and Work (1996) and the Sunbridge International Collaborative (2013). The Brightmoor Maker Space began its community work in 2009 under the name of Entrepreneurship in Action, and we inaugurated our official home in a 3,200 square foot brick garage on the campus of Detroit Community Schools in 2013. Our funding arms are Detroit Community Schools and the Sunbridge International Collaborative. You can view our hands-on work on Instagram (@sunbridgecollaborative) and also the Brightmoor Maker Space website established for our collaborative work with the University of Michigan Penny Stamps School of Art and Design. We are currently participants in the 21st Century Community Learning Centers grant, which is a federal grant serviced through the Michigan Department of Lifelong Education, Advancement, and Potential (MiLEAP).

Returning to Detroit

It was in the spring of 1982 when I was a participant at the Centre for Social Development, as I began pondering my "next steps" that I heard a voice say to me, "Bart, you are going back to Detroit and you are going to work with young people!" The voice seemed like a command that I couldn't ignore, but I confess to hearing my own feeble response by thinking out loud to myself, "But I don't know anyone in Detroit!" Soon thereafter, I was invited to return to the Waldorf Institute to become a participant in the emerging Center for Life Studies and my fate was "sealed." Before returning, though, I had an opportunity to visit Arta in Zeist, Holland, which was a drug rehabilitation clinic for youth that was using the sheaths of the human being as a pathway of healing in both an inner and outer way. With great enthusiasm, I recall thinking to myself, "Wow! Anthroposophy really does have practical ways of bringing the spirit into matter while at the same providing a healing impulse to the societal organism and the human being!" At the Centre for Social Development, we had learned how to diagnose organizations by using the physical, etheric, astral, and ego to identify problems and solutions, and, most of all, to gain a sense of the "being" (identity) of the organization. It was also during this time that I began to think that if you could activate the sheaths for organizational development and individual healing, then why not for a Healing Pathway of Work and the Healing of the city of Detroit?

I felt like I was "on fire with possibility" when I returned to Detroit in the early summer of 1982, and occasionally, there seemed to be signposts along the way that would reignite the spark if it began to falter. One such occurrence happened shortly after I had met with a group of African American youth from Detroit who were part of an initiative sponsored by the American Friends Service Committee. As our connection developed, I invited them to come to the Waldorf Institute (then in Southfield, Michigan) for a get together. While we were touring the campus, we entered one of the classrooms where a picture was hung above the blackboard. Before I could say anything, a young man looked up at the picture and exclaimed, "Oh, that's Kasper Hauser!" It took a few decades for me to digest the impact of this event, but over time I have realized that the Kasper Hauser experience relates to the life and wellbeing of the young people in the city of Detroit. Like Kasper Hauser who was cut off from the world in his youth, our young people have been subjected to their own prison-like conditions in that they have been denied resources essential for a healthy livelihood, they have been "boxed-in" to an educational system which denies their creativity, and they have been channeled into a track that is commonly called the "school-to-prison" pipeline. But the greatest impact of this story lies in the fact that Kasper Hauser was deliberately imprisoned so as to be unable to fulfill his destined mission, just as an entire culture has been marginalized with the intent to eclipse its meaning and purpose. We can all remember the "War on Drugs" in the 1990s, which led to the incarceration of generations of young black men, and we can all remember the "fear" of the young men from the "streets" that arose in those of us who stood at a distance. Some will even say that the "crack-cocaine epidemic" that devastated the inner city was deliberately engineered, but that is the subject of another essay, because the real message behind all of this must be filled with hope for the future of all and not just a few.

Not too long ago I had a dream, and in that dream, I had the feeling that Hope was everywhere, that one could sense it in the air, in the shrubbery of front lawns, and in the work that we do among each other. It was the same feeling that I had when I stood in front of abandoned houses and empty lots on the streets of Detroit so many decades ago, because I felt that the air was full of "possibility," and that it would be possible to redeem that which had been so damaged, neglected, and abandoned on a soul-body level. But the real question arose when I asked myself, "What are the forms (vessels) that will come to meet these spiritual intentions?"

Gone were the days of the "Great Society" and the hosting of many programs that worked for the betterment of the community. The Reagan years began with the cutbacks in social spending, and it appeared to me that if we were going to work with the youth, especially through the practical arts, then we would have to create our very own high school, and thus began a long journey with many twists and turns.

First, I knew that I had to return to school to obtain a teaching certificate and master's of arts in teaching. Second, I had to accept the fact that to fulfill this dream, I had to do "1–8" at the Detroit Waldorf School as a preparatory step, and, finally, I had to realize the difficulty of creating a high school with no funding. In the meantime, I had been working with a group from the Presbytery of Detroit, and we had created the Barnabas Youth Opportunities Center near downtown Detroit as a seed for the future high school with no clue as to how it would happen. However, and most amazingly, when I was teaching the 5th grade at DWS, the charter school movement was beginning to flourish in Michigan and a ray of hope began to dawn in me. With my colleague and friend, Candyce Sweda, we made our pitch to our friends, the community and the charter school authorizing body (Saginaw Valley State University), and we were granted a charter to operate in late '96, and thus began our adventure at Detroit Community High School and Kindergarten.

Detroit Community High School and Kindergarten

It was never our intention to create a "Waldorf" charter school, but we were very clear that what we were trying to do was to build a school that harmonized the educational archetypes—thinking, feeling, willing—as presented by Rudolf Steiner. A major objective was to gradually discern what the neighborhood and community needed and to design our curriculum to meet that. This was to be achieved by working within the "system" of traditional public-school education and finding ways to enliven it, particularly through the arts and hands-on activity. Initially, we offered wood shop, metals, gardening, and the arts as part of our daily curriculum, but ultimately this came face to face with the Bush administration's No Child Left Behind, and then Race to the Top from the Obama administration.

With the handwriting on the wall, and the dismissal of the arts and hands-on from the daily schedule, we were forced to discover new forms by which to keep the arts and craft work alive, while continuing to be active within the Detroit Community High School. This was in the years 2007 and 2008.

Detroit, Brightmoor, and Spirit Park

Our first step was to participate with organizations within the Brightmoor community that were working out of the spirit of community building. In the meantime, we became a program provider for the Grow Detroit's Young Talent program for summer youth employment. Our first community project in the summer of 2009 was to work with Leland Missionary Baptist Church in Brightmoor on two empty lots across the street from the church. We were fortunate to have made a connection with Johannes Matthiessen from Stuttgart and his Sacred Landscapes initiative, so with the help of about a dozen Detroit Community High School students we undertook the design of Spirit Park on behalf of the elders from the church. Over the course of the next two summers, we realized that we had actively been working with the "being" of the city of Detroit through a process of Earth healing.

To backtrack for the moment—by the late 2000s, Detroit had become a city that had collapsed upon itself. There were thousands upon thousands of abandoned homes, twice as many vacant lots, the transportation infrastructure provided only unreliable and intermittent service, there were few streetlights, the public schools were graveyards for forgotten and misguided youth and "Devils Night," as it was known, showcased the torching of hundreds of buildings in the city. This is foretold in the "Seal of the City of Detroit," also known as the Greek Phoenix. The emblem features two women dressed in togas with one of them with her head down, weeping and wearing tattered clothing while the city is up in smoke behind her, and the other with her head upright and a thriving city behind her. This is known as the Greek Phoenix and its motto reads: "We hope for better things; it will rise from the ashes."

Although the seal predates the 20th century and belongs to another era, it is certainly a prescient portrayal of the dire consequences that were to come and the "hope for better things." In our imagination, we conceived that we could do something on behalf of the city that might bring some Hope and act as a leaven for the neighborhoods, and thus we began in 2009 with Spirit Park where we dug a spiral pathway with plantings in the empty lots. This brought us to 2010 with more youth when we built a spiral bench around an immense cottonwood tree on another lot and in 2011 when we invited the community, friends from around the country, and international partners to participate in what Johannes had called the Children's International Tree Dome Park. In some small way, we realized that we had traveled on a pathway through the sheaths of the city and had (as was our wish) touched the hidden "being of the city" and ever so carefully nudged it into a resurrected form of what might eventually come into being.

The Brightmoor Maker Space

It just so happened that in 2011 we were working next to an abandoned garage, and this led to the reclaiming of the idea of our wood shop at the Detroit Community High School, when we cleaned up the garage, built workbenches, and began to chisel handcrafted signs for the community. In the fall of 2011, we reopened our space at Detroit Community High School, worked to renovate a 3,200-square-foot garage on our campus and began to work afternoons and weekends with the young people who were flocking to us. This became the launching of the Brightmoor Maker Space and our year-round connection with community-based organizations in the Brightmoor and Cody Rouge neighborhoods.

Many people think of a maker space as a place where folks can learn to make things that interest them and that is true, but on a deeper level I have heard people describe it as a place where young people can come to "fashion (their) identity," and in this regard it is very much different than a regular classroom. This is because the instructors stand next to the youth with whom they are working and form a heart-to-heart connection. Maker work allows the young people to be able to explore experiential learning situations that relate to their inner will impulses, and to self-initiate their own ideas as they awaken their creative and innovative spirits. In The Apocalypse of St. John (lecture 10), Rudolf Steiner said: "There is a saying well known in spiritual science, which runs: Man will only produce living organisms in the experimental laboratory, as he now produces mineral products, when the laboratory table has become the altar and the mixing of substances a sacramental act. This is a saying which has always been found in occult circles."

The Brightmoor Makers have made its own adaptation of our "experimental laboratory" and have acknowledged that the wood-shop workbench has become a sacramental altar for self-discovery, ingenuity and focus. There have been moments over the years when the only sound that is heard in the wood shop is that of the rhythm and cadence of mallet and chisel on a piece of wood while the entire atmosphere of the workspace is magically altered! It is in these moments when it becomes possible to grasp the performance of a sacramental act of young people completely immersed in work, a truly amazing moment of eternal truth.

Earlier in this essay, I asked: What are the forms (vessels) that will come to meet these spiritual intentions? And this question is one that deep down, underneath our young people are asking, and that is: What is my Place and Purpose in the world? For it is out of Purpose that the young person finds his or her meaning, and it is out of Place where the "house" is built that will provide the nourishment, strength and growth forces so that these great human ideals and spiritual archetypes might incarnate together through the appropriate forms. And a maker space is a Place, if rightfully energized, that will become a Sanctuary Space. Orland Bishop in his book, *The Seventh Shrine: Meditations on the African Spiritual Journey,* provides us with so much to cherish and contemplate in his thoughts on a Sanctuary Space. "Sanctuary is a sacred space whereby the inner intentions are manifested in real time; Sanctuary is the creative space to receive the Gift; Sanctuary is a Place outside of time where there is always time for what is needed; and Sanctuary is a Place of beginning, of faith, healing, forgiveness, imagination and intention."

The Brightmoor Maker Space has become a place of "possibility" over the years, and we are currently offering wood shop, carpentry,

T-shirt design, sewing, filmmaking, audio, and a combination of bike repair, electronics, robotics, and jewelry making. When possible, we provide our youth with a stipend, but when the times get rough, we focus on sales from youth made products as we strive for program sustainability. During summers, we are a site provider for Detroit's Grow Detroit Young Talent program, and they are paid at a going rate which is currently $12.50 per hour. Like a class teacher at a Waldorf school, we have an opportunity to work with our young people for multiple years. On occasion, we have worked with youth who have graduated from Detroit Community High School. I would also like to mention that the young people with whom we have worked are ultimately Waldorf youth. It may take longer for them to get there because there are many factors that they must surmount on their journey into adulthood, but they are also guided by the identical inspirational spirit that is offered to the Waldorf-educated students. Our work at the Brightmoor Maker Space asks us to meet the young people where they are and to slowly build from there. Much of this involves the installation of a work ethic through the opening of genuine interest into a new world of possibility. It is the unfolding of the latent and natural gifts that they have brought with them into this incarnation. I will now turn our attention to a young man who has worked with us for nine years and who embodies the Spirit of Detroit through a phenomenal series of life challenges and changes.

JY's Story

JY began to work with us during the summer of his 9th-grade year, and he was recommended by a former superintendent who understood that the traditional classroom situation was not working for him. When I first met him, his hoodie was always up, while his gaze was directed downward. He barely spoke and rarely made person to person contact. JY had suffered an immense tragedy as a middle-schooler when he heard the screams of two of his siblings from his home that had caught on fire. They were calling his name as he stood outside, and it was impossible to rescue them. When he first began to work with us in the wood shop, his responses to questions and directions were barely audible, but after he had worked with us for a while, we noticed that he became receptive to one young lady who showed him how to correctly carve wood and paint the sign that he was making. As small as that may seem, it became a giant step for JY, and to see him today, nine years later, one would never have guessed that he had been through such severe trauma. He has become our master sign-carver and to watch him at work is a thing of beauty as chips fly away while he carves the wood. He is now a member of our staff and teaches the youth who first enter the woodcraft-carpentry program the basics of sign carving. All of this is a testimony to the healing power of craftwork, learning to work with one's hands and developing the self-confidence and will power to create high-quality products. He will always carry with him the trauma of the middle school tragedy that he experienced, but he is learning to manage his life circumstances in a very uplifting way.

Youth and Trauma

About seven years ago, the Brightmoor neighborhood's local organization, the Brightmoor Education Action Team (BEAT), took a survey amongst its residents, and it turned out that trauma was the number one issue, and the residents were looking for ways to heal it. Family and generational trauma is endemic in the community, and our young people bring so much of that into their school life. Sometimes this leads to severe disturbances during the school day with fights and inappropriate behavior. However, and we are asking ourselves this question, over the past 15 years of maker space activity, we have never experienced a fight. Why is this? I think there is a hidden power in craftwork to heal deep seated trauma and disturbances that occur in the developing teenager. Observation suggests to us that when a young person is fully immersed in their work, and if that work resonates with their latent creativity, then the outcomes lead to both an inner and outer sense of belonging to themselves and to the world. It seems that the awakening of creativity leads to the discovery of that which inspires the self-confidence and courage to explore new worlds, both inner and outer.

Part of the on-going research into the sheaths is associated with the creation of the Developmental Pathway of Work and four levels of activity that exemplify stages of development. They are known as apprentice, journeyman, master, and entrepreneur.

- **Apprentice:** An apprentice must be capable of and willing to learn tirelessly as well as be willing to strengthen their effectiveness as a worker. They hold the position "doer of common tasks" and must dedicate themselves as a student and follower. However, they must also take the initiative to drive their own learning experience and to seek out the understanding they need to accomplish the task(s) at hand.
- **Journeyman:** A journeyman must stand out as a skilled and capable worker, while showing the judgment and openness of a leader. They hold the position "doer of complex tasks" and must find the balance in the application of their skills—i.e., knowing when to push and when to pull, and when to step forward as a leader and when to follow in support of someone else.
- **Master:** A master must excel in organizing, doing, and teaching complex work projects. They hold the position of "doer of complicated tasks" and must organize the overall flow of many smaller tasks as well as ensure that the means are provided for the output of quality work. They must possess expertise and know-how within the field of their endeavor.
- **Entrepreneur:** An entrepreneur sees the shortfalls and gaps within a group or an organization and turns them into strengths. They navigate obstacles, innovate solutions, and open new horizons. They are responsible for understanding all work on all levels of the organization. An entrepreneur has the skills that are transferable to multiple disciplines. As a collaborative leader, the entrepreneur finds their place and purpose in the community as part of a broader collective effort. They hold the position of "innovative initiative taker."

The four levels provide a framework of what we are looking for in our youth, but we do not follow a rigid pathway. There is a much more organic flow to the four levels with us being able to acknowledge "signposts" along the way. Our work is best described as being an Apprenticeship training with a wide variety of activities that serve to awaken both creativity and initiative.

And on a final note, I would like to return to the young man who inspired me way back in the summer of 1983, when I first began working with young people through the Barnabas Project. His name is Orlando Robinson, and I met him when he was a fifteen-year-old from "the hood" and was placed with us by way of the City of Detroit Summer Youth Employment and Training Program. He was a young man filled with life and mischief who challenged us in every possible way. I soon learned that his older brother had been shot and killed in a drive-by shooting in the spring, and we knew that he was grieving tremendously. I had a red Toyota pickup truck at that time, known as Sparky the Rooster, and one day I invited Orlando to drive with me to Duns Scotus to pick up a load of biodynamic compost and to transport it back to the city to become part of our vacant lot garden. This compost had been carefully nurtured by Alan York and Hilmar Moore when they gardened at the Waldorf Institute. While we were out there loading the truck, Orlando began to tell me about his brother, and he told me with much emotion that he still heard his brother speaking to him. Since he had provided the opening, it was possible to talk with him about life after death and how we can still receive solace and comfort from those who are on the other side.

The summer ended and Orlando returned to Murray-Wright High School, but by the early fall, we began to find him coming to visit us at Barnabas when he should have been at school. There were occasions when he seemed listless and would come by to sleep on a workbench. In late summer, Orlando had experienced another tragedy in a drive-by shooting that had left a second brother paralyzed from the waist down. It was obvious to us that he was experiencing a downward cycle of grief and despair, and it became a situation that could not be cured by talk. During the next couple of years, we saw less and less of Orlando until we heard in March of 1987 that he had suddenly passed away. His passing did not occur through street violence or suicide, but of a massive heart attack. In other words, he died of a broken heart.

It is now 2025, and nearly 40 years have passed since Orlando's needless death. The streets are calmer now, but the trauma still exists. The city is looking up with the rebirth of the downtown, and yet the neighborhoods have been left in their wake. Some folks are "going somewhere" others are still "there." Public education in the city has not changed much, and standardized testing still runs the show. Young people yearn for more, while the "old-timers" bemoan the dismissal of the trades and home economics. And, yet here we are, and it's only the beginning! Despite it all, there is Hope! Hope is in the air; it's everywhere...and it heals despair!

I will end with a tribute to Orlando who has been with us all these years. I would like to share with the reader a verse that was written for him long, long ago. It is a tribute to those on the other side who may have had their destiny usurped, but who, nevertheless, are still with us and continue to inspire.

Orlando

Beyond the Threshold,
You see our dreams.
Here we know you for your own.
Inspire Us! Guide Us!
Toward the youth of today.
That we may create
~Those Forms~
~That Speak~
The Truth, The Beauty, The Goodness
To the youth of our day!

Back to the Land, but with Purpose

Alice Groh

The year 1968 was a rough and tumultuous year throughout Europe, but perhaps especially here in the United States. We experienced the assassination of Reverend Martin Luther King Jr. in April, civil unrest throughout the summer, coupled with being the year of the highest casualties in the Vietnam War, a second political assassination, this time of Robert Kennedy in June and then in August the Democratic National Convention violence in Chicago, in which I briefly participated. I was sixteen years old at the time, and like so many of us, was looking for some sort of sense and reasonable future amid the chaos. Having grown up in a Jewish family, I was exposed much earlier to films of the liberation of the death camps; the mid-sixties being a time when the Shoah weekend celebrations began to commemorate those who had died in the Holocaust of World War II. We were told to "never forget" so that such a thing might not happen again. Then also the early 1960s was a time of the Cold War, the Bay of Pigs incident, lots of talk of bomb shelters, and the absurd practice of having students prepare for air raids by crouching under their desks or sitting in the hallways, with backs against their lockers. By the time the Kent State University massacre took place my anxiety levels were peaking. So, it wasn't at all surprising that these experiences of fear and chaotic social conditions led me to feel very sympathetic toward the ideas blossoming in the late 1960s of going "back to the land," to lead a more peaceful, safe, and fulfilling rural existence.

The alternative imagination for my future lay with social justice issues. I was certainly aware of, if not directly involved in, the many issues of social injustice and inequality that existed (and continue to exist) in and around life in the Chicagoland area. I definitely toyed with the idea of becoming a civil rights lawyer but, quite honestly, I think I knew that I was too lazy to put myself through the rigors of law school and somehow the idea of spending my life in the city was not so appealing. I kept the decision in abeyance but somehow already knew the answer. And yet I wondered, was there a way that I could both live in the countryside but also be active in societal change?

I was always one of the younger members of our group of hippie friends so I could watch while the older ones tried out different experiments, in both living arrangements and diverse behaviors, so to speak. One group did actually try to go "back to the land" but came home defeated, mostly because none of those involved possessed any of the requisite skills needed to prosper, or even to survive rural life. This was all wishful, fantasy thinking and not much more. Their example led me to a resolve: if I ever attempted to live a rural life, I would first somehow seek training in alternative agriculture so that I would stand a chance of being "successful" in my project.

In the meantime, in the autumn and winter of 1968, two of my older friends introduced me to a place called The Occult Bookstore on North State Street, a rather seedy neighborhood on the north side of Chicago. The friends had previously gone on a drama department trip to England with their high school class and had visited Stonehenge. I remember being very interested in hearing about their experiences. And then they also told me about later being in the fabric section of a department store where an elderly woman came up behind them and started telling them things about the "meanings" of all the colors. Upon hearing this story, I felt something physically "move" in my head, and I said to them, "You must tell me EVERYTHING you know about such things." This led them to take me to The Occult Bookstore, but I have no idea how they found out about the place.

I have strong memories of spending snowy Saturdays at the bookstore that winter, sitting on the radiators and reading all sorts of strange books about magic, tarot, astrology, various paths of spiritual development, and occult groups like the Golden Dawn in London. One day, Russell, the bookshop manager, a tall, dark-haired young man with an ample mustache, handed me two books at exactly the same time. They were *The Rosicrucian Cosmo-Conception* by Max Heindel and *Knowledge of the Higher Worlds: How Is It Achieved?* by Rudolf Steiner. My first glance into *Knowledge of the Higher Worlds* told me "this is what I am looking for"—but I also felt that I didn't have the discipline to tread this path at the time and wanted to first enjoy my time as a teenager. So, I kept the books and eventually took them with me to college out at University of California Santa Cruz in the fall of 1971.

In autumn 1969, my older sister began studying at the University of Wisconsin in Madison. I was bored to tears with high school so I began to go up on weekends to visit her there. She started to take some astrology courses at the Free University and came to know Richard Koepsel, a physics professor, who also ran the Microcosm Bookshop. A group of my sister's friends and I would often hang out at the bookshop late into the evening. Richard had a large array of books on Western occultism, including things by Helena Blavatsky, Max Heindel, and Rudolf Steiner. I started to read many other things, such as the novel *Zanoni* and another called *Brother of the Third Degree,* a story of 19th-century occult groups in Europe, as well as several other lecture series by Steiner on inner development. One evening I overheard a conversation about there being a "Steiner school" out on Long Island. Based on what I had read by that time, my 17-year-old imagination conjured up pictures of a place where people walked around in white robes and got "initiated." At that time, I had never heard of any daughter movements stemming out of anthroposophy and had only read some of the esoteric development writings, so this wrong conception can perhaps be forgiven.

A pivotal moment came in the spring of 1973, while on a leave of absence from college I was told by some visiting friends that they had spoken with a young man at the student farm at UC Santa Cruz. He had just returned from a place in England where he had done a training in a certain type of organic agriculture. This place was based on the work of Rudolf Steiner, whoever he was. But I knew who he was, and I was astounded, delighted, and very excited that Steiner had something to say about agriculture. I very soon afterward wrote to the folks at the college and told them that I had to come!

On the first evening after my arrival at Emerson College in the fall of 1974, I went up to the library on the second floor of Pixton House, the main administrative building. I more or less blindly pulled a book off the Steiner shelf and the title was *Nine Lectures on Bees*. I burst into tears. "Finally," I thought, "here is someone who can explain the world to me!" A year in the agriculture course with Dr. Herbert Koepf followed. Afterward, I finished my degree at UC Santa Cruz with a joint major in environmental studies and religious studies and then went on to graduate school at UC Davis for a degree in international agricultural development.

A return visit to Emerson College in the spring of 1978 connected me with a young German man who secured a position for me at the Research Institute for International Agricultural Development in Heidelberg, Germany, which sent me on a journey to West Africa. Later that same year I also traveled with my parents on one of the first trips for Americans to China with the International China People's Friendship Association (May 1979). Both trips gave me insights into different cultural and historical approaches to agriculture as well as much to ponder in terms of so-called development work. Some questions emerged as to which concepts of "development" one was working with and who would actually benefit and in what way from the array of concepts I saw being put into practice. Many of my fellow students at graduate school already had experience working throughout the world, including with the Peace Corps or projects sponsored by the US Agency for International Development (USAID). We were all deeply skeptical about the so-called Green Revolution package that was being pushed onto people in "developing" countries. As far as we could see, their having to purchase the whole package of hybrid seeds, irrigation, fertilizers, and pesticides also—or even mostly—benefited those who were the purveyors of those commodities. The promises and benefits of larger crop yields were also a topic for discussion as these yields seemed to be aimed for mostly the export market, and therefore were not feeding the local populace. These debates brought up social as well as farming method questions for me. On various levels, this was certainly not biodynamics, but as yet my ideas about how to partner biodynamic practices with social ideals had not quite congealed.

Autumn of 1979 saw me move to Wilton, New Hampshire, in order to find anthroposophical community life while still being engaged in some sort of agricultural pursuits. In October of 1984 I signed the papers to buy a small farm property with a house and barn. Fifteen days later Trauger Groh, a German biodynamic farmer, arrived in town to advise some local farmers who in turn had gotten him the invitation to be the main speaker at the annual biodynamic agriculture conference, "New Social Forms for Agriculture." We began a year-long exchange of letters, which resulted in our marrying one year later, in October 1985.

Now came the challenging question of how we were going to support ourselves and build up this small farm that I had purchased. An opportunity for Trauger to work for the Biodynamic Association as their field advisor fell through, so we were thrown back to thinking about selling vegetables and dairy products locally.

Trauger brought with him a whole world of experience, both in the farming and in the social realms. He had come from a farm in northern Germany where three independent farmers worked together, on land that had been donated into a land trust. All the households on the farm lived with adults with special needs,

Trauger's former wife carrying the largest number of residents and the responsibility for the Social Therapy program as a whole. This program contributed very needed income into the farm budget, especially in the early years of the operation. The farm itself produced milk and a variety of dairy products, an array of vegetables, meats, and freshly bread baked on the premises from grains grown there. All goods were sold in an on-farm shop and additionally were distributed through a box scheme to customers in Hamburg, using one of the Waldorf schools around the city as a distribution point. Thirty families who felt closest to the farm agreed to work with the GLS Gemeinschaftsbank eG, the anthroposophically inspired "ethical" bank originally located in Bochum, Germany, to form a kind of support circle for the farm. Each of these families was granted a line of credit from the bank, which they in turn made available to the three farmers as their working capital for the year. In addition, each of the families pledged to back up the farmers to a maximum amount of 1,000 deutsche marks in any given year, if the farm ran a deficit. (Trauger told me that they had only needed to call upon these extra pledges once.)

This was an interesting system, but we in New Hampshire did not have a bank that would be willing to do something similar for friends of our farm. So, what could we do instead?

The Temple-Wilton Community Farm is Born

We started to hold conversations with more than twenty families we knew were interested in having biodynamically grown vegetables and high-quality dairy products. Trauger spelled it out in simple terms: "Do you want this? If so, how are we going to make this financially possible?" He also said, *you need to want the farm, not just its products.* Several months of conversation followed, with Trauger speaking to us all on biodynamic themes but also urging us to feel that we were all farmers in a way, at least to the degree that we wanted to take responsibility for how the food we were eating was grown. He also pointed out the many benefits to the community of having a farm in its midst. (These ideas eventually took the form of a lecture to a Waldorf teachers conference held in June 1987 at High Mowing School in Wilton, New Hampshire. The topic of the conference was "Life Skills," and his lecture was titled "The Farm as the Teacher of Humanity.")

Our conversations settled into a willingness to try something new. Our group would take on the whole budget of what it would take to run the farm for one year, each person or family taking on as much financial responsibility for this budget as they were able. We did not care if everyone gave the same financial contribution; what we cared about was that everyone felt responsible for the wellbeing of the farm and that we met the full budget for the year. Most contributions were given in monthly installments, with one or two families eventually paying in larger, less frequent amounts. The point was to create a situation in which the costs of the farm were met, and then the so-called Active Farmers (those who did the actual farm work in the name of all the rest of us "farmers") could concentrate their efforts on growing the highest quality vegetables, specific to the needs and wants of the members group, instead of growing crops that had high market value but were grown at risk and, hopefully, sold to an unknown set of consumers. What was grown and how many cows and other animals the farm supported was therefore dictated by the ecological conditions of the land plus the needs and wants of the animals and the human stewards involved, rather than by anonymous markets and the need and desire for profits. We were glad if we could cover our costs (and in several years this was very challenging), but our costs were well thought through and included experience-based calculations in terms of what was needed, both to run the farm and to support the farmers.

In the beginning, our member group met frequently, both to discuss and pledge toward the budget but also to celebrate festivals together. Most of us had young children at the time, and this was a chance to bring these young families together. Trauger never failed to take the opportunity to speak at these occasions on some inspirational theme, be it of a biodynamic, social engagement, or anthroposophically inspired theme related to the festivals of the year. Certainly, all the gatherings had their positive community-building effects.

In the early years, our budget and pledge meetings were particularly interesting. We insisted that all families who wished to be part of what came to be called the Temple-Wilton Community Farm (as our land was located in the two towns of Temple and Wilton) be present at two meetings a year. During the first meeting, we reviewed the budget that the Active Farmers had prepared for the coming season. Trauger always encouraged us to see the budget as "the footprint of our intentions." Everything we planned to do that season had a line item in the budget. If it wasn't in there, we couldn't do it (outside unexpected emergencies, of course). This took very careful planning, which improved as we went along.

The second gathering was the pledge meeting. The member families sat in a circle and, initially at least, voiced their pledges out loud, so that everyone witnessed what the others were giving. This method involved a certain amount of soul restraint, since we all knew each other and, to some degree, the details of our personal circumstances. The pledge amounts were then added up. If we came up short in comparison to the total budget, then we went around again. As the years went by, we eventually had processed goods like yogurt, eggs, and cheese available that we could sell to ourselves and to outside customers, so this added an income stream that helped keep the needed pledges lower.

The trials and triumphs of the community farm need not be spelled out in great detail here. Suffice it to say that we, in 2025, are now headed into our 39th season, serving 85 families. This year we have deliberately reduced this number from 100 families in order to improve our crop rotation and thereby honor our ecological responsibilities toward the land that has served us so well for so long. This last year saw a wonderful anonymous donation that helped us pay off the mortgage for the farmstead, and we are in the middle of deliberations to change some of the legal structures that underpin our land holdings and how we are viewed both at the local, state and federal levels. Succession issues on the farmer level are in process, and maintaining an informed and enthusiastic member community remains both a challenge and a joy. Some long wished-for educational projects are in the wind and we are on the lookout for those who want to take up these tasks. And lastly, cooperation and interaction between all the institutions on Abbot Hill, namely the farm, the cafe, the Waldorf school, and the Wild Rose after-school and summer-camp programs for children, are only starting to evolve. Community building, with an emphasis on nutrition and education, is what this community is gifted with and what it can give, as a training ground, to the world. I envision a very fruitful, if still, in many cases, only potential, future for this particular place, and for our greater southern New Hampshire community. Through my work with the farm and through the anthroposophical adult education work we have sponsored in the Garden Room of our home, as well as in the wider community, I feel quite blessed to have such grist for the mill for our social practice.

The CSA Movement

Within a few years of our founding the Temple-Wilton Community Farm in 1986 and especially after the publishing of the book *Farms of Tomorrow: Community Supported Farms—Farm Supported Communities* by Trauger Groh and journalist Steven McFadden in 1990, the idea of community-supported agriculture (CSA) started to spread quickly throughout the organic farming network in this country and abroad. Why was this new relationship of producers and consumers suddenly so popular? To get a perspective outside of my own Wilton farm experience, I turned to my long-time friend Sonya Dagovitz, who has been a leader in the organic food industry for more than forty years. Among her many other activities within the organic-food distribution networks, her experience of CSA was to be a distributor of produce from the Angelic Organics CSA in western Illinois, to urban drop-off centers throughout the city of Chicago. This was certainly a wider perspective than I was able to glean here in New Hampshire.

Sonya partnered with urban gardening groups and co-ops in places in the city that are bordering on being what are now termed "food deserts," that is, where access to fresh produce is extremely limited. Bringing fresh food into these neighborhoods was part of a larger effort to educate about and support better nutrition in these areas. And this connection with a particular farm gave these people, although perhaps not always first-hand, a connection with a particular spot on the Earth, for which they felt responsible and which in turn fed and supported them.

Other rural-urban connections were made in this way—I know of situations around Boston and certainly New York City where these connections were created. This was easier and more efficient for both farmers and customers, according to those involved, than farmers selling wholesale to distribution companies and then supermarkets. Also, this membership system avoided a lot of the waste involved in farmers coming to farmers markets and spending all day at a stall. Not that these more conventional distribution systems are "wrong" in any way; only that CSA broadened the options for connecting people in the cities to healthy food, with the added benefit of their feeling in some way involved with "their" farm. Some families in these situations did manage to come to visit "their farm," while of course most did not.

From the farmer's end, CSA provided both challenges but also a certain sense of relief. Trauger always said that a community of people would only enter into a CSA relationship with a farmer that they already knew and could trust to care for the land in such a way that the community could be fed. This usually meant a longer conversation between farmer and community, both a kind of getting-to-know-you process and also giving the group a chance to assess what was wanted and needed in that community. And, more often than not, it meant finding people in the community who had access to usable land if the farmers themselves did not already have a farm to work from. Growing for a set market community with set wishes is quite a different experience than choosing what to grow or how much milk or meat to produce based on the maximum financial return these products could yield and then hoping that—through various market outlets—indeed these things would produce the needed income. Also, having a regular income *throughout the year* through monthly member pledges is a more balanced and less stressful economy for the farm. But again, community members need to be able to trust that the farm is indeed going to feed them and that they are willing to risk that part of their household budget that goes to food to support this particular farmer's efforts. Suddenly, through sharing the economic "risk" with the farmer, community members also began to share in the concerns about the weather, the health of the animals, and if the vegetables are getting properly weeded or not. And farmers could turn their attention to doing what was best for the farm as a whole, instead of looking down a row of carrots and calculating their financial return, or choosing to grow only specialty crops that were sold at the highest prices.

Some CSA farms have widened their activities to include nutritional education, food preservation classes, and festival celebrations, all of which are community building in their own way. Children grow up feeling a part of their farm, getting to know the cows, helping harvest the carrots and collecting vegetables with their families on farm store days. Hopefully this helps them to ever more consciously experience a sense of responsibility and gratitude toward the Earth and her creatures and a growing camaraderie with the world of nature as a whole.

With the publication of the book *Farms of Tomorrow: Community Supported Farms, Farm Supported Communities* by Trauger Groh and Steve McFadden in 1990 and the sequel, *Farms of Tomorrow Revisited,* published in 1997, the idea of CSA spread quickly. Indian Line Farm CSA in the Berkshires was started in 1986 at the same time as the Temple-Wilton Community Farm in New Hampshire, and the two places have served as models and sources of inspiration and information for what has become a real "movement" within the alternative agricultural networks. Our home and the Community Farm were flooded with visitors, farmers with intentions to start their own CSA, as well as mere curiosity seekers. The community risk-sharing model was very attractive to young farmers, but as Trauger would always point out, it was a matter of building trust between the farmers and the community. And being at the center of this trust was not always an easy and comfortable position for a lot of farmers. Our partner and vegetable grower Anthony Graham shared his feelings in this context: "People ask if the farm budget is already 'met' (at least in pledges) before the season starts, then what is the motivation for the farmer to do any work? The motivation comes from the fact that people have entrusted you with their household food budget and you had better get out there and make sure that they are properly fed!" As with so many things, it's the angle at which one looks at things that dictates what one sees.

Another aspect has come from my friend Aonghus Gordon in England, founder of the Ruskin Mill Educational Trust (rmt.org). He has characterized the CSA movement as having de-commodified food. That is an interesting concept. Rudolf Steiner spoke about three things that should not be treated as tradable commodities (and which still are), namely land, labor, and capital. Perhaps one could see the de-commodification of food under the umbrella idea of taking land itself off the market. Trauger often spoke of trying to find the "final buyer" for any particular piece of land, having that piece from that time forward held in trust, with various rights of usage being dictated by the community or at least by a group of people acting as trustees on behalf of the community. This is certainly a fertile topic for deeper exploration.

Nutrition and Education

One afternoon many years ago, I was shopping at the discount store in Peterborough, New Hampshire, and was struck by the unhealthy and unhappy appearance of most of the shoppers. A thought then came to me that the two most important issues in this country (and probably worldwide) were nutrition and education. Without decent nutrition, a person cannot think properly and without a decent education, the ability to exercise independent judgments becomes severely compromised. This thought reaffirmed my desire to dedicate my efforts to support both biodynamics and Waldorf education.

The work in biodynamics has involved mostly a constant attempt at improvement and understanding on our own little farm, but also was expressed by my being involved for several years as a board member of the Biodynamic Association in America, and of course, helping the Temple-Wilton Community Farm and the wider CSA movement to evolve.

The dedication to good education came through sending both of our children to the local Waldorf schools and eventually in my being on the board of trustees for six years each for Pine Hill Waldorf School and High Mowing School, being board chair at Pine Hill for three years. These board experiences deepened my respect for all the challenges that are involved in educating children in such a way as to give them the best chances to bring their highest intentions to fruition in this life.

I have also taken a strong interest in what might be called the general anthroposophical adult education work. Trauger and I built a large room connected to our house back in 1989 which has served as a gathering space for a whole spectrum of activities. The Anthroposophical Society has held meetings here, the School for Spiritual Science Class lessons are now read here, we have hosted many kinds of workshops, lectures, and study groups, and for a number of years The Christian Community children's services took place here once a month. We have also hosted the whole range of human celebrations, from christenings and birthdays, weddings and funerals, and celebrations of life. Also concerts and festival celebrations and board meetings for various groups. The Garden Room, as it is called, has indeed been a vessel to hold a whole range of cultural events in our area. During the years of Trauger's illness and after his crossing the threshold in the summer of 2016, I have tried to remain in a hosting mode for the community.

How this will continue is unclear at the moment. Board meetings, study groups, and First Class lessons continue to be held here, with only a few intermittent Anthroposophical Society-sponsored events having been organized since the end of the so-called Covid era. Having this meeting space be an extension of a private home has had its advantages in the past, but it could complicate the succession picture in terms of who would like to take on the support of the Anthroposophical Society work here in Wilton. There have been several iterations of supportive planning groups for Society events over the years. It is time to bring together another one, with an eye to the future of the anthroposophical cultural life in the area, one that especially engages with the farming and Waldorf school but also with general adult educational interests. The age range of those involved in study groups and Class lessons at the moment is encouraging: we have people in their 70s and 80s all the way down to several people in their early 30s. We even have a few people in their 40s and 50s, although not too many. A new wave of people arrived in the community post-Covid, and I am hopeful that among them we will find folks who wish to continue to foster anthroposophical cultural life in the area. I remain willing to play an adjunct and supportive role in all that wishes to take place here.

Anthroposophy and Catholic Worker Activism

Neil Golder

"There is only one question—how to love this world."
—Mary Oliver

There are many ways to love this world, to act in it for the good of all beings. I take this quote from Mary Oliver as an inspiration and as a touchstone for the following thoughts.

The following is a very personal account. It is an attempt to deal with a question I have lived with—and that has plagued me—for some years. It does not offer answers, but perhaps some possibilities.

I came of age (my early 20s) in the late 1960s to early '70s, the time of the US Vietnam War and the American Civil Rights Movement. In 1966, while I was in Peace Corps training in Berkeley, California, I came into contact with radical (left wing) politics, the "love revolution," and mystic revelations through the use of hallucinogens. At that time, I had no knowledge of Rudolf Steiner and anthroposophy. I became interested in Hinduism, Buddhism, and Jewish mysticism.

At this time (mid-'70s), I had dropped out of graduate school and any intention of a career. But I did decide to finish my dissertation on "Borges and Qabalah." At that time, I was exposed to and got very interested in the writings of Owen Barfield. They opened up a new perspective for me that penetrated and enhanced the Mystery.

In the '80s, I went on a harvest brigade to Nicaragua, in support of their revolution and to help counter US aggression against the Nicaraguan people. That's when I came into contact with the Catholic Worker Movement, which I describe below.

Over the next 20 years, I was involved in protests and civil disobedience as a way of publicizing and countering US war-making, especially against Iraq. I served some brief periods in jail.

It was after 2003 that I got more involved with anthroposophy. I had been in a life-threatening automobile accident (I was run over by a car), and after I recovered, I decided it was time to deepen my study and commitment and joined the Anthroposophical Society in America (ASA). I then got a mailing about a speech formation workshop at the Threefold Community, which I attended, leading to my taking many speech and eurythmy workshops up until the present time. During this time, I helped to finance the purchase of a house in Ithaca for use by the Ithaca Catholic Worker.

The Catholic Worker Movement began in 1930s New York City when Dorothy Day, Peter Maurin, and some of their friends noticed that many people in their neighborhood were going hungry. Seeing this, they simply invited people to their meals and began feeding and housing poor people.

Dorothy Day was a reporter with communist leanings. In the early 1930s, she had a conversion experience to Catholicism. The impulse of the Catholic Worker Movement—to offer hospitality and fellowship to poor people and to live with them—is based on the social teachings of Jesus Christ.

The other thread of the Catholic Worker impulse—based again on Christ's life, actions, and teachings—is to bring to light and confront nonviolently the worldly powers and systems that create poverty and oppression in the first place. The two strands are sometimes referred to as doing the Works of Mercy and confronting the Works of War. It has been said that the job of the Catholic Worker is to "comfort the afflicted" and "afflict the comfortable."

This impulse has grown so that there are now hundreds of Catholic Worker Houses all over the world where people live in voluntary poverty and serve the poor. Many of the Catholic Worker communities put out newspapers, and some members engage in civil resistance to raise awareness in an attempt to change the system of oppression. There is a complete commitment to nonviolence, especially as practiced by Christ, Gandhi, and Martin Luther King Jr. Thomas Merton is also an important source for the thinking and actions of Catholic Workers.

I met several Catholic Workers in the 1980s, when I became involved in nonviolent direct action to stop the US from supporting violence against the Nicaraguan people and their 1979 revolution—which has since been grossly betrayed by Daniel Ortega.

In the 1990s, some of us in Ithaca, New York, came together to offer hospitality to Central American refugees and to oppose the violence of the US empire in Central America. Eventually we obtained a house, a former church, that continues to provide housing and food for those in need.

I came to the Catholic Worker not as a Catholic, nor even as a Christian, having been brought up Jewish. What motivated me was that there I had found, I believed, a marriage between spiritual life and compassionate action in the world. Not having been brought up Christian, it was nevertheless not difficult to translate in my mind some of the unfamiliar terms and names to make sense to my humanistic Jewish and Buddhist perspective. I had been strongly practicing vipassana—insight meditation—for a number of years and was especially influenced by Thich Nhat Hanh. I feel I went from loving kindness meditation to engaged Buddhism to anthroposophy. Now I'm wondering what an engaged anthroposophy would look like.

The Catholic Worker provided me then—and still does—with a sense of community and close friends. But mainly, at that time, the activities of the Catholic Worker, especially the activism part, spoke to my sense of truth—the sense I had from previous experiences in the 1960s and '70s—with consciousness-altering substances and through all my reading and practices—that there is a hidden reality far richer, more sacred and more real than what the culture was offering, as well as from my love of the mystery as it is portrayed and manifested in literature and the arts, which led me to Owen Barfield.

I could say that my sense of truth also drew me to anthroposophy for similar reasons, and that I have also had to translate and ponder the meaning, the significance, the living reality presented there in images and words.

From the perspective I have now, after some years of anthroposophical study and practice, work for good in the world clearly has to do with inner work, with accessing my "I" and living from it with heart awareness, with prayer, meditation and exercises (such as the six subsidiary exercises), and with coming together with people of similar interests.

I also became interested in conversation as a way toward illumination and a way to impregnate action with holiness. I had been noticing that in our Catholic Worker meetings, some people were more controlling and others did not get heard. I also learned about conscious or living conversation and became convinced that so much good and positive change can come from a conscious conversation. This I have pursued in reading, study and practice, and leading groups in the senior center in Ithaca and at the Threefold Community. I am gravitating toward biography work.

It has seemed to me for quite a while that the Catholic Worker approach to life and work—voluntary poverty, hospitality, protest—is somehow rather different from the life and work of anthroposophists whom I know (including now, myself). The meat and potatoes of my Catholic Worker friends involved actions such as bringing into the public eye world events of violence and injustice, with a view toward righting wrongs, through organizing, vigils, rallies, demonstrations, and nonviolent protests against war, injustice, and nuclear arms build-up. These do not seem to be the activities of most of the anthroposophists I know. On the other hand, my take on most of the people in the Catholic Worker movement is that these, in general, do not seem to have a perspective which includes things such as the evolution of consciousness, repeated earth lives, inner development, and supersensible worlds and beings. Having said this, I wonder if it matters.

Granted, these are large generalities and the sample is limited by my experience. My desire is not to label any person or group, not to say that this is "good" and this is "bad" but to find a way of understanding and a way of living that satisfies inner and outer work. Might there be a way of bridging the (perceived) gap between the two groups, of having them cross-fertilize each other for the better of each and the world? This is more than an academic question for me. It has to do with where and how I see myself working, what I do, where I live, and with whom I associate.

Right now, as I explained, I am more focused on anthroposophy, believing that activism of soul and spirit will have a more real and lasting effect on the world. But I also still have a great attraction to my Catholic Worker friends and what they do.

Over the years, I have made some attempts to bring a wider (anthroposophical) perspective and practice to the Ithaca Catholic Worker. I have taught them some eurythmy and have written about meditation for their newsletter. I have brought them speech formation through poetry recitation. And when I am at meetings, I try to be present to the angels and the so-called dead, to the spirit and soul being of each person there, and to what actually goes on during the conversation.

Sometimes I wonder if this "gap" is all in my mind. After all, there are wonderful anthroposophical endeavors doing the Works of Mercy: for example, the Camphill movement, education for children with special needs, and many I am not familiar with. And these impulses have good and lasting effects on individuals and society.

And the Catholic Worker movement has its deep thinkers and practitioners, a theology and practice that may not be so far from anthroposophical insights. Are these two separate streams that have their own domains and ultimately complement each other in bringing love and justice to the world?

Here is a possible positive change of perception: I have described a relationship of polarity or contrast. Could that be transformed into a relationship of relatedness, or even wholeness? The one heart that we all share manifests as thinkers, doers, inner workers and outer workers. Some people gravitate toward one, some toward the other, or one person may switch from one to the other depending on mood, circumstance, and understanding.

One challenge I see—certainly in myself—for a possible merger of understandings and actions is the great urgency of the times. What does one do in the face of such vast and terrible injustice and violence such as we see in the world today? What does one do in response to the genocidal nightmare of Gaza? Stand on a corner, hold a sign with others, express grief and outrage publicly so that some hearts may see and be moved? Attend a eurythmy performance, where the grief of current events may be transformed into an invisible force of beauty and love that permeates the ether? Write and lobby US government representatives to stop arming Israel? Practice Loving Kindness meditation? Delve into the mysteries of the Word? Do not all of these have their place in the scheme of things?

The world and its beings are in great peril, yet there is the ever-present help of the spiritual worlds. And that help may sometimes manifest as works of depth and beauty in the human form and voice. And it may also manifest as creative and nonviolent denouncement, disruption and disobedience, as Thoreau, Gandhi, and Martin Luther King Jr. taught us. I believe that the wealth of insights, practices, and the arts in anthroposophy could be brought even further into the world. Here are a few suggestions that I have thought about:

- Eurythmy and speech formation workshops and performances brought into prisons, hospitals, mental institutions, assisted living and nursing homes, and to neighborhoods of marginalized people;
- Speech artists performing at local open mic poetry readings;
- The Christian Community people getting involved in interfaith groups, initiatives, including in Black communities;
- Study groups in anthroposophical communities which deal with world events, such as the situation in Gaza, nuclear proliferation, etc.

Let us be open to true cooperation, to the sacred flow between us, to the transforming power of love in its many forms. To love this world means to know it and all its beings and all its joy and suffering more deeply. And to find ways—from that perspective—to change the world, to make it better, while still loving it.

> What we would like to do is change the world—make it a little simpler for people to feed, clothe, and shelter themselves as God intended for them to do.... We can, to a certain extent, change the world; we can work for the oasis, the little cell of joy and peace in a harried world. We can throw our pebble in the pond and be confident that its ever-widening circle will reach around the world. We repeat, there is nothing that we can do but love, and, dear God, please enlarge our hearts to love each other, to love our neighbor, to love our enemy as well as our friend. —Dorothy Day

Searching for Threefold in Thinking and Willing

Gary Lamb

Beginnings

I grew up in a small iron ore mining town located in the Adirondack Mountains of New York State, sometimes called the "North Country." For a child it was in many ways an idyllic place to grow up because of the beauty of nature and the rhythms of the seasons. As a boy I did a lot of hunting and fishing with my father. It was part sport, but also provided a significant amount to our family food supply.

Our village was mainly Irish, Lithuanian, and Polish folk with most people attending one of the two Catholic churches. Going to church every Sunday was a family activity that I participated in until I left for college. While baseball was my favorite activity growing up, I also participated in track, football, wrestling, and bowling. I'm the oldest of three children, four years older than my sister and six years older than my brother. Because of these age differences I participated in more activities with my father than my siblings.

After leaving high school, I went to a two-year technical college with a focus on civil technology, which included highway design and large construction projects. My goal was to become a licensed civil engineer.

When I graduated from the two-year technical college in 1968, I was facing being drafted into the Army during the Vietnam War. One option was to transfer to a four-year college, obtain a draft deferment, and obtain a bachelor of science in civil engineering. Another option I explored was to enlist in the Navy's Seabees, the construction division of the Naval forces, to gain practical experience in the construction of naval bases. An added benefit of taking that route was that at the same time I would qualify for the GI Bill of Rights to help pay for attending a four-college at a later date. I went to a local Navy recruiter office to explore the naval option at a time when the military branches were desperately seeking recruits to support the war in Vietnam. Much to my surprise, the recruiter firmly told me not to enlist in the Navy but to transfer to another college and get my bachelor's degree first. I thought, well, that's strange, I've been rejected in the middle of a war from joining military service. I did end up transferring to the State University of New York at Stony Brook on Long Island, where I ended up being a mathematics major.

Awakening Social Interest and Meeting Anthroposophy

When attending Stony Brook, the interest in social issues really awakened for me. The focus at that time was the Vietnam War and the Civil Rights Movement led by Dr. Martin Luther King Jr. During my time there, I was surrounded by student and faculty protest marches in opposition to the war along with narcotics agents posing as students and arresting students for possession of illegal drugs. Classes were routinely canceled by professors to make time for discussions on the war.

In the midst of this turmoil, I had exchanges with a fellow student who was a passionate Marxist. The theory of Marxism interested me greatly since I had recently begun reading about Rudolf Steiner's social ideas, including his critiques of Marxism, as will be described in what follows.

Around 1969, I met Joel Kobran, a student of Steiner's work, who was also a math major at Stony Brook. Several times he handed me notes in very small handwriting with Steiner book titles after class. As we went our separate ways to our next classes, I would crumple up the lists and litter the halls of Stony Brook with Steiner titles.

My engagement with social issues and my meeting with anthroposophy happened at about the same time when I was 20. (Yes, I did eventually read one of those books that Joel recommended and went on to be an avid student of anthroposophy.) I initially didn't see the outer connection of anthroposophy with social issues. Besides being surrounded by the turbulence of outer events, I was also experiencing a kind of inner vacuum. I no longer had any inner relation to Catholicism, and the rampant atheism prevailing on campus did not appeal to me either. I felt an emptiness of soul and was looking for something that would connect the different experiences of my studies and life—for example, what was the connection between philosophy and science and how did that relate to me? Initially, I didn't realize that anthroposophy had a strong social dimension. But within a year, I did realize it as I read *Towards Social Renewal*. And I remember taking that book and going to my Marxist friend and saying, well, why don't you try reading this, but he had no interest whatsoever. I would say that Steiner's *Philosophy of Spiritual Activity* and *Towards Social Renewal* were the two main pillars of my studies of anthroposophy during those years.

Once I finished college and was again subject to the draft, I struggled with the question of whether I was truly a conscientious objector, or did I just want to get out of the draft out of fear? I knew that one of the questions that the members of the draft board might ask would be, "if you applied for conscientious objector status what would you do if your country is invaded by a foreign country? Would you fight or not? I struggled with this question. I ended up reading Tolstoy's short story, *Ivan the Fool*, and that gave me a moral imagination for objecting to war. I ended up going before a draft board of five or six elderly men who had all been in the military. Looking back, I felt I was more prepared for that meeting and more sure of myself than any other meeting in my life. And they gave me the conscientious objector status. I ended up working as a medical technician at the Albany Medical Center Hospital as an alternative to entering the military. One of my duties was to work with doctors who did autopsies in the morgue. My responsibility was to process autopsy specimens and convert them into microscope slides for diagnosis purposes. Oddly, I may have seen more blood and guts at the hospital than if I had gone to Vietnam. But at least I was still alive.

Following my Two-Year Conscientious Objector Duty

During my college years and my two-year conscientious objector duty, my mother was struggling with terminal brain cancer. As it got worse my father could not both work and provide the necessary physical support for her. Following my two-year duty just mentioned, I returned home and became my mother's main caregiver five days a week for the last eight months of her life. My father, with help from my sister and brother, took care of her on weekends.

I was 26 years old when my mother died. At this point I did not have a clear idea of what I was going to do next in life. However, I was certain that I wanted to work practically out of the insights of anthroposophy. The only two practical vocations I knew about in relation to anthroposophy were Waldorf education and biodynamic agriculture. I decided to explore the master's degree in Waldorf education at Adelphi University in Garden City, New York, which was connected to the Waldorf School of Garden City. When I went to visit the school, Ina Barton, a school administrator, gave me a tour of the classrooms from kindergarten through high school. I was awestruck and devastated at the same time. I realized what I had missed in my own education. When she asked me whether I wanted to enroll in the teacher-training program, I said, "No, I want to enroll in the kindergarten."

Emerson College

Upon hearing about Emerson College in England, which offered a foundation year as part of the teacher training, I decided that I would try to counterbalance 12 years of public education with an intensive art and craft experience for a year, after which I would consider doing the Waldorf teacher training program. I was accepted to the Foundation Year program at Emerson College starting in September 1974. That was a fantastic year for me, 1974–75. I met a lot of people, made many friends, and experienced arts and crafts as never before. The following summer I went home to make money so I could return to England and take more courses at Emerson.

When I did return to England, I felt really on top of the world but the thought came to me, this is too good to be true. And sure enough, five weeks later I got sick with flu-like symptoms and remained ill on and off for the next four years.

I had really enjoyed the speech work at Emerson, so I decided to spend a third year in England at the London Speech School, but that was clearly too much for me and I regressed in health. It was during that time that I met the Hassells, Jade, and Chris, and I ended up convalescing in their home. But I didn't really get better, so I ended up returning to the States.

Returning to the US: Recovery, Spring Valley, and Weleda

After seeing six doctors about my health situation, I ended up being treated by Paul Scharff in Spring Valley who began treating me for having a liver disease. He was right and I slowly began to improve. As my health improved, I began to see Jade and her children more, and eventually we got married and moved to Spring Valley where I began working for Weleda. I learned a lot there with Christine and Finbarr Murphy, the owners. I began by packing boxes but ended up being the production manager of the toiletry division. This was my first intensive experience in business life; the production, distribution, and sales of products. As the business was small, I also went to trade shows around the country and experienced the intricacies of the cosmetics business.

Weleda was a good schooling in business and economics for me, and I was happy there and in the Threefold Community in Spring Valley. I became good friends with Owen Holder, the director of the

Threefold Foundation, and I learned about the social ideas behind the Threefold Community, including its experimentation with a local currency. I also learned about the history of Weleda and Der Kommende Tag, the joint stock company that Steiner founded shortly before his death in 1925 and of which Weleda was part. This insider's view was largely due to the fact that Christine Murphy is the granddaughter of Emil Molt, the founder of the first Waldorf school in Germany.

Hawthorne Valley

For nearly seven years things went well at Weleda until I became ill with pneumonia and couldn't get out of bed for a month. Even though I loved my work at Weleda, something told me I wasn't going to recover and get out of bed until I figured out what I was meant to do next in life. While I was sick in bed, I surrounded myself with books by Steiner. I felt somewhere in one or more of those books was a message of what I was supposed to do next in life. And what came to me, vaguely at first, was that I needed to work in some way with Rudolf Steiner's social ideas, in particular with cultural freedom. More specifically, I needed to somehow challenge New York State's highly restrictive religious exemption of its vaccination law regarding school age children.

A very specific idea came to me. I should move to Harlemville with my wife, Jade, and step child, Emily, and start a small business to help fund a small school. A small school that would refuse to enforce New York State's religious exemption law regarding the vaccination of children, which schools are required to enforce.

But just as I was contemplating this, a New York State Court overruled the vaccination law, which allowed families with spiritual beliefs that are in opposition to state regulations regarding vaccinations to not vaccinate. And I thought, wow, this is really great. Parents need to know about this court case and the resulting change in the vaccination law. I called the Department of Health and asked them when they were going to let parents know about this change.

They said that they were not under any obligation to inform families about the court decision.

Since Joel Kobran and I had just incorporated the Margaret Fuller Corporation (around 1987) to publish *The Threefold Review*, we decided that our first current events communication would be to notify elementary and secondary schools in New York State about the court ruling and the resulting change in the religious exemption regarding the vaccination of children. We did so by sending out several thousand announcements to schools in New York State, including folding letters, addressing and sealing envelopes by hand, and taking them to the post office.

At this point I was working as the farm store manager at Hawthorne Valley, because I had wanted more experience in retail business. Joel and I had also started the Northeast Threefold Group with between twelve and fifteen members meeting regularly. The group initially focused on studying the US Constitution, the Bill of Rights, and the Federalist Papers along with studying various publications by Steiner related to the threefold social organism. Each time we met someone would also present a biography of one of the Founding Fathers. It was a rich experience for all of us.

I was also involved in organizing conferences on freedom and funding of education. The largest of these was a conference called "Goals 2000: Educate America Act: A Critical Review and Dissent." This occurred when Bill Clinton was President of the United States. We brought together a wide spectrum of people from homeschoolers to independent school teachers and administrators, as well as professors from colleges and universities. We had fourteen different speakers, all critical of the federal government's efforts to impose uniform testing and curriculum on both public and private schools. It turned out that the editor at that time of the *Holistic Education Review*, attended the conference and published the full proceedings of the conference, and sent copies to every member of Congress.

School Vouchers or Tax Credits? Efforts to Increase Educational Access

During my time at Hawthorne Valley, I switched from being the farm store manager and became the development director of Hawthorne Valley School. This was in the mid 1990s and I served in that capacity for about seven years. Because of my position I ended up on the Tuition Assistance Committee of the Waldorf School and was sometimes the person of last resort for desperate families to talk to who could not keep their children in the school with the amount of financial aid being offered to them. I would really try to help every family with school children to figure out a means for them to afford having their children remain in school and for the school to take into consideration all extenuating circumstances, all the while keeping within the school's financial guidelines. I experienced the pain and suffering caused by not having education financially accessible to all, of not having a free cultural life supported by economic life.

This led me to begin a scholarship program working with thirteen schools, helping families in financial need to send their children to the school of their choice. I ran that program for about five years in the late 1990s. I also studied the whole area of funding independent education, including education vouchers and tax credits. I reached the conclusion that educational tax credits come closest to Steiner's suggestions of how to safely finance independent schools without government regulations.

I also began meeting with non-public school representatives. They told me to meet with Jim Cultrara, a lobbyist for the Catholic schools in the state, which I did. We became collaborators in efforts to pass education tax credit legislation in New York State that would provide financial support to families who want to send their children to non-public schools. There were two attempts over a nine-year period to pass education tax credit legislation, but the powerful teacher unions were instrumental in thwarting both efforts.

Working with Waldorf Schools and Publishing

When Joel Kobran became ill and unable to help any further with publishing *The Threefold Review* and hosting the Northeast Threefold Group meetings, I did not have the energy to carry both initiatives by myself, and so they came to an end. I continued writing and editing and published two books on Waldorf education: *The Social Mission of Waldorf Education* and *Wellsprings of the Spirit: Free Human Beings as the Source for Social Renewal* and also a volume on *Associative Economics,* both of which are distributed by Waldorf Publications. Later, Sarah Hearn/Mecca and I edited *Steinerarian Economics,* a compendium of Steiner's indications on economics with explanatory text, now distributed by SteinerBooks. This book has since been translated into Spanish and Portuguese and published in South America by Stay True Organic.

I also collaborated with Bob Munson and Mary Roscoe for a number of years in developing an Accessible to All (ATA) tuition approach in which no Waldorf school family is turned away from sending their children to a Waldorf school for purely financial reasons. While I was involved, there were approximately 35 schools employing the ATA model.

The Avalon Initiative

My interest in accessibility and accountability in education continued, and together with Patrice Maynard at the Research Institute for Waldorf Education began The Avalon Initiative, a kind of educational think tank. We had the idea of bringing together people from different educational philosophies and backgrounds; teachers, administrators, parents, and academics to discuss pressing issues in education in an open, non-politicized, and caring environment. We held four conferences over four years. The first conference was on Accountability in Education, which was well attended by people from public, private, and homeschool initiatives, along with university professors. The conferences ended around 2016 with the election of Donald Trump and the polarization which occurred around the issue of the funding of education at that time.

Even so, there was a unique quality and atmosphere surrounding these events. A public-school teacher with no connection to anthroposophy that I know of visited me one day. She had just attended one of our gatherings a few days before our conversation, and told me, "I don't know exactly what you intended to achieve at those conferences. I can only describe my experience of them as 'sacred' events. They are really special, so I wanted to thank you."

Further Work

I have continued writing under the auspices of the Hawthorne Valley Center for Social Research. Currently, I am in the process of completing volume 2 of *A Road to Sacred Creation: Rudolf Steiner's Perspectives on Technology*. The first volume was published by SteinerBooks in 2021 and volume 2 will be published in 2026. As a result of my research on group work and collaboration, I published *On the Wings of Words: Conversations and Human Relations: Inner Aspects of the Fundamental Social Law and the Threefold Social Organism*, in 2024. I am currently preparing two further areas of research: politics and the American Constitution, Rudolf Steiner's perspectives on race, and the issue of racism in the United States. With these projects I intend to employ collaborative "conversation-based" group research and development techniques.

Based on an interview with Gary Lamb by Christopher Schaefer

Section V

Leading with Spirit: Supporting Communities and Organizations

Vignettes from a Career in Coaching and Consulting

Gordon Collins

Formative Experiences

I met anthroposophy while I was at university and exploring different spiritual paths and practices. After receiving a degree in psychology, I decided to go to teacher college (when you don't know what you want to do with your life—more education provides a path of least resistance!). While there I began to search for an educational approach that acknowledged the spiritual dimension. I found a book on Waldorf education and began to learn more about it. When my time for a teaching practicum arrived, I asked if I could have a placement in a Waldorf school. I vividly remember my conversation with the head of the department (highly regarded by many), who refused my request, but even more striking was that in that moment I was convinced that he had no idea what Waldorf education is about!

Years later my wife and I were beginning to explore options for a kindergarten for our son. A sign in a local health food store announced an upcoming meeting for any parents interested in Waldorf education. We went and at the end of the meeting five sets of parents stayed to ask questions and someone asked, "What do you have to do to get one of these schools started?" We launched an initiative and started the Lakeshore Waldorf Kindergarten and participated in a study group in support of the school. I remember thinking how peculiar this was and that it must be an old person's spirituality, belonging to a previous age: "Just look at the fonts they use on their books and the titles." About 18 months later I had a realization that

I was being a dilettante in my approach to spirituality! I had been arrogant in my judgments about what we were reading and now this was seriously looking like it was going to become my path. This was further confirmed when the leader of our study group gave me a paper written by Bernard Lievegoed from the Netherlands Pedagogical Institute (NPI) and I discovered that there were other consultants working out of anthroposophy—I had found my home!

One day while driving on one of the twelve lanes of Highway 401 in Toronto, I was overcome with a feeling of euphoria. Why am I feeling so good? Why is it so intense? And then a line from the back cover of Steiner's *Knowledge of Higher Worlds and its Attainment* flashed in my mind ("discover true self-confidence"), and this was exactly what I was experiencing in this moment—a true confidence! This was not a confidence I had in a particular expertise or skill; it was much more of a foundation of confidence—for meeting what comes toward me and actively engaging in life!

A Research Opportunity—Discovering the Theme of my Career—Conversations

> *Conversation and dialogue between human beings is the archetypal social phenomenon.* —Rudolf Steiner

Permeating the interactions and transactions of business are deeper levels of encounter, relationship, and validation of each other's humanity. The world is evolving in many ways that are faster than our capacity to adapt to it—let alone to understand and consciously direct it. Technology is a big part of this acceleration from instant global communications to algorithms making choices for us and the ever growing "promise" of AI. But let's not lose sight of what is at the heart of human beings being their best—cooperating and collaborating with others for noble purposes!

Fortunately, early in my career opportunities came my way. I was introduced to a senior manager at a large telecommunications company who had a question about how she could develop more creativity in the team of engineers reporting to her. We immediately connected with each other, and it resulted in a project which we called the IT (Innovative Technologies) Project. I essentially had a lab to work on this challenge with 30-plus engineers for almost two years. We explored various processes, competency building exercises, and approaches. I noticed that much of what we initially introduced was transformed into rigid structures and processes—a set of instructions or steps to be followed. The phrase nonlinear was a derogatory term that over time took on positive connotations as we challenged the engineer's mindset—especially when it is applied to human beings!

We began to gain traction when we started exploring different ways that people could collaborate with each other and create value. We realized that we needed something new, something that would allow us to take bold action into a future that neither of us had experienced yet. We couldn't fall back on being the expert or giving advice. We had to create a new path together, not follow an existing one. We needed a new conversational form—a new social form!

We worked intensively with listening and trust, linking creativity to producing effective action and this led to a simple structure—one person having a question or challenge they were facing and the other person supporting them by establishing trust and through careful listening and questioning, assisting their learning partner in finding their own solution. We ended up calling this process coaching—as it so happened, the idea of coaching was just emerging from the world of sports into the business world at this time.

Employees volunteered to participate as a coach or a learning partner and we provided developmental learning paths for both roles. The coaching process essentially moved through four phases and would tend to last from 16—20 weeks.

1. Warmth—Building trust and relationship
2. Light—Inviting insight through enlivened thinking
3. Movement—Exploring the horizon of possible actions

4. Form—Committing to a course of action and following through to achieve a desired outcome

We recommended that coaches and their learning partners weren't in a direct reporting relationship—i.e., as a coach, I would be coaching someone who reported to a different manager within a different team or department. We also discovered that many employees had issues they wanted to address with their own manager but didn't know how to have that conversation, so this gave them a safe place to plan their conversation, practice it, and build the confidence for action! We ended up calling the initiative a coaching network, and I started a new company called The Coaching Network. The initiative kept evolving and spread to different departments within the organization and eventually to other organizations in North America and Europe.

Working Consciously with Freedom, Equality, and Brotherhood

The coach would constantly strive to leave their learning partner in freedom—in choosing what they would do and how they would do it. All participants chose freely to participate, no one was sent by their manager because they "needed coaching." Freedom also came with responsibilities—e.g., each participant was responsible for the consequences of their actions (or lack of), their full participation in the program, and to bring the coaching relationship to a successful and amicable conclusion. Working consciously with freedom encourages productive dialogue around what freedom is and isn't, and how responsibility-based freedom (which has an emphasis on leaving the other free vs. a more singular focus on "my freedom") differs from freedom permeated by egotism (which really isn't freedom at all!).

Equality was built into the culture of the program—the coach and their learning partners were equal even if their organizational titles suggested otherwise. In some cases, we had people lower in the hierarchy coaching others that were higher up in the hierarchy and other coaching partnerships reflected more of a peer coaching relationship. Hierarchy was there, but in the background. In all cases, we were striving for a real "I"-to-"I" meeting of the participants.

Collaboration (brotherhood and sisterhood) emerged as people energetically volunteered their time and energy to organize, promote, and track the results of the initiative throughout the organization. Giving of their time, energy, and talents—and receiving the benefits of participating—brought a warmth and liveliness to the community of participants.

Living and Working with Anthroposophy

If we are going to make progress with the threefold social organism (3FSO), it will require that we effectively engage in dialogue and conversations—especially outside of the anthroposophical community. We will need to socialize ideas, encourage initiative taking, and practically demonstrate the value and legitimacy of the 3FSO ideal! However, an ideal like the 3FSO can seem daunting—"too large for me to deal with" or be seen as the responsibility of those with power. However, like many things, often the real question is "What within my sphere can I influence?" The example above shows that we can make real progress by being inspired by ideals like the threefold social organism and take action in our immediate circumstances—even if it is just a beginning. Where can we influence the conditions for creating greater freedom for others? Where can we influence greater equality and fairness in opportunities for all? How can we collaborate with a generosity of spirit in both our giving and receiving? I believe that we need to prepare the conditions—develop the capabilities to provide a foundation for an idea whose time has come.

> *Nothing else in the world... not all the armies... is so powerful as an idea whose time has come.* —Victor Hugo

Working Consciously with Conversation

You are your attention! —Georg Kühlewind

Our attention is so close to us that for the most part we don't even notice it—we simply attend to what we are paying attention to—our focus, the content, etc. There are moments when someone tells you you're not paying attention. Or you have a realization that you have been distracted for the last while. Typically, then, we just go back to the conversation or whatever activity we were engaged in and think nothing more of it.

What if we were to take this more seriously? And actually, pay attention to our attention, not just what we are attending to...

I was having lunch with a colleague one day when they asked me "Gord, what is your vision for yourself?" I immediately experienced a change of state—it was as if time slowed down and everything went into slow motion—the temperature in the restaurant seemed to become cooler and at the same time my mind was racing wildly, trying to find something meaningful to say...when he then said, "If you don't have one then don't just make something up!" I was flabbergasted as I realized that this was exactly what I was trying to do! I felt like I had been seen through—was I that transparent? So how is that possible?

My Reflections on this Conversation

On Him: He was calm, relaxed, focused (there was a noticeable absence of distraction), and serious—not in a heavy way but clearly not in the pursuit of trivial, small talk. He was also centered in himself and very attentive to me—simply present!

On Myself: I was feeling good—quite normal, but my attention wasn't grounded. I was actually a little on edge, perhaps not sure what to anticipate, engaged but not centered.

But what if I had paid attention to my experience—the moment that he asked me the question, it disrupted the flow of my "normal" state and I panicked! I was overwhelmed by my experience and a chain of events unfolded. My attention became identified with being overwhelmed—and I became exactly what I was experiencing at that moment—overwhelmed!

Now, what is possible when I notice my attention? The act of noticing itself frees up some of my attention and suddenly, I begin to have the possibility of "acting in the middle of the act" of making a choice—how do I want to respond in this moment, navigate in the conversation? Is this not just another step in the direction of becoming free?

I also realize that this kind of insight can occur at any moment in the conversation, in reflection after the conversation or perhaps even years later, but the point is that there is a capacity here and it can be developed. What difference would it make if I could develop my capacity for freeing up my attention? I want to be clear that by this capacity I do not mean an analytical intellectual exercise but what some traditions call an observer or a witness.

We can strengthen our attention through concentration exercises and meditation practices, and I believe the connection between freeing up our attention and the true meaning of freedom will become increasingly important for us.

The Power of Not Knowing

I was asked to contribute a series of articles to the Leadership Network of the Canadian federal government. I remembered a phrase we used to work with—"knowing is the enemy of learning"—and many times I experienced the challenge of truly listening to another person when I felt I knew where this line of thought was going. I also witnessed the arrogance and certainty of many leaders and managers (as you know, it is always easier to see arrogance in others) and the consequences it had in their conversations. People would feel shut down or the conversation would veer off course and the potential creativity that lay below the surface never had the chance to see the light of day and get socialized. Below I share an excerpt of a paper I wrote with leaders in the public service as the intended audience.

In the beginner's mind there are many possibilities, but in the expert's, there are few. —Shunryu Suzuki

How much of the work that you do takes place in conversations? Face to face, Zoom calls, written communications, e-mails, etc. Daily we are engaged in conversations—helping others in their planning, setting direction and goals, providing feedback, making decisions, solving problems, etc. At the same time as leaders and managers we have been through many of these conversations before and through our experience and learning we have built confidence in ourselves, in particular in our knowledge and expertise.

Being an expert can be quite attractive. Our expertise is also a source of satisfaction for us. We often equate the value we bring to our role with our expertise. People often come to us with an expectation that we will use our expertise to help them with their questions, problems, and decisions. We are often acknowledged and rewarded for being an expert. In some cases, we identify so strongly with our expertise that we might say that we are our expertise!

Our intention is not in any way to devalue expertise, but to point out a potential blind spot in its overuse and to reveal a complementary insight and practice we call "the power of not knowing."

When we over-rely on what we already know we can fall into an automatic mode of operating. Our attention relaxes, as we already know where the conversation is going—what the right answer is. We can easily slip into listening to our own internal dialogue, confirming, and strengthening what we already know. This can further lead to making judgements about our conversation partner or looking for the right moment to make our point. It is also important to notice the role our emotional state plays in this situation. Our comfort and confidence are often tightly coupled to our competence (what we know and what we do). This "good feeling" that comes from the coherence of our comfort, confidence, and competence often produces an attitude of certainty, and certainty is not conducive to openness, genuine interest, and the spirit of inquiry.

By contrast, being in a state of not knowing is initially emotionally unsettling. We have left the comfort and familiarity of the known behind and stand facing the present, emerging moment without our familiar security. How will we respond? Will we retreat to the known, the familiar or will we step forward into the unknown, into the possible? Being in a state of not knowing is not denying our knowledge, experience, and expertise, but utilizing it in a new way.

Our expertise is still there; however, it is in the background, available to us but held in reserve. By holding back on providing an answer to their question or the solution to their problem we are encouraging two important developments. First, we are giving our conversational partner an opportunity to both develop and express themselves, to extend their thinking or logic to the point where it "breaks down" and allows a moment of insight or the possibility of their true question to emerge. Second, we are developing our own power of restraint and in so doing, allowing ourselves to further develop our sense of timing! This ability to sense or create the learning moment in the conversation and intervene appropriately is the essence of "timing." Our experience at The Coaching Network strongly supports the notion that this is what our direct reports, colleagues and our bosses really want in our conversations with them. They have a deep desire to "break through" and discover their own insights, answers, and solutions. The difficulty lies in that we don't always know how to ask for what we deeply desire, but the good news is that we can often recognize it when we experience it, as indicated in the following comment by one of our participants—a performer recalling a confidential moment of insight:

> It wasn't what my coach said! It was what I said! I know I have known this for years, but it wasn't until my coach helped me see it so clearly that I now know exactly what I need to do. I am very grateful!

Final Thoughts

Anthroposophy has been an ongoing inspiration for me in my client work with individuals and teams. Work and life in general seem to be intensifying and asking more of us—more patience, more restraint, more flexibility in our soul. If we are going to meet this challenge in a healthy way, we will need to develop new capabilities to be able to effectively engage in conversations with others who may see the world very differently than we do!

The Association for Social Development

I would like to acknowledge the role the Association for Social Development (ASD) has played in my life and career. The ASD is an international group of consultants that work out of anthroposophy. It was founded out of the Netherlands Pedagogical Institute and inspired by the work of Bernard Lievegoed.

We hold an annual conference in different locations around the world and guests invited by a member are welcome to attend. Each year we adopt a theme related to emerging phenomena that affect our work, our clients and the evolving world situation. We also work on our own development—e.g., a few years back we worked with Arthur Zajonc over a four-year cycle on meditation and its vital role in our consulting life.

Having a community of practitioners to share ideas and practices with and correct our one-sidedness is invaluable.

Current Ongoing Research

Christopher Schaefer and I offered a workshop on Sacred Conversations—the Social and Spiritual Dynamics of Conversations at the last ASD Conference (2024) held at the Royal Agricultural College in the UK. Our goal was to develop a new guiding imagination for our encounter with others.

We shared experiences of when there was a felt shift in consciousness and a "star-filled" space opened in the conversation—even if for just a moment. We continued to explore how we can best meet or allow for these moments of grace to appear. The group continues to meet to share our questions and research findings.

> *We begin to develop an understanding of the spiritual world only when we wake up in the encounter with the soul-spiritual element of the other.* —Rudolf Steiner

Reflections on the Path to Social Awakening

Michael Soulé

Life as Dialog

The beginning of my social awakening happened at a very young age. I had the sense that everything was connected to everything else, though I wasn't sure how. Years later, with the advent of the ecological movement in the 1970s, this feeling was affirmed when I heard "everything is connected to everything else" articulated as one the four basic laws of ecology. I knew inwardly that this reality applied not only to nature but was relevant to all of life—everything from our thoughts to what we said to what we did, past, present, and future.

In reflecting on the topic of this essay—how did anthroposophy help shape, illuminate, or lead my work in social development—anything I recalled from my life seemed to be entangled with everything else.

I came across a piece by Arthur Moor from the 1965 issue of *Art of Education.* In it he is describing a typical botany= lesson in a Waldorf school:

> You cannot really pick a dandelion—for a dandelion is not a thing that exists all at once. It is a performance. And it only happens when the sun and earth, the sky and water are all working together. The pattern may be in the seed as the pattern of music is in the score, but it doesn't come to life till the players play it, or the singers sing it. The score becomes music only as the players and singers pour themselves into the performance,

> just as the sun and earth and air and water pour themselves into a dandelion. And every plant, and every living thing is really a world performance—even you. Every living thing is a world performance. That is the heart of it—a realization that illuminates not only botany but every human being and action.

This thought helped me see how my understanding of social phenomena unfolded throughout my life. It is clear that it was there all along and that both my life experiences and growing relationship to anthroposophy called it into consciousness through an unfolding dialog with life and the world around me.

In her booklet on community building, Marjorie Spock recounts a scene from Goethe's fairytale, "The Green Snake and the Beautiful Lily": A king asks the Green Snake—who loves gold—about her experience:

> "What is more glorious than gold?"
> The snake responds, "Light."
> "And what is more quickening than light?" asks the king.
> "Conversation," replies the snake.

My version of this exchange goes like this:

> "What is more glorious than experience?"
> "Understanding!"
> "And what is more quickening than understanding?"
> "Insight arising from Dialog."

Reflecting on My Journey

With the ever-increasing pace of life, it is difficult to find the time and space to gather life experiences and reflect on them to find deeper insights that might lead to a greater sense of one's life purpose. We are hardwired for daily reflection in our diurnal rhythm, but life often offers so many distractions that it is easy to miss the opportunity. Rudolf Steiner repeatedly pointed to the importance of daily reflection and offered ways we could prepare for and use the night to gain life insight. I remember first hearing about this in my

20s. I already had an active dream life, but the idea that I could use the night to process one day and prepare for the next was intriguing. Immediately I started taking time before sleep to ponder the day and a few moments in the morning to listen to any reflections from the night.

Gradually, I became aware of the more specific aspects of this practice that Steiner offered. Especially thinking backward. It made sense. It just was very difficult to do. The main thing about this practice was that when first I heard about it, it immediately made sense, became a practice, and yielded results. It seemed so simple and yet so profound and it intrigued me enough to continue to explore Steiner's suggestions for other practices. Could I really follow Steiner's suggestions and be my own teacher in developing my capacity for spiritual insight? Developing the discipline to do it regularly was a slow and gradual process. But this practice planted a seed for a time 30 years later when life gave me an opportunity to take a reflective break for a longer period.

Twice in my life, circumstances unfolded such that I could step back from my profession for an extended period. The first time was just after working for five years in my first Waldorf school job. My wife and boys and I planned to take a gap year and travel the world. This was really a year to explore and experience the world, less so to reflect on my life. We circumnavigated the globe, visiting Waldorf schools and meeting Waldorf colleagues everywhere we could. In addition, I spent a semester at the Social Development Centre in England. These experiences added layers of understanding to my experience in Waldorf education and at a Waldorf school. The second time came 20 years later. By that time, I had worked in two more Waldorf schools (one teaching and one as administrator), spent seven years on a Waldorf school board, directed an educational nonprofit and worked for six years as an executive in the Association of Waldorf Schools of North America (AWSNA). I had visited at least 50 schools, completed Developing School visits to dozens and participated in accreditation, membership, and a whirlwind of activities supporting schools. I was grateful to have time to look back and reflect on what I had learned.

From Experience to Understanding

It was 2014, and I had just completed two years as administrator at a small Waldorf school in rural Idaho. My wife and I were committed to staying another year in Idaho and our life circumstances provided me an opportunity to take a sabbatical. I had years of experience working in ecological nonprofits, teaching, being an administrator, board member, and advisor in Waldorf schools, working in teacher training and traveling. I wanted to see if I could discover how all this experience could be integrated into the next phase of my life.

One thread I reflected on was woven through much of my life. I have always felt drawn to group work. Whether it originated by being born into a large family in a neighborhood of large families, or whether I had chosen that situation for my own development, it was definitely a theme in my life's work. Even as a child, and certainly later through my professional life, I felt most alive working in groups and found a sense of purpose as a facilitator. While I generally found myself in leadership positions, it wasn't leading that motivated me. It was being able to help a group find its way. Understanding the dynamics of group work was a passion, even before I met anthroposophy and began to understand the dynamics of group processes from a higher level.

Another thread was what opened up for me through my first job in a Waldorf school in 1986 when I began learning about Rudolf Steiner's insights about social processes. Through the years since that first job, I have studied a lot about group processes. I have had many mentors and teachers that helped me, and equally as many people who offered resistance and challenges. I had read a lot of Steiner, followed the work of Bernard Lievegoed, Christopher Schaefer, Gary Lamb, and others on social development. I had worked in many different groups and organizations in various roles.

I had spent time at the Social Development Centre at Emerson College. Despite the variety of my experiences and study, I had a nagging feeling that I needed to go deeper.

What I wanted to understand more deeply was the nature of collaboration—how can people work together in ways that each individual and the group as a whole grow and develop and that the work of the group can be healing to the organization or community around it? And how could a deeper understanding of collaboration, illuminated by anthroposophical social insights, provide a foundation for building healthy collaborative organizations where the whole structure and function of the organization rested on, and derived from, insights into and practice of collaboration?

The biography of Waldorf schools in the world offered a great wealth of experience related to how collaboration might work, or didn't work, and what conditions were needed—what practices, what understandings help create a truly healthy organization. What I had experienced firsthand in many settings and many groups was the potential and power of collaborative leadership. I had also experienced how a lack of understanding of collaboration created major challenges to organizational health.

I began my exploration by returning to Rudolf Steiner's basic insights about the evolution of consciousness and especially what he called the consciousness soul. Steiner's insights (echoed in my own organizational experiences) pointed to the reality that this phase in humanity's development was the time of learning to work together—in both our inner life and our social development. What Rudolf Steiner called the time of the consciousness soul or heart soul, rang true for me. The tools he gave—including his social laws, mantras, verses, and the College of Teachers' imagination—were already touchstones in my understanding and work.

In groups, communities, and in outer culture, we are being called to learn how to practice collaboration—the ability to recognize the other and share leadership in finding healthy creative solutions to emerging local and global challenges. We are being asked to learn how to think, feel, and act together as free individuals.

It was clear to me that the age of singular inspired leadership is past and evolving to the age of inspired collaboration. It was the huge paradigm shift that Rudolf Steiner pointed us to 100 years ago. It is what Waldorf schools have been practicing (more or less successfully and more or less consciously) for 100 years. It was what was emerging in new thinking and writing across the globe—from insights in writings like Christopher Schaefer's *Partnerships of Hope*, to Otto Sharmer's *Theory U,* and Frederic Leloux's *Reinventing Organizations*. We were just at the beginning of a cresting wave of new imagination and insight about the path of collaboration. And there are many pioneers who have laid down the path.

From Understanding to Insight

My first work during my sabbatical was to explore the basic elements of successful collaboration. After much research and pondering, six key elements emerged. Success in organizational collaboration is fostered when individuals and groups have a commitment to:

- Clearly articulate a common concern and goal, including a vision and sense of direction;
- Individuals bring their best and most aware self to the group—open minded, empathic, enthusiastic, with equanimity, and knowing their biases;
- Support others and their participation in the group—recognizing their qualities, styles, capacities, and needs for support;
- Work in a healthy way together through rhythm, clearly defined roles and responsibilities, hygienic meetings with facilitation, building trusting spaces, and active recognition and reconciliation of conflicts;
- Practice reflectively as individuals and as a group—to consider, learn from, and grow with your work together;
- Create generative dialog through which new ideas, inspirations, and insights may arise.

With this as a foundation, I set about gathering a group of people who might be interested in building a community to deepen our understanding and strengthen our capacity to put into practice, and coach others in putting the emerging art of collaboration into practice.

We named this new research project LEADTOGETHER. It was conceived as a virtual space where people could connect, share ideas and research, exchange resources, and build a circle of collective wisdom about collaboration in light of the spiritual understanding of the human being and the cosmos. It wove together my initial experience of being part of a large family and community, my deep connection to a living spirit, my awakened ecological consciousness through my university studies and post-college work in environmental education, and my long growing appreciation of Steiner's insights on social development.

Initial conversations among long time colleagues from throughout the movement built an imagination of a networking space where like-minded individuals could gather and converse. After six months we had created a platform that would house resources and host online exchanges, especially between people working in schools who were striving to understand and practice creative collaborative governance. The project included online monthly newsletters, occasional blogs, and a collection of about 100 articles related to collaboration, organizational development, leadership, and building community. We also created an online forum for sharing ideas and resources. People visited the site from around the world and signed up to be part of the community. It felt exciting and alive. A few people offered comments and positive feedback. Our hope was that it would become a living network of people sharing, creating and researching together and it seemed to be off to a good start. I was excited to see how many of the social ideas and insights Steiner gave us all could be realized in this small project.

At the end of that year, my time for a sabbatical was over. We moved back to Seattle, and I became the administrator in a small

Waldorf school. At the same time, I was invited to help lead a Waldorf school management course in China, and I was called to do advisory work with numerous schools. With new work unfolding in numerous directions, the LEADTOGETHER project took a back seat. After its first year, it gradually became more of a resource collection and regular newsletter than a living community. Something important was missing. Gathering resources, creating an imagination, and sharing ideas was important, but didn't generate the kind of dialog that I thought it might.

From Insight to Dialog

It was more and more clear that the LEADTOGETHER project needed a greater sense of common ground and stronger connection between people if it was going to become a real community. And I knew from everything I had experienced and absorbed of social life that community could only be really built from dialog. This idea of the power of dialog was at the heart of all the work I had done in the different groups and organizations I had been working with. It was a foundational idea within everything I had learned of social development. I remember how the light went on so brightly for me when I first heard Christopher Schaefer speak about the three dialogs of life and of organizations and then read about it in *Vision in Action*. It both made immediate sense and illuminated my experience. As I mentioned before, it was an idea that wove together and provided an integrating context for three themes in my life—seeking contact with the spirit, feeling connected to the earth in a holistic ecological way, and finding like-minded colleagues. While I had found aspects of the three dialogs in every setting along my life path, I found myself longing for a new group with which to work

In 2015, Christopher Schaefer reached out to a group of four colleagues and invited us into a conversation about the possibility of recreating a training for Waldorf administrators like the one he had created at Sunbridge College. All of the group had been through his training program and had a good feeling for its structure, format, content and the transformative learning that it offered. By the next summer, we had developed a new admin training program and launched it at Hawthorne Valley, New York, and then both there and on Whidbey Island, Washington. Since then, we have had a steady flow of participants through the program's summer weeks with some participants joining an ongoing certificate program extending over the two years. Through the course we began to build a network of people in the schools. This new training within the Art of Administration we named Leading with Spirit.

It was through this course that I had a new opportunity to work with groups directly with the insights of anthroposophical social development. In each week of the course, we go deeply into one aspect of individual and school development. Through the Leading with Spirit training and advisory work, a new sense of purpose for LEADTOGETHER came to life. We had gathered resources and created the means for people to connect, but the real dialog needed to create a vibrant community between Waldorf board members was what was needed.

So, we refocused our effort toward a new goal: to get every Waldorf school board member a Waldorf specific board training. It is important for the future of Waldorf education that board members understand the unique educational approach, spiritual foundation, and social mission of Waldorf education. To develop the board training, we invited a team of colleagues, conducted focus groups with experienced board members, co-created a curriculum, and a basic workshop format. After our first few workshops we developed a guidebook with all the resources we use in the training.

From Dialog to Community

Since that time, we have had 230 board members from more than forty schools participate in the training. One of the outcomes from the training is that many people asked for additional courses—how to be a better board chair, Finance 101 for boards, the art of philanthropy, and fundraising for boards. And this common experience is laying the groundwork for a new level of dialog between schools and boards in the movement. The work is ongoing.

One of the gifts of this essay is the realization of how the path to social understanding unfolded in my life. The seeds of social understanding and social action were always there. At each step, there were four elements present. First there was a situation where I felt called to help some social cause. Second, there was a like-minded companion interested in the work. Third, I found an experienced guide-teacher-mentor who helped guide us. Fourth, the living being of anthroposophy was always there inviting, nurturing, and illuminating my journey. For all of these, I am deeply grateful.

And so, the dialog continues.

Threads of Destiny: Seeking the Healing Social Life

Christopher Schaefer

Motto of the Social Ethic: "The healing social life is found only when, in the mirror of the human soul, the whole community finds its reflection and when, in the community, the virtue and strength of each one is living" (Rudolf Steiner).

Themes in Life

There is a phrase by Rudolf Steiner that I have come to appreciate in my later years. It is, "As we grow older, we begin more and more to love the wisdom revealed by life."* I have taken this to mean that in our later years we can look back at our life and see patterns and themes which we were not aware of at the time while we were floundering, trying to decide what to do next, but which in hindsight, reveal the themes of our destiny. From this perspective the chance encounters and conversations leading to our life decisions do not appear random.

I can look back on a long life, having been born in Germany in the middle of World War II, in 1942, on a family farm owned by my father's family for many generations. I still experienced the War's aftermath—many widowed families, veterans with lost limbs and psychic trauma, and in some places bomb craters, rusted tanks, and hunger. What perhaps went most deeply into my subconscious was a daylight air-raid on Frankfurt in the spring of 1945, with the sky black with planes and the ground trembling as I ran for shelter. This early memory made visible one of the themes in my biography,

* Rudolf Steiner, *Love and Its Meaning in the World*, SteinerBooks, p. 179.

namely a deep concern about war and conflict and the human tragedy it causes. I also had many nightmares as a child about warfare from an earlier historical time, and when I was 19, I arrived in Berlin just in time to experience the building of the wall and the massing of Russian, American, French, and British tanks and troops at Check Point Charlie.

A second theme in my biography has been my interest and love of people, and of different cultures and languages. My grandmother used to call me *Herdenmensch*, meaning a lover of people and crowds, as I was always roaming around the neighborhood with a group of four or five boys, and I delighted in telling them long tales of made-up stories. I have lived in four countries for various amounts of time: Germany, the US, England, and Holland.

In addition, my career as an adult educator and consultant has given me the opportunity of working with many people, in many countries, often in connection to Waldorf education, including in the US and Canada, many European countries, Latin America, and in China, Thailand, and Mexico. This interest in people and cultures also inevitably led me to an interest in bringing people together and in family, community, and organizational life.

A third theme revealing the "wisdom of life" is my lifelong connection to anthroposophy, to Rudolf Steiner's teachings and insights. I did not need to look far in order to become aware of his work, my parents sending me to a German Waldorf school for a year and they themselves being engaged with his teaching. I also, much later became a faculty member at two Anthroposophical adult-education centers, Emerson College in England and Sunbridge College in Spring Valley, New York.

A fourth theme that also runs through my life is my connection to Waldorf education, first as a student in Germany and then later in a Waldorf boarding high school, High Mowing School in New Hampshire. This was followed by helping to start what was to become The Waldorf school in Lexington, Massachusetts. Later I was also a parent in three Waldorf schools and worked extensively as an advisor and consultant to Waldorf schools in community and organizational development.

One further theme I need to add to this reflection on my life is that I have been involved in starting things, in taking initiatives, usually in collaboration with others, all of which had a grounding in anthroposophy. This included helping to start a Waldorf school, the Centre for Social Development at Emerson College in England, an international consultancy company, Social Ecology Associates, and initiating and promoting the Social Science Section work in North America. I also assisted in the further development of the Waldorf Institute into Sunbridge College as an accredited master's degree-granting institution in New York State, as well as then developing a long-running program in Waldorf school administration and community development.

A Growing Social Interest

I remember coming to the US on a military transport in 1950 and seeing the sun setting behind the Statue of Liberty as we steamed into New York harbor, wondering what life would be like in a new country with a new language and a new life. My father was working for the US Navy as the head of a laboratory in submarine and space medicine, having spent some time during the war on a German U-boat.

My siblings—an older brother, a younger sister, and brother—and I learned English quickly and became American in no time, in part to avoid the understandable prejudice against Germans since the war had only ended five years earlier.

Being an immigrant family, my siblings and I all went to elite private colleges as education was seen as a prerequisite for success. I took a year off after my sophomore year and went to Berlin to study at the Free University and to travel through Europe. This was a truly formative time for me as I arrived just as the Berlin Wall was being built. Tension was high and troops and tanks were massed along Check Point Charlie and the demarcation lines separating

East Berlin from West Berlin. Since I had an American passport and spoke German well, I got involved in helping people escape. This led to many political and philosophical conversations with students and older people about World War II, the Nazi period, communism, the Soviet Union, and the Cold War. I was waking up to the social, political, and economic issues that would preoccupy me for the rest of my life. The assassination of John F. Kennedy during the year after my return to college in 1963 further shocked me into thinking more deeply about politics, conflict, and social reform.

I finished college with a major in history and philosophy, writing a thesis on the German resistance movement to Hitler and then went on to study international politics and economics at the Fletcher School of Law and Diplomacy at Tufts University. I was particularly interested in finding alternatives to war and focused on the history, conceptual background, and development of the European Union (EU).

It was at Tufts that I also met Signe, my life partner. We would soon marry and begin our joint journey. We first lived in Washington while I was on a fellowship at the Brookings Institution. When we first met, I told her about Waldorf education and the little of Steiner's work I knew about and, as we were both interested, we began a study group reading the *The Philosophy of Freedom*.

In 1968, Martin Luther King was killed, leading to riots in most American cities. I remember walking through burned-out sections of downtown DC and being ever more engaged with both civil rights and the Vietnam War. After the year at Brookings, I spent another year working in inner city neighborhoods evaluating the impact of the Model Cities Program on the lives of predominately Black communities. This was an eye opener for me as I experienced something of the poverty, discrimination, and lack of opportunity which so many Black communities suffered, despite the passage of the Civil Rights Act and the Great Society programs of Lyndon Johnson.

In 1969 we moved back to Boston and I began teaching International Politics and American Foreign Policy at MIT. By this time, we had a young daughter and were adjusting to family life in a small apartment in Somerville. We were also busy opposing the Vietnam War, demonstrating and going to teach-ins.

A Deepening Connection to Anthroposophy and Finding My Work

It was in 1970 that we made the decision to attend the Anthroposophical Youth Conference in Spring Valley, New York. This was life changing for both of us as we met soul mates from around the world and experienced a vortex of human and spiritual energy which was to change our lives. For me two events stand out, a conversation with Alan Howard and Diana Hughes from Toronto about the possibility of starting a Waldorf school in Boston and a meeting with Bernard Lievegoed and some of his colleagues from the Netherlands Pedagogical Institute (NPI), a Dutch research and consultancy institute based on Steiner's work and devoted to community development, team work, and conflict resolution. These meetings led to two decisions for us, first to start a Waldorf school in the Boston area, and to then spend some time studying and working in Europe, if at all possible.

While I had intended to work on questions of peace between nations while in graduate school, I now realized that work in the State Department, the U.N., the International Monetary Fund or the World Bank was not likely to meet the needs of my youthful idealism. It would require years of working in an international bureaucracy before I could make a difference, and the institutions to which I was initially attracted were so bound up with the existing power structure that it was unclear to me that they would be able to do much good. Also, I realized that war and conflict not only existed between nations, but within organizations, groups, and individuals as well as within me. This realization was important because I saw how much of conflict was the result of projection, feelings of inadequacy and prejudice, and the reality of antisocial forces within us all. And I wanted to find work which would connect my desire to work for peace and social healing with my growing interest in anthroposophy.

Full of idealism and youthful energy and not burdened by much insight or knowledge about Waldorf education we threw ourselves into starting a Waldorf school and engaged in community living, sharing our first house with friends. The school started as a small kindergarten in a church basement and we spent endless meetings raising funds, having fairs, and hiring teachers. We soon realized that we had a lot to learn and decided to go to Europe, Signe to attend the Waldorf Teacher Education Program at Emerson College, and I to work with the NPI in Holland. Fortunately, the school survived our desertion, and we headed to Europe with our two young children.

England and Holland

We lived in England and for a short time in Holland between 1973 and '81, although we had only planned to go for a year. This was an extremely rich and challenging time for both Signe and me as we found our directions in life and an ever-deepening relationship to Rudolf Steiner's work.

Arriving in Holland in August 1973 I remember visiting the offices of the NPI for the first time and, when facing the front door, having the feeling that I had in some sense come home. When entering, I saw a man coming down the stairs, knowing I knew this man although I had never met him. It was Coenraad van Houten, with whom I would later partner in starting the Centre for Social Development at Emerson College and, with others, Social Ecology Associates, an international consultancy group with colleagues in the UK, Sweden, and Australia.

We lived in Holland as a family in the winter and spring of 1974 and I learned passable Dutch and was taken along on consultancy projects to Germany and England. The other part of my learning process was to spend hours reading the hundreds of stencil research papers in the NPI archives and library that had been written by

Bernard Lievegoed and his colleagues. What impressed me deeply was that the advisers at the NPI would spend three weeks of the month doing their consultancy projects and one week together doing research and sharing their insights and experiences. Central to this research and the orientation which the NPI brought to their work was a detailed description and understanding of the individual phases of human development and biography and also of the phases of group and organization development. I still remember Lievegoed saying that our task in social inquiry was to develop middle-range concepts which were true to spiritual archetypes on the one hand, and also to human experience so that anyone could recognize their validity out of their personal experience. I also remember giving a talk to a group of supervisors at Ford Motor Company in Cologne about the phases of human development and having an older man approach me afterward, saying, "I wish I had known this before; it helps me to understand myself and my daughter, it's a whole new outlook on life."

The following summer we returned to Forest Row, where we had also lived in the autumn and winter of 1973/74, and I began working to help start the Centre for Social Development. I spent the next six years teaching adults at the center and doing consultancy projects in England and Germany with corporations such as Ford Motor Company, Imperial Group, and Trebor-Sharps, as well as with nonprofit organizations. The work involved team-building, organization restructuring, conflict resolution, and helping organizations move into a new, more human oriented phase of development.

I was also very fortunate to be able to meet and teach adult students interested in anthroposophy and social questions from around the world. There is perhaps no better path to learning more about social life than having to teach subjects such as learning theory, conflict resolution, group facilitation, and courses on human centered approaches to leadership and community development. From the ages of 33 to 39, I was given the opportunity of helping to bridge a healing social impulse from its continental Dutch base into the more international world of English. I also greatly benefited from having developed close friendships with some of my colleagues at Emerson College and also with my colleagues at the Centre. I learned much about family life with our children Karin and Stefan and through negotiating roles and responsibilities of being in a marriage with Signe, who was deeply interested in what it means to be in a conscious relationship and the question of being a woman in the present age.

Developing a Practical Social Understanding: A First Step

When working in urban centers and teaching at MIT, I had the sense that the concepts and methods I had learned in graduate school did not really help me to see and understand people and social situations. I had not developed much practical social understanding, as Steiner called it. This was my study at the NPI—a deepening engagement with Steiner's social thought, teaching at the Centre for Social Development, and ongoing consultancy work. Understanding the phases of human development and of group and community development, of temperaments, the seven soul types, of social and antisocial forces in the human being, and the threefold nature of all social life helped me to see more of the living nature of what we create together in dialogue, of the great karmically linked reality of the social world. Martin Luther King Jr. put this so movingly in his letter from a Birmingham jail, stating: "We are all caught in an inescapable network of mutuality, tied in a single garment of destiny. Whatever effects one directly effects all indirectly."

It was this period of my life and my learning from it that led to the publishing of my first book, written together with my colleague and friend Tÿno Voors, *Vision in Action: Working with Soul and Spirit in Small Organizations*.

Returning to the US

By 1981 it became clear to us that if we stayed any longer in England our children would become English and we had, after all, only planned to stay for one year. But departing was hard as we had close friends and loved our work—Signe teaching in the Foundation Studies at Emerson College and my work at the center and consultancy work with Social Ecology Associates. We began looking for a situation in the US where we could both find meaningful work and were offered an opportunity to join the Waldorf Institute in Detroit, with my working part time at the Institute and Signe full time in the orientation year. So, we moved from rather idyllic Forest Row to a city in the Midwest, which was in a state of crisis.

Part of our intention in returning to the States was to share what we had learned from our rich time in Europe and to work on social questions and issues of human development. So in addition to teaching at the Institute, Signe and I started the Center for Life Studies, giving courses and workshops on biography, relationships, questions of masculine and feminine, group work, conflict resolution and community development. We also joined other parents in attempting to develop a high school at the Detroit Waldorf School, and with others, MOMO's Café on Woodward Avenue as a meeting space for diverse groups of socially engaged individuals.

Spring Valley, 1985–2007

While living in Detroit I had already begun working more intensively with nonprofit organizations, in particular with Waldorf schools and, to some degree, with Camphill communities. What struck me was that these institutions had high ideals based in anthroposophy and had non-hierarchical social forms but often needed the social and leadership skills to make these communities work more effectively. This experience was quite painful for me and I resolved to help in any way that I could, steeping myself in Steiner's work on social questions; self-administration, group dialogue, and threefold principles in social life.

I had been a member of the international Social Science Section Collegium in Dornach while living in England and so I also began preparing to initiate Section work in the United States, which culminated in 1986 with founding the Section Conference in Chicago, followed by annual section conferences throughout the 1990s. This work also helped me to deepen my understanding of Steiner's profound insights into the challenges of building community in this age as so clearly expressed in his lectures on *Awakening to Community.*

The move from Detroit to Spring Valley was accomplished with most of the faculty relocating to the East Coast. Werner Glas, who had been the main founder of the Institute became quite ill right after the move and so the main faculty had to step up to carry the college and its courses and students. This was done through creating a core group with the responsibility for creating a creative, warm learning environment for students new to anthroposophy and those wishing to become Waldorf teachers or early childhood educators.

Deepening My Social Understanding: A Second Step

From this experience and my ongoing work with groups I began to more clearly sense the ongoing presence of spiritual beings linked to the psychological forces of interest, empathy, and love and those of annoyance, fear, and egotism. I now began to know that all social entities—couples, families, groups, and institutions—were the abodes of spiritual beings who went through their own development process with us, and that crises were opportunities for the growth of both human and spiritual beings. In the same way that we as individuals have a higher self and a double, so do groups and organizations. And so, I increasingly practiced asking the good spirit of the group or organization I was working with for guidance, for what was needed now, especially when I was stuck, which was often.

Developing Sunbridge College and Working with Waldorf Schools

My work with Waldorf schools increased dramatically after returning to the States in 1981. I spent many weekends from the early 1980s through the first decade of the new century traveling to many parts of the country seeking to help schools work more effectively with principles of self-administration, consensus decision-making, Waldorf school governance, and with the often tension filled relationships between faculty, board and parents. This work led me to develop a part-time course for Waldorf school administrators, pedagogical leaders, and board members at Sunbridge. In my experience, schools tended to hire administrators who were either former teachers with limited administrative skills or nonprofit administrators with no knowledge of Waldorf pedagogy or anthroposophy.

The course provided school leaders with a basic grounding in anthroposophy, insights into the social mission of Waldorf education and an understanding of the many challenges and opportunities of non-hierarchical social forms. Only half-joking, I used to say that Waldorf schools were compost heaps for mutual development—creative, life-filled, and a bit musty.

The experiences from the course and the advisory work with schools led me to publish my second book in 2013 called *Partnerships of Hope: Building Waldorf School Communities.*

My work with the college had a number of components: teaching in the Foundation Studies Program; the year-long introduction-to-anthroposophy course; the teacher training; early childhood education courses; teaching in and running the Waldorf School Administration and Community Development Program; and doing much of the college's fundraising work after Werner Glas became ill. I also helped the college gain a charter from New York State as Sunbridge College, allowing us to offer accredited master's degree programs.

9/11 and the American Empire Project

Having taught American Foreign Policy in the Political Science Department at MIT, 9/11 shocked me deeply as it did the country and the world. I could not accept the relatively simple explanations given by the Bush administration and the rationale it provided for war in Iraq and Afghanistan. So, I began to research more deeply into what happened and the history of what I came to call the American Empire Project. I also became deeply concerned about growing income inequalities in the United States exasperated by the financial crisis of 2008. I began to think that a radically unequal society in which corrupt financial institutions and politicians deprived average citizens of reasonable opportunities for well-being would in time undermine our democracy, as has happened to an ever-greater degree. Thus began a period of giving talks, workshops and writing articles on these themes and an ever-deeper study of such Steiner works as *The Fall of the Spirits of Darkness; From Symptom to Reality in Modern History*; *The Karma of Untruthfulness;* and other lecture courses. The resulting articles eventually led to the publication of my third book, *Re-imagining America: Finding Hope in Difficult Times* (2019).

Dialogue as the Archetypal Social Phenomenon: A Third Step

- The natural world is a divine creation, but we human beings are the creators of the social world. The world of families, shops, schools, companies, towns, and nations is created by us; reflecting our nature, consciousness, values, and intentions.
- The archetypal social phenomenon through which the social world is created is the meeting and dialogue between two or more people.
- What is revealed through dialogue, through encounter, is the reality of the mutuality of our karma, the foundational principle of all social life. We can only find our destiny through our relationship with others.

- The first spiritual experience we have is through conversation with another in which we experience something of the soul and spirit nature of ourselves and of the other.
- In meeting and conversation, we have three soul experiences which form the basis of a healing social life; freedom of expression and opinion in our thinking life, experiencing the desire for equality with others in our feeling life, and wishing to serve the other and the community in our will life. These experiences are the basis of both a healthy human being and a healthy social order, which Steiner described as the "threefold social order."
- In speaking and listening we can experience aspects of the social and antisocial nature of each other. Rudolf Steiner describes the antisocial nature of our times as manifesting in doubt and skepticism in our thinking life, likes and dislikes in our feeling life, and egotism and fear in our will life. He also suggests that these forces are manifestations of imbalance and evil in our times, calling them the three beasts of modern consciousness. Truly finding ourselves in right relationship with others comes from developing interest in their thoughts, empathy for the other in our feeling life, and the volition to love and serve the other in our will life. In this way, human encounter is a path for transforming evil in our time and finding a way to the being of the Christ.

These statements paraphrase different statements of Rudolf Steiner's and show why our relationship and dialogue with others is a modern mystery school, fostering our inner development and working toward a healing social life.* Relationships and what I think of as the life world offer hope for the future because they are the road to peace and a gift of Sophia to our time. The path of relationships, of friendship, needs constant practice, patience with self and others, and recognition that we are all on Parzival's journey, needing to develop interest in the other and asking the question: Sister and brother, what ails you?

---

* See Gary Lamb, *On the Wings of Words: Conversations and Human Relationships, Passages from the Work of Rudolf Steiner*, SteinerBooks, 2024.

Leaving the College, Experiencing China, and a Slow Retirement

Unexpectedly, questions from some of our former Chinese students in Waldorf Teacher Education led Signe and me to experience a totally new culture through the burgeoning Waldorf school movement in China. I made five trips to China from 2009 to 2013, developing the Waldorf School Administration and Community Development program, while Signe helped in initiating biography work there.

I continued doing advisory work with schools and other institutions inspired by Rudolf Steiner's work for a period of time and finished two of the books previously mentioned.

A Final Reflection: Step Four

It has taken my whole life to come to full recognition that nonviolence toward all living beings is the only proper relationship to cultivate toward others and all life forms. War and violence are a disease of our times and I can now fully recognize the truth of what Martin Luther King Jr. said when accepting the Nobel Peace Prize:

> Nonviolence is the answer to the crucial political and moral questions of our time—the need for man to overcome oppression and violence without resorting to violence and oppression.... Sooner or later, all the people of the world will have to discover a way to live in peace.... The foundation for such a method is love."*

For Martin Luther King Jr. and his friend Thich Nhat Hanh, nonviolence was based on the imagination of the Beloved Community, a recognition that we humans are imbedded in a world of interrelationships with the natural world, the human life world of karma, and with the spiritual world, the source of our creation. I

* See Marc Andrus, *Brothers in the Beloved Community: The Friendship of Thich Nhat Hanh and Martin Luther King Jr.* (Parralax Press, 2021), p 55.

have begun to see all of anthroposophy, the story of human and cosmic evolution, as a description of this Beloved Community.

And so, I find myself increasingly and haltingly asking the question in daily life: Is this the path of love? It is the path we all must travel as the social world is a modern mystery school in which we are called to be awake, to be interested and to learn to love.

Section VI

Peace is the Way

Creating a House of Peace

Carrie Schuchardt

The stages of biography have been very powerful for me as they are for all of us in our life. My first stage started in Montreal, Canada, where I was born the third of four children. I had two older sisters, and at a very young age moved to Newtonville, Massachusetts, outside of Boston, due to my father's work. Ours was a lively Irish Catholic family with a very strong sense of calmness and presence and working toward the good.

From a fairly early age it was discovered that my sister, Mary Ellen, had suffered injuries at birth, leaving her with some cognitive differences. So, I grew up in a family that not only accepted, but worked in a very realistic way to transform this apparent scar into something precious. My parents refused to accept the all-encompassing advice of those days that "nothing can be done—take her home and keep her happy."

My parents were soon surrounded by others with an array of offspring with all kinds of disabilities. I became a kind of activities director for all their kids while the parents would huddle in the living room and participate ultimately in the founding of the Boston branch of a national and international group for people with disabilities. It was very challenging, all quite amazing.

I quickly learned to fight Mary Ellen's battles. In the first six years of schooling, she had no special classes, and children unfamiliar with such differences would taunt us. I would give it right back and then come home and just cry on my mother's lap: *Why do they say my sister's sick?*

In the midst of it, I remember someone coming to the house for the many Irish parties we had, and taking me aside after having been with Mary Ellen, and saying to me, "What is it like to live with an angel?" How that mystified me. She was my challenging big sister, but somewhere I knew that the angelic lived in her. That was such a confirmation. That awakened me early on to this enormous world of people with special needs, with so-called impairments, with so-called disabilities and handicaps. It awakened in me—I don't know if it's too strong to say—the cosmic significance of what these special people were meant to be in this world.

In 1962 I went off to college. This was during the Vietnam War and the anguish of that unending slaughter of innocent people entered into my soul very deeply.

After graduating in 1966 with majors in sociology and philosophy, I came into a new stage of life and work that flowed from what one might call a kind of religious stream. I had been led at an early age, through a spiritual director, to a path of meditation that gave deep focus to the questions and hopes of life.

An inner call began to deepen, and I was able to enter a monastic community for two years. During this time, I continued my study of Teilhard de Chardin, theologian and paleontologist, a process I had begun in college under a professor/associate of Teilhard. He was a deeply committed builder of a bridge between the spiritual world and the material world, describing a Divine Milieu in which we all live and breathe.

Back in Boston in the catastrophic year of 1968 I established a center for adults with impairments who had no program outside their homes. It was during this time that I encountered the community of Camphill Village and recognized in total astonishment that I had met what I had long sought—a way of life-sharing with people carrying special gifts into this world, often masked by special needs.

After completing a master's in special education and having pursued an interest in curative education and social therapy, I set sail as a newlywed for Camphill Community Glencraig, a flourishing Camphill center in Northern Ireland.

It was 1971, and in Glencraig there was a combination of the highest level of true community living, with each person valued with an equality that was essential. But at the same time there were constant explosions in the background because we were just eight miles from Belfast...and "The Troubles" were raging. With family roots in the south of Ireland it was especially devastating for me to see the ravages of this war: tanks and guns, terrified children, suspicious adults, all in an atmosphere of violence and oppression.

One year later I returned to America having had this experience of the handicapped person in an environment of war. I then began to seek what the next steps were. I knew with deep conviction that war is immediate. War is in you. And war that claims the lives of mothers and children is your war, and you are not separate from it in any way. And throughout all of this, the presence of anthroposophy offered its light, ever deepening and taking hold, with its summons to create, in the face of world suffering, true knowledge of the world of spirit.

For me Camphill embodied this. In my soul I encountered the being of Dr. Karl König, founder of Camphill, who so revered the destiny of handicapped people, experiencing in them our true humanity. Through Dr. König I also met the incredible being of Kaspar Hauser and the knowledge that there had come to live in a being in Nuremberg, Germany, a profound spiritual essence clothed in unbearable pain that comes with those who are meant to be born with destiny differences in this world.

In 1975, together with my husband and little son, Colum, soon to be joined by brother Kieran, I arrived at Camphill Village Kimberton Hills in Pennsylvania.

Here one could share in the intense spiritual striving of people working actively in many areas with the riches and challenges of anthroposophy—all in a beautiful agricultural community where people with special needs were thriving!

During this time there came a powerful call, perhaps shaped by the tragic aftermath of the Vietnam War. I knew I had to offer the mantle of my own motherhood to those who had lost their mothers in the conflagration of war. And so, in 1980, with the trusting approval of the community, our family welcomed two boat refugees who had fled Vietnam and spent one year in a crowded refugee camp. In 1986, two younger brothers and an older sister of one of these boys came to join us. My little daughter, Ethna, had been born and now we were a large family, finding our way to the true bonds of spirit that would transform us all.

As these traumatized children began to heal and flourish, I came to realize that the healing for these uprooted people who had lost their family, their culture, their language, their country, their religion...these true healing forces were flowing from a wonderful mosaic of intertwining lives within the community of people with special needs from their unconditional hospitality.

I realized: you have to know all this, and meditate all this, and work with this with all your forces because that's what Dr. König and Rudolf Steiner and anthroposophy are saying we are meant to be. Through Anthroposphia, we are meant to be a presence, a Christ-Sophia presence in the world that touches this suffering and calls down the forces of transformation and healing.

With this all reverberating in my soul, I carried a question to a pilgrimage to Iona, sacred isle of spirit presence: Am I meant to build a soul-house—even a physical house—where this community magic of people in need of special care can give special care to those victims of the wars of this world?

On Easter Sunday 1989, I had the inner experience: Yes, this is your task. The work began. Now a single mother, I faced the uprooting of all my children into an unknown new life. And they were more than prepared, as it turned out! The Camphill friends rallied to the cause, and we were supported by help all around.

At St. John's time, 1990, we loaded up a U-Haul truck and all these beautiful children. We were accompanied by John Schuchardt, who I had already met ten years before, through the peace movement. He is a mighty leader, nationally and internationally, with a passion for peace and justice. I was living in community, trying to serve and heal victims of war; and he was out there—in prison, at the Pentagon, and all over the world—crying out for the abolition of the weapons of war, above all nuclear weapons. He had come and met Camphill and anthroposophy, and he was deeply moved by it. He was discerning his path into that, just when I was discovering the extreme change in my own path. But with great trust and selflessness he joined this endeavor.

We arrived at the 300-year-old Rogers Manse in historic Ipswich, the purchase of which held its own miraculous mysteries. With its central location, large carriage house for meetings, and four acres of beautiful land it was the perfect place for us. Soon the refugees came: at first unaccompanied minors fleeing wars and violence. Then came streams of refugees from Bosnia and Kosovo, Sudan and Somalia, Pakistan, early Afghanistan, Iraq, and Syria.

We formed lasting lifelong friendships. Families moved on to independent living and continued to connect with us. Referrals came through Catholic Charities, the major resettlement agency in Boston, along with the International Institute and then through other smaller agencies, as well as word of mouth. Hospitals began to refer children to us—burn victims, amputees, and victims of depleted uranium poisoning from US weapons. Right up to the present such children come, each with a caregiver, for the duration of their medical treatment at Boston hospitals.

The House of Peace grew. At its heart was the work with anthroposophical friends on the North Shore. We became a center for study groups, First Class lessons, lectures, concerts and more...all in the hope of creating healing community. Veterans of war found their way to us, as well as peacemakers engaged in bearing witness for years. Gatherings of young people for work parties and retreats, volunteers offering every kind of service, collaboration with others offering support for refugees... all this and so much more have filled these 35 years.

War is the ultimate handicapping condition. To live in a community where people with special needs can address the needs and handicaps of victims of war is a great revelation and fulfillment of the goals of true social therapy. That's what the House of Peace in its own small way has tried to be: a place for that to happen.

How should we meet the world through anthroposophy is an ongoing question. We ask: Can we meet the challenges of our time? We have to. We can no longer ask: Can we...? We have to! That's what Rudolf Steiner suffered and died for. That is what the flames of the first Goetheanum burned into the world: Dr. Steiner's passion for putting it right and making holy places on mountaintops, holy places in valleys, and holy places in every single one of us so that the healing can happen.

The House of Peace owes everything to this Christ-imbued reality, the being of Anthroposophia. We owe everything to those who nurture it and stand for and with it in a time of unprecedented anguish. At every festival gathering we have, and every study group, every class lesson and ritual, we feel the summons: *Come together to the fullest of your capacity so that this world, so hungry and so broken, may experience this work as truth-bearing.*

On June 1st, 1990, when we signed the papers that transformed the old Rogers Manse into the House of Peace, I remember saying to our small group that the pillars of the House of Peace are gratitude and trust. And I can only express from everyone who has ever lived here the most profound gratitude for all that's been given us and the humblest trust for everything that is still to come toward us.

From an interview with Carrie Schuchardt
by Signe Eklund Schaefer

In the Belly of the Whale
Untruthfulness and the Confrontation with Evil

John Schuchardt

This fifth post-Atlantean age has the task to go into the inevitable battles with the most manifold forms of evil.
—Rudolf Steiner, *The Problem of Faust*

In the present epoch of the Consciousness Soul two mysteries are of particular importance for the evolution of mankind—the mystery of death and the mystery of evil.
—Rudolf Steiner, *From Symptom to Reality in Modern History*

When I look at my biography, I might give the picture of Jonah on the way to Nineveh to shake and wake people up. The kingdom of God is at hand. It's all around us. It's right here—Paradise, the Garden of Eden, this spring, and every spring. We just need to step across the threshold of materialism into the reality of God's creation of beauty, abundance, healing, accepting God's law that we harvest what we sow, those who live by the sword die by the sword. Untruthfulness, war is always the spawn of the Father of Lies.

I was swallowed by the Leviathan. I've been in the prisons with the poorest, in the belly of the whale. I've witnessed for peace amidst the wars of cynical, criminal US invasions "for democracy." The House of Peace has lived life in community with the terrorized families from 30 some countries fleeing for their lives; attended to the burned and dismembered children maimed by the US bombing of Vietnam, Iraq, Syria, El Salvador, and so much more. Between 80 to 95 percent of all victims of US bombing are defenseless mothers and their children.

The whale is the unitary state, with its ideology, law, and murderous exploitation of peoples and resources. It's possible that not many anthroposophists have been in the Belly of the Beast. Everything looks different when you are secure and benefiting from the top or the victim on the bottom. If you're enjoying income, education, and opportunity, the world looks all right. But it looks quite different when you're a prisoner or an innocent family being bombed.

My history-centric biography is such that I think it contains the challenge of our times, as Rudolf Steiner suggested, to know evil and to be a witness for truth and to unmask and name the spiritual forces of our age of the consciousness soul. "The first task of the honest seeker after truth today is to convince oneself of the existence of these evil forces." Steiner observed during the catastrophe of 1914 to 1918, "People flee from the truth." When protective myths and lies are proven unreal, this shattering of illusions is very painful. And I can say this because I was blind and uninformed about the very existence of the Leviathan, of the violent unitary national security state that is the United States of America. I was blind to the spiritual ground of the world, deaf to the cries of the two-thirds of the world suffering in hunger and deprivation while being killed by the multiple wars of neocolonial Western powers.

I volunteered for the Marine Corps and was proud to be "185 pounds of romping, stomping fighting hell." I was schooled to execute legalized, normalized murder in the name of "serving my country." I hadn't heard Dr. King's truth that "the US is the most violent perpetrator of violence in the world."

My first marriage was into the Jim Crow South, the segregated, absolutely "Whites Only" South. I had no questions, no interest in Reverend Dr. Martin Luther King Jr. I was blind to the repression and humiliation of Black Americans. Every Southerner I met was nice to their servants, yardsmen, and cooks. I visited the family's "nanny" living in a kind of shack with no basement, no second story, on a neglected piece of land. I was blind to the injustices and evils of racism and the evils of poverty which Gandhi named "the most extreme form of violence." Not many years later I was the one being repressed and humiliated in the belly of the beast, standing as one condemned and imprisoned for seeking to abolish war, to abolish prisons and to abolish poverty.

Now we see daily the atrocities of Gaza, with US weapons, money, and propaganda, while the Trump administration pursues its strategic goals of oil, gas, pipelines, and real estate. The soul-sickening bombing of homes and hospitals, targeted murder of children, doctors, medical aid, humanitarian staff, first responders, and journalists is in fact mind blowing, while the people of Gaza succumb to extermination by starvation. On Ash Wednesday, a priest in Bethlehem said, "Gaza is the moral compass of the world." How do we as people and as students of anthroposophy relate to this compass?

Dr. Steiner said that Jerusalem is the physical-spiritual center of the world because of the "Mystery of Golgotha." Do we feel this? Can we in the US read the signs of the times or even try? Where are the retreats, the workshops, the lectures, the books on unmasking and confronting Evil, the giant triplets of Evil named by Dr. King as racism, militarism, and economic exploitation—and "war, the most colossal of all evils."

The mystery of evil is the challenge of our times. Dr. Steiner's profound insights into invisible spiritual forces indicates the necessity of the polarity of evil in the evolution of humanity. But evil is temporal; the good is eternal. It is the central moral purpose of our lives to unmask, name, and resist evil. If we do not have a No, we do not live a Yes. Our silence gives consent and by our indifference we are drawn down by the destructive forces of technology, violence, and money into the realms of subnature. *The Transformation of Evil,* by Sigismund von Gleich, has been helpful, for "we must rise in spiritual knowledge at least as far into extraterrestrial super-nature as we have descended through the technological sciences into sub-nature."

Early Beginnings

I was born in rural northern Illinois, a region of small, self-sufficient diverse family farms, soon to be paved over by highways and cookie-cutter subdivisions. What "farming" remains is corporate industrial agriculture. World War II came home to us there. I remember vividly Jillian Millar and her mother being given refuge in our home from the bombing of London. We had blackout drills. My older brother Bob and I were also in awe of Uncle Bob, Navy chaplain on the *USS Augusta,* command ship for the Normandy D-Day invasion. So, we naturally wanted to be naval officers.

Isolated, insulated, homogenized—that was basically grade school, high school, and then I went off to Swarthmore College at the height of the Civil Rights movement. Yet I had no interest in it. I thought Dr. King was an "outside agitator." Even though my children think I was a hippie at that time, I was a buttoned-down square.

Waking Up

While in college, I took any job to pay my way—$25 a month to give out free samples of Winston, Camel, and Salem cigarettes. I began reading about cancer and smoking and began to kind of protest handing out dangerous products. I was eager to be accepted into a fraternity that had a selection process whereby a member could insert a black marble to prohibit a freshman from joining. I participated but began to think: Who am I to blackball anyone?

In my last year at University of Chicago Law School, President Kennedy was assassinated. Initially I didn't have questions but I soon read the Warren Report and 26 volumes of "evidence" asserting that JFK was killed by a bolt-action rifle. As a Marine marksman I knew you couldn't aim and rapidly fire a bolt-action rifle and hit anything. I recognized this was a coup d'état, ending the pretense of democracy. Robert F. Kennedy's murder sealed our destiny, leading in a straight line to where we are today.

In law school, I learned the difference between legal and criminal, what's legitimate self-defense and what is not. That, coupled with singing lullabies to my infant first child at night and acting like a homicidal maniac in USMC training during the day, tore my soul asunder, leading me to resign my commission. I knew then that killing another human being was soul suicide and Vietnam was a criminal war of aggression.

I resigned my first lieutenant commission, and people told me I had ruined my life. I believed they were probably right. So, I was absolutely thrilled and indebted to Swarthmore College for hiring me as Assistant Dean of Admissions. That was followed by Director of Orientation with the Experiment in International Living in Putney, Vermont, led by idealistic returned Peace Corps volunteers and internationalists. Vermont was a beautiful and extraordinary place to live in during the ferment of the 1960s.

Into the Wilderness

However, it was at that time that I had an inner and outer crisis. Like Paul on the road to Damascus, I was "knocked off my horse." My marriage collapsed. I was limping with physical pain, troubled and sleepless for seven years. I heard this strong message "to find yourself you must lose yourself." I had no idea what these contradictory inaudible words meant, but they gripped my waking and sleeping consciousness week after week; they drove me into the wilderness to literally lose myself. I went into the Vermont mountains in winter without food or shelter to see whether I would live or die. But instead of sinking to the bottom I floated up to the true, beautiful and good.

I had never before really seen the Sun rise, nor had I ever concentrated on the Sun all through the day. Then I saw the Sun set and the full moon rise, and I began to realize that we were in the kingdoms of beauty, nature, goodness, healing that surrounds us all, and that forces of the universe are life-giving, healing, guiding, and sustaining. For the first time, I was just filled—I mean, literally filled physically and spiritually filled with awe and joy. So, I survived and came out of the wilderness and back to the world.

I began to practice law. I found my way to the Weston Priory community of Benedictine monks and began reading Thomas Merton and the Bible. I had not really been inside a prison before and was shocked to experience the barbaric, truly medieval conditions when I became a public defender for Windham County, Vermont. I discovered the most disadvantaged, maltreated, and neglected people of our society: prison inmates. Because of that experience in the prisons, I saw the injustice and cruelty of the legislative and judicial systems, imprisoning mainly the poor and making them scapegoats for the sins of our society's violent systems. I felt I had to take a further step. So, in 1975 I heard of the Bruderhof and joined Woodcrest Bruderhof Community in Rifton, New York. I was soul sick, in constant pain, but at the Bruderhof I was spiritually and physically healed. The Bruderhof, founded by refugees from Nazi Germany, had decided to follow the Sermon on the Mount with their whole lives.

Working for Peace

In fall 1976, I felt compelled to seek further. I went to Mary House Catholic Worker in New York City, saw Dorothy Day and met Daniel Berrigan, who told me about the nonviolence movement of Jonah House in Baltimore. I became part of the peace movement, working with giants such as Revs. Philip and Daniel Berrigan, who had used homemade napalm to burn hundreds of 1-A draft files at Catonsville, Maryland, in 1968; Daniel Ellsberg, who released the Pentagon Papers; and many draft resisters who had suffered long imprisonments, as well as World War II, Korean War, and Vietnam War veterans.

Beginning in 1976, I also became a devoted participant with the Japanese Buddhist Order Nipponzan Myōhōji in innumerable world-embracing pilgrimages, peace walks, fasts, demonstrations, and building Peace Pagodas—the first of which was inaugurated in 1985 on Turtle Island in Leverett, Massachusetts. Through our mutuality in Spirit with these extraordinary activist Buddhist monks and nuns we have realized the seeds of a merger of Christianity and Buddhism (see newenglandpeacepagoda.org).

Four years later, a small group of experienced civil rights and peace activists protested at the General Electric Plant in King of Prussia, Pennsylvania. They were building the nuclear warheads for ICBMs, M-X, and Trident submarines there, each warhead 35 times larger than the one detonated at Hiroshima. On September 9, 1980, our community of eight, formed through scripture study and prayer over nine months, disarmed two Mark 12-A nuclear warheads and poured vials of our own blood on official documents. We were on trial for two weeks, ending in felony convictions during Holy Week and given three- to ten-year prison sentences.

It was during the trial in 1981 that Carrie and I first met each other. She was well acquainted with Revs. Philip and Daniel Berrigan and came to give support. That was a moment of destiny where Carrie's life and mine intersected. I would occasionally visit her in the intervening years at Camphill; my sister Ada Lorette lived in nearby Doylestown. Meanwhile, after release from Western Penitentiary, my life work as an activist continued, including witnessing in many peoples' countries—Russia, Japan, Iran, Iraq, Palestine, and Nicaragua to name a few. Carrie and I also saw each other at the ReThink Conferences organized in Denver by Rev. Diethart Jaehnig, a priest of The Christian Community and a Waldorf school co-founder. At the age of five, Diethard was dug out of the basement rubble of his home, which had been bombed by British and US planes, following Churchill and Roosevelt's January 1943 Casablanca Directive for bombers to prioritize destruction of cities and civilian populations.

Chris Schaefer's childhood was, in the same manner, forever marked by the coldest, cruelest barbarism of the 20th century, his first memory being as a three-year-old looking up to see the heavens black with bombers, Frankfurt reduced to the rubble, as we now see daily in Gaza. In a life forged by subhuman forces, Diethart brought forth John the Baptist's cry to repent, change one's thinking, in the Re-Think appeal. The conferences always spanned the August 6th and 9th dates of the Hiroshima and Nagasaki bombings. One year we were part of an entire encirclement of the many thousand-acre Rocky Flats nuclear warhead production.

The House of Peace

Through visiting Carrie and Camphill Village Kimberton Hills I was drawn powerfully to anthroposophy. Dr. Karl König, a Jewish refugee from Nazi Austria, founded a new community movement to establish sisterhood and brotherhood between all peoples and all abilities. It was in opposition to euthanasia and brought about a huge transformation of relationships.

By this time Carrie had taken in a number of refugee children from Vietnam. This led her to discover that people with so called "disabilities" had a remarkable capacity for helping refugees to overcome fear, distrust, and bitterness. And she had an imagination that she should create a House of Peace as an independent initiative. So, she began looking for a place to do that. By this time, she was single, had three children, a number of Vietnamese youth and several residents needing special care, including her sister. Somehow Carrie found a house in Ipswich, Massachusetts, with ten bedrooms, a meeting hall, and land. I urged her to give up her vision. It was impractical, she had many children, no money, mortgage rates of 12 percent, and the house needed a lot of work. No surprise, Carrie was undaunted. That was 35 years ago. Soon after, the House of Peace board was formed and purchased the 1727 Rogers Manse. We were married in our chapel on Nov. 12, 1990, the day after a massive Armistice Day protest in Boston against the "Desert Shield" preparations to destroy Iraq, the cradle of civilization.

Building community is essential to effective and enduring activism, to witness, to actively oppose the evils of war on the one hand and to build healing relationships on the other. That is what Carrie and I are dedicated to, building community, doing constructive work, while trying to diagnose the "signs of the times" and penetrate the illusions, thereby bringing into light the extreme manifestations of evil in our time.

Since our founding in 1990 the House of Peace has, with the Anthroposophical Society of Cape Ann, organized biweekly study groups, monthly First Class readings, festivals throughout the year, a summer lecture series, and a multitude of cultural, artistic, and dramatic offerings. We are part of The Christian Community, with priests' retreats and events here from time to time. We benefit from close relationships with Camphill, North American Council, the Catholic Worker, Fellowship of Reconciliation, and the Veterans for Peace communities. Anthroposophy is the foundation and lode stone of The House of Peace.

Jonah and the Whale Again

Let me return to our beginning, Jonah and the whale. Given that Steiner enlightened us in the truth that unmasking, naming, and transforming evil is the central task of the consciousness soul age, I believe it should be evident that anthroposophy is a revolutionary movement for the abolition of war and prisons, a radical witness to the necessity to overturn the tables of the money changers and create a society where the use of money as power and usury is named as ahrimanic and creates parasitic tumors in our society. Steiner urged humanity to recognize the cancers, the tumors that have invaded our culture, for it is only from this diagnosis that the remedy can be found. In Dr. Steiner's last of 12 heartfelt lectures, given on Armistice Day 1923, *The Harmony of the Creative Word*, he names cancer twenty-one times! No matter how difficult and unpopular it is to denounce the profound evil of US money, weapons, propaganda, and strategy carrying out the massacre of the innocents in Gaza, we must find our voice and our witness. "Moral passivity is the greatest danger of our time," Thomas Merton observed.

In Steiner's lecture courses, *The Karma of Untruthfulness*, *Towards Social Renewal*, *The Challenge of the Times*, and throughout his many lectures and books, we are called toward the healing of social life and to recognize, name, and resist the destructive counter-forces. Steiner's work is brought forward and made contemporary for our times by Tom Raines, *New View* (Edinburgh), and T. H. Meyer, *The Present Age* (Basel). These publications and *Truth, Reality, and Evil* by T. H. Meyer (2005) are, from my point of view, indispensable for our movement.

I believe that we as anthroposophists must focus and prioritize bringing into the light the Leviathan of the destructive unitary state which has caused limitless pain, human suffering, death, and destruction throughout the 20th and 21st centuries. I aspire for a more active stand for our central mission: "good news for the poor" and "woe unto those who are rich now." A total transformation of what Dorothy Day magnificently called "this filthy rotten system." An inspiring example is Anthroposophical Prison Outreach, a bright torch of warmth, justice, and healing in a dry, cold season.

Unless we as anthroposophists have our feet in the earthly, in the mud of assassinations, torture, Guantanamo, deportations, prisons, propaganda, "the grey magic of the media," false flags, Gaza—in short, Evil, the lure of Lucifer will lift us into blissful heights of creativity, blind and deaf to the American empire of violent exploitation and its flood of innocent victims. Work without our feet secure in earthly daily world events becomes luciferic.

If anthroposophy is not recognized as a committed peace, economic justice, and environmental movement, why would it be of any interest to the rising generation? Why would the public consider it even relevant in our current choking atmosphere of lies? Truth is the only force more powerful than lies; Gandhi called it Satyagraha, Truth Force. Consider the consequences of the assassinations of our four moral leaders in the 1960s; 9/11 World Trade Center implosions, the most successful false flag in history executed to fabricate the Global War on Terror, an endless war against invisible enemies. Truly in 2025, the 100th year of Dr. Steiner's death, "truth is on the scaffold and falsehood on the throne." It should not be so. We have profound resources in the works of Dr. Steiner and the anthroposophical movement. May we find the Michaelic courage to use them to their fullest potential that the good may become.

From an interview with John Schuchardt
by Christopher Schaefer

Know Evil, Grow Love

Rosemary McMullen

I discovered Rudolf Steiner in the 1990s, when I was in my 50s. I see that two streams of activity flowed regularly during my adult life—war resistance and justice activism alongside social arts and "soul work," or inner development—that accorded well with my gradual transformation throughout 25 years in the Anthroposophical Society and movement. "Know evil, grow love" have now become guiding principles, intertwined and strongly alive in me. Rudolf Steiner stressed these capacities as particularly important for working in the social realm.

Know Evil: Strive to Know the Truth behind Outer Events

> Man must assimilate these forces of evil which are operative in the universe. By so doing he implants in his being the seed which enables him to experience consciously the life of the spirit. The purpose of these forces of evil which are perverted by the social order is to enable man to break through to the life of the spirit at the level of the consciousness soul. If he did not open himself to these tendencies to evil he would not succeed in developing consciously the impulse to receive from the universe the spirit which henceforth must fertilize the whole sphere of cultural life if it is not to perish. (Rudolf Steiner, *From Symptom to Reality in Modern History,* lecture 5, October 26, 1918)

Since my early twenties, my understanding of "what is really going on" in world history and current events—of anti-human social systems; the military industrial complex looming in the "free world" of the late 1950s—has expanded and become more nuanced. The activist communities confronting, exposing, and attempting to transform social ills often included an ongoing geopolitical-economic-cultural educational component, regular analysis sessions, formal and ad hoc. Most of us were lifelong learners from the start; we learned a lot from each other and from working in the world together.

John F. Kennedy was shot the day after my 20th birthday: November 22, 1963. I am 81. On January 25, 2025, the Trump administration declassified sealed JFK assassination documents. I will not be surprised when later this year the US confronts a darker set of facts than 1963 could abide. From the Vietnam War era to the present, ideals needed to resist and learn from evil were being forged not only by my soul, but by the world at large.

My parents were exceptionally free thinkers compared to the rest of their family members. They met each other in the Young Catholic Workers—a Chicago branch of Dorothy Day's movement. My father was exempt from military service because of a chronic stomach ailment. They married in 1940. I am the second of four siblings.

Along with making a living and raising their children, my parents were active in the Christian Family Movement, supporting needy families and volunteering in civic groups. I can see clearly now that my parents were warm buffers between us growing children and "the authority" of the church and the USA. They searched for and found—and sometimes instigated—communities of like-minded people with whom to practice their understanding of living a truly Christian life. The limits and flaws of Roman Catholicism—one way of looking at what evil really is—knelt beside us celebrating the sacraments, studying scripture, practicing the yearly liturgy.

My mother went back to college to finish her degree when I was a toddler. Thereafter adult study groups, subscriptions to progressive bookstores and magazines, as well as friendships with professors, intellectual clergy, survivors of death camps and war were parts of home life. Most of Teilhard de Chardin's books were purchased as soon as they were published shortly after his 1955 death released him from his Jesuit vows. His *The Divine Milieu* and *The Future of Man,* and Simone Wiel's *Waiting for God* were all sitting on the crowded bookshelf for me.

Ah, the late 1960s! Draft resistance was the issue that started my social activism. My comrades in Students for a Democratic Society (SDS) also studied the dynamics behind the military industrial complex, revealing that poor people of color had few ways to avoid the draft, whereas college students were deferred. The Black Panthers and SDS crossed paths often. Previously I had rarely encountered blacks, let alone eloquent social leaders. Franz Fanon's *Wretched of the Earth,* Eldridge Cleaver's *Soul on Ice,* and other contemporaries tore my ignorant complacency to shreds. I noted white privilege and middle-class behaviors in my own and others' reflexes with repulsion. Feminism was another shocking awakening, but we women took it up in mostly warm circles of sisterhood. I loved our feelings of unity and shared possibilities for a better social future—beyond race, gender, class distinctions. As a graduate assistant, I taught English 101 to veterans older than I. Before the internet, we studied three or four news reports of the same incident trying to deduce what the truth was and what interpretations of events were being advanced by the media and why.

But fear of narcs, internal spies, police—and then military—crackdowns set in. On a beautiful spring morning in 1970 I gave a speech on white privilege outdoors in the Southern Illinois University quad. Armed military were on the roofs. May 1970 of course is memorable for the Kent State University killings of unarmed students by National Guardsmen. At a massive Panther/SDS rally in Chicago that June, we were all patted down for weapons and drugs before entering. I found the rhetoric and the atmosphere repellent. In shock, fear, and loathing, I resolved to exit the affiliation. When my degree requirements were finished, I left the campus and association with SDS.

As a college instructor at the Pontifical Catholic University of Puerto Rico (1971–1976), I experienced the downstream effects, not only of militarism but also of institutional racism with student veterans. They had been drafted, trained, deployed, and survived combat, even though Puerto Rico was not a state and they were not allowed to vote. The VA could not heal their inner wounds. My most promising student suffered nervous collapse and could not continue his studies. He had been the point man for his squad in 'Nam. In 1972, I advised my boyfriend—a 1-A in the draft—to declare himself a conscientious objector at his sleepy village draft office. He was not called up.

I let myself luxuriate in the belief that antiwar resistance was part of the reason Nixon signed a ceasefire on January 27, 1973. No—too many tactical mistakes had been made in the region and the conflict continued until the fall of Saigon in 1975. Active conscription in the United States also ended in January 1973; however, all men between 18 and 25 were still required to register with the Selective Service Commission.

I am convinced that demonstrations and protests serve important functions. Those who plan and participate receive power from expressing publicly—however briefly—their moral rejection of authorized systems of power. Exhilaration from solidarity with masses who share your ideals is an unforgettable tonic for soul and spirit. Those on the sidelines—perhaps amoral or numb—watching social conscience enacted by their neighbors and fellow countrymen, perhaps are moved to ask: what am I missing?

Protests continue around the world, firing up the hearts of millions. In February 2003, BBC reported that over the weekend of February 15 and 16, between six and ten million people took part in protests in up to 60 countries on every continent—including Antarctica—against the US invading Iraq. May we say those millions called out the "evil empire"? The false weapons-of-mass-destruction argument pushed their governments to go along nevertheless. In September 2024, tens of thousands of Israelis marched in Tel Aviv against Israeli military action against Gaza and the West Bank: the soul of Israel "demonstrated" for all to see.

I last took part in a formal peace and justice march in September 2009 when the G20 met in Pittsburgh. I moved to Pittsburgh in 2005 to teach at the Waldorf school. Looking for community, I had joined the Network of Spiritual Progressives and then the Thomas Merton Center, a peace and justice organization started by Molly Rush—one of the Plowshares Eight, which also included John Schuchardt, peace advocate and lawyer, later anthroposophist and currently of the House of Peace in Massachusetts. I worked with police accountability groups and attended Black and White Reunion over many years, meeting and working for social renewal with an array of locals. One of the best initiatives, One Hood, gives media, digital, and financial literacy training to youth. The Whites Challenging Racism working group that met over three months in 2007 was a next level for me of self-analysis and inner unravelling of racism USA-style, deeper, more transformative than I had experienced as a student in the late 1960s. By the time George Floyd was murdered in May 2020 and the Black Lives Matter movement caught on world wide, I believe millions started to or continued to remove more blindspots around systemic racism.

In late September 2009, during the meeting of the G20, we local activists put on an alternate conference—the G6 Billion, with speakers and activities educating on the truth of what was really going on. Nicanor Perlas' colleague from the Filipino threefold movement, and co-recipient of the Right Livelihood Award in 2002, Walden Bello, was a keynote speaker. We hosted Howard Zinn via satellite only a few weeks before his death.

September 25, 2009, the Pittsburgh police did not stop or interfere with our march, but later that evening nineteen were arrested in places where protesters were gathered. The Merton Center gave legal support. While on the board of the Merton Center I had met Noam Chomsky, Dennis Kucinich, and Vandana Shiva—recipients of the Merton Award. I had been following Chomsky's analysis particularly, since my twenties. He was in his mid-eighties when he journeyed to Pittsburgh; the awards event was sold out. By the way, no local Pittsburgh anthroposophists were disposed toward peace and justice activism.

By then, 9/11 and the financial crisis of 2008 were behind us. I had read T. H. Meyer's world historical take on the incidents of 9/11 and the beginning of the war in Afghanistan and Iraq—*Reality, Truth, and Evil* (2005)—around the same time as Hans Werner Schroeder's *Necessary Evil* (German, 1984; English translation, 2005). These anthroposophists and Terry Boardman's articles in *New View* helped me apply Steiner's wide view of human and Earth evolution to recent history and current events.

From September 2011 to March 2012, I once more reentered the activist mode with Occupy Pittsburgh. A camp was built and sustained over five months in the heart of corporate Pittsburgh. We met with Occupy Wall Street and followed news of other Occupy camps. In my view the Occupy movement was another huge surge of mass education, raising financial and economic questions into the light, perhaps for the first time for many. While those in the movement had another blast of solidarity with like-minded idealists from across the world, noncommittal "others" witnessed from the sidelines.

No local anthroposophists were interested in joining me, but by then I had connected with others elsewhere. In August 2010, Gary Lamb organized a meeting in Spring Valley, New York, of the Social Science, Natural Science, and Agriculture sections. I met Luigi Morelli, Mack Mead, many from Think Outward, as well as John and Katie Stubley of Australia on their way home from six months in Dornach. In September 2012, I attended Threefold Bootcamp in Ghent, New York. Facilitators were Gary Lamb, Seth Jordan, Sarah Hearn, and Travis Henry. Seth and Travis had visited Occupy Wall Street several times. The Threefold Bootcamp leaders were good examples of "know evil." I found their diagnosis of contemporary systems spot-on, having flipped high ideals—health, justice, safety—to dysfunctional or, in some areas, blatantly evil versions. I encountered another savvy anthroposophist, Christopher Houghton Budd, his team, and their publication *Associate!* through friendship with an anthroposophist who lived in Pittsburgh (2015–2016).

MysTech, an anthroposophic initiative founded in 2016 started offering free online study groups in 2017. Andrew Linnell had gathered Rudolf Steiner's many indications for present and future developments in technology. I was in the first group and then co-hosted with Andrew for two years. The basic beginner's text is in Steiner's *Challenge of the Times*, lecture 3, "The Mechanistic, Eugenic, and Hygienic Aspects of the Future." I bring you first this quote:

> You will recall that I drew a map here two years ago that is now becoming a reality, and I did not show this map only to you. I presented the map at that time to explain how the impelling forces are moving from a certain side, since it is a law that, if we know these impelling forces, if we take cognizance of them, if we grasp them in our consciousness, they may be corrected in a certain way and given a different direction. It is important that this should be comprehended.

By directed human "cognizance," "grasping in our consciousness," negative forces "may be corrected in a certain way and given a different direction." This is precisely the activity I mean by "know evil."

Steiner foresees that in our epoch abilities will be growing among humans that these secret societies are already molding to their own ends. Steiner was convinced in 1918 that Anglo-American brotherhoods were maneuvering for mastery long term.

Later in the same lecture Steiner says:

> ...the goal striven for is to establish a caste of masters in the West and a caste of economic slaves in the East, beginning with the Rhine and extending eastward all the way into Asia. This does not mean a caste of slaves in the ancient Greek sense, but a caste of economic slaves organized in a socialistic way to take up all sorts of impossibilities in the social structure that then shall not be applied among the English-speaking peoples. The essence of the matter is to make the English-speaking peoples into a population of masters of the world.

Since 2017, MysTech has given free online study groups to hundreds around many of these present and future indications. "The Mystery of Evil" course was launched two years ago; new hosts facilitate each year. The internet has made it possible to find at one's fingertips in minutes critiques and ongoing questioning of systems in power. MysTech co-founder Andrew Linnell administers several online groups of 40 or 50 thousand members filtering this content every day.

Has a critical portion of the world's population awakened to reality since 1918 to exert the rectifying counterbalance? Steiner points hope in this direction at the end of the lecture:

> ...you see it is discretion in forming judgments that must also be attained. If this discretion in forming judgments can be gained it will be a great help toward the development of those latent capacities of which I have spoken to you today, which must develop in the future of humanity, differentiated in a threefold way in the various parts of the world. You will then discover that what I described to you a week ago [the threefold social organism] as the only justifiable solution of the social problem so far as we can speak today in the sense indicated of such a solution, was by no means developed from mere intellectual ideas as an abstract program.

I hypothesize that the widening critical and awake response to various implosion points in the 20th and 21st centuries marked by resistance, awareness, consciousness-raising, and community building has curtailed the victory of adversarial forces.

Grow Love: Create New Social Forms of Agape and Take them Into the World

The citation at the beginning of the first section of a lecture that same year about the necessity to know the evil of our times, then turns to cultivating interest in other human beings.

> When one speaks of these things one must touch upon the very core of human evolution. At the same time, they are related to

> the calamities that have overtaken mankind at the present time and will still befall it. For those disasters, like flashes of summer lightning, are harbingers of quite other things that are destined to overtake mankind—lightning flashes that today often reveal the reverse of what is destined to happen. These observations are not a reason for pessimism, but rather should serve to arouse us and stimulate us to action.
>
> Perhaps we shall best achieve our purpose if we start from a concrete phenomenon. I spoke yesterday of an important impulse in the epoch of the consciousness soul—the development of an active concern on the part of every man for his neighbor. This mutual concern for each other must grow and develop in the course of man's subsequent evolution on earth, especially in four domains. First, as man prepares his future development, he will see his fellow man in a progressively different light. Today, when a little over a fifth of the epoch of the consciousness soul has run its course, man still shows little inclination to see his fellow man as he will have to learn to see him in the course of the epoch of the consciousness soul, up to the fourth millennium. Men still ignore the most important element in others, they have no real understanding of their neighbor.*

"The way I used to love feels obsolete," I said during an online Warm Circle group early in 2025. I was not the only participant who had realized just then: we have been growing into and practicing new ways of loving, especially socially. Cultivating the social arts with more directed consciousness, both to strengthen our esoteric communities and to take new forms of agape—community love. Rudolf Steiner called for ever-widening love capacity, along with ever-growing understanding of the Christ.

> No one today stops to think that if outward harmony and a life steeped in love are to be realized, the Christ impulse must have penetrated to the utmost depths of human nature, *so that human love becomes something entirely different from what it is at present, even among the noblest spirits. The impulse*

---

* Rudolf Steiner, *From Symptom to Reality in Modern History,* lecture 5, October 26, 1918. See the "Note" on page 255.

> *which was foretold, and then entered the world, is only at the beginning of its work*, and an even deeper understanding for it must be shown.*

Steiner expanded that idea for anthroposophists in Zurich at the start of the threefold movement:

> Christ said: "Inasmuch as ye have done it unto one of the least of these my brethren, ye have done it unto me." The Christ never ceases to reveal Himself anew to men—even unto the end of earthly time. And thus He speaks today to those willing to listen: "In whatever the least of your brethren thinks, you must recognize that I am thinking in him; and that I enter into your feeling, whenever you bring another's thought into relation with your own, and whenever you feel a fraternal interest for what is passing in another's soul. Whatever opinion, whatever outlook on life, you discover in the least of your brethren, therein you are seeking Myself."
>
> So does the Christ speak to our life of thought—the Christ Who desires to reveal Himself in a new way—the time for it is drawing near—to the men of the twentieth century...so that it may be known: Christ is the God for all men. We shall not find Him if we remain egotistically bound up with our own thoughts, but only if we relate our own thoughts to those of other men, if we expand our interest to embrace, with inner tolerance, everything human.**

Preparing this autobiography, I realized that in the second half of my life I kept encountering groups engaged in therapeutic social healing, creative witness involving inner work, conscious heart exertion. I did not call these practices "social arts" or "new kinds of agape" then, but I do recognize them as such now. I can also testify that they did work effectively for me and my fellow participants.

In New York City, 1987, I was on staff with the Children of War, a project of a coalition of Christian ministries that brought

---

* Rudolf Steiner, *The Gospel of St. John,* June 29, 1909 (my emphasis).

** Rudolf Steiner, *Inner Aspects of the Social Question,* Feb. 11, 1919.

together teenagers from war-torn countries for a week of healing through fellowship. Besides meeting program sponsors Yoko Ono and Harry Belafonte, I witnessed skilled counselors helping the kids create new thinking and feeling through friendship, alliance, and new understanding. Such healing is certainly a way to define agape: community love in action.

The facilitators were international, with a variety of backgrounds and training: co-counseling, nonviolent communication, indigenous heritage. A Protestant cleric from New Zealand remarked during an orientation session: "I learned a long time ago that if there was a woman or indigenous person in the room, I should keep my mouth shut until they had their say." Remembering this remark from 1987 makes me realize for how long the dying systemic coils of patriarchy, militarism, racism, and colonialism will be unwinding.

In the early 90s in Washington, DC, I pursued a two-year certification program in poetry therapy. As an English major even in college, I appreciated having a direct line to higher soul capacity any time I cared to open a book of poetry. Williams three—Shakespeare, Blake, Wordsworth—were my reliable mood-altering voices. If one dead poet can re-charge one person's flagging soul, how much more nuanced would be the spiritual refreshment engendered in a group?

My practicum—poetry appreciation and composition sessions in mental health outpatient clinics—demonstrated that the process of reframing difficult feelings and memories really works every time to engender "soul refreshment" for the participants. More precious than the words, however, was the array of faces around the table, revealing new feelings of joy, appreciation, seeing and being seen. The first seeds of agape—full attention to others and deep listening—were being laid.

Wonderment glimpsing the beauty and virtue alive in the souls of others—another stage of awakening agape—occurred pointedly in the peer poetry groups for the trainees. A leader would choose a poem for the group to read together; then everyone would write something spontaneously, which generated another round of fresh recognition of each other. Fleeting but unique and real soul friendships grew between us over the course of the training, something I had never experienced before.

In years that followed, I was able to bring groups of friends and acquaintances together in peer poetry circles. A few were college professors of literature doing this for the first time. They, too, were exhilarated to discover their beloved poets "forged" anew in a contemporary "social meta-word smithy." I now see this experience as a new form of agape, with the "loving community" including poets we have not met in person. Thus was the ground of social love cultivated, life refreshed, and souls steeled among middle-aged female academics well-schooled in current social evil.

James Hillman's and Robert Sardello's archetypal psychology soul work and David Whyte's poetry process practice in the mid-1990s created multiple contexts for inner work, body work, as well as poetic speech. Weekends with all three of these gifted soul researchers, delving into truth and beauty with like-minded peers, opened vistas of future love in this lifetime and beyond!

Another new dimension of social healing arose through my participation in one of the first Bert Hellinger Institute Family Constellations Trainings in the United States over two years, from 1999 to 2001. The same group of two dozen trainees met on intensive weekends and a few week-long sessions in Washington, DC, and New York City. Bert Hellinger (1925–2019) and several of his first students helped us build skills in facilitating, practicing, assisting the processes of diagnosis and treatment of family entanglements manifest in an individual's physical or mental health crisis. In essence, Hellinger's method assumes there is hidden trauma in the family that can be discovered and given its first treatment in a group session.

A Family Constellation session usually takes several hours. The client explains his or her complaint to the main facilitator. Representatives for family members from the audience are next asked to stand in the circle in a beginning configuration. Then various subtle shifts start to take place with movement promoted by the facilitator, the client, or spontaneously by the representatives. Having served as a representative many times, I can testify that a "field" comes into play in the center of the circle—an invisible crucible or bubble—and motivates the family representatives to shift position, gesture, sometimes cry, speak, or otherwise signal. From these the skilled facilitator interprets and poses possible traumas, crimes, exclusions. Once such scenarios come to the client's attention, new awareness starts to work. It can filter through the family as a whole, not only the client.

Bert Hellinger was a military veteran of the Third Reich, drafted as a teenager in the last years of the war. He later became a Catholic missionary priest in Africa, then left the priesthood and studied psychology. The tribal healing methods he witnessed in Africa inspired the family constellation method. Psychosocial aftershocks of World War II were then and are still rippling in every veteran's family. Family Constellations has grown by leaps and bounds over several generations, now internationally. Another enormously successful version—called Collective Trauma Healing—was developed by Austrian Thomas Hübl (b. 1971) beginning in the 2000s.

Among the trainees with me were two very close friends whose family history was known to me in some detail. We also became close with six others. Each of us had at least one session devoted to us and our family. We all agreed after the whole course that our own family had healed in some significant way—forgiving, reconnecting, getting a liberating explanation—a new form of agape for sure. We were still buzzing with amazement that we experienced a healing social phenomenon repeatedly over two years, activated simply by the good will of those who showed up and participated. I did not know then why this was so. Now I am able to connect family constellations with what Steiner called *bringing warmth into the social field.*

> Man brings into this world of centripetal forces cosmic forces that dwell within his inner being. When we grasp clearly in our mind's eye what it is that lives as forces in man's inner being... *it is an element that we can call love, warmth, warmth of soul; the human being carries this soul warmth into the cold domain. This is preeminently his cosmic task. He is the source of warmth for this sphere... particularly those that have to do with the social field so we may realize what mission men's social life on earth has for the whole cosmos.**

Whereas Family Constellations was in person, MysTech has been carried mostly online. Communication on the internet became a large part of my spiritual community in the 21st century, especially after I retired from teaching.

From its inception in 2015 I participated in ULab, a free online open course offered by the Presencing Institute out of MIT's Sloan School of Business. The basic dynamic of an online ULab session is: through conversation a circle of people, trained and prepared to be wholly present and to listen, generating pictures and ideas from the social field pertinent to the group's collective focus. Further sessions working with the emergent ideas follow.

I believe Family Constellations, poetry and other art therapy circles, and ULab are early forms of the "Royal Art of the future which will be a social art."

> Through this Royal Art, man must acquire control of something similar to the force which sprouts in the plant, the same force that the occultist uses when he accelerates the growth of a plant in front of him. In a similar way, *a part of this force must be used for social salvation.* This power, which is described by those who know something of the Rosicrucian mysteries, as for example did Bulwer-Lytton in his futuristic novel *Vril,* is at present still in an elementary, germinal, stage. In the Freemasonry of the future, it will be the real content of the higher degrees. The Royal Art will in the future be a social art....

* Rudolf Steiner, *Spiritual Science as a Foundation for Social Forms,* Aug. 28, 1920 (my emphasis).

> Humanity is unaware that it is dancing on a volcano. The revolutions beginning on our earth make a new phase of the Royal Art necessary.*

With MIT tech support, ULab was able to do what small scale training could not do: connect with huge numbers of people in multiple countries and languages. My experience in guided meditations with several thousand people around the world seeking a healthy social future feels like yet another entirely new phenomenon I was privileged to encounter: tapping into and distributing agape—social love. In 1906, when Steiner brought the Royal Art, including women in a Masonic lodge, was a progressive first. In July 2020, a group poem was generated by over 10,000 international participants registered for the GAIA journey—a ULab online event over several days raising hearts in community during the world pandemic.

I started a group blog called SocialSculpture USA in 2007. Michael Howard, David Adams, and Anne Mendenhall contributed several times. We were interested in instigating something for anthroposophy in the USA comparable to what Joseph Beuys and his students did in Germany in the 1960s. A few members of the Social Science section were briefly interested. In 2011 I started another blog called *Liminal Weaver* with some of the Social Sculpture themes taken to a next level (https://timesculpture2021.blogspot.com). Through this blog I document many promising discoveries of critical thinking and social arts promoting agape in the English-speaking world: Charles Eisenstein, Bayo Akomolafe, *Urphanomen*/Matthew David Segall, Jonathan Rowson and *Perspectiva,* Iain McGilchrist, John Vervaeke, and more.

In 2019, I proposed on *Rosemary's Substack* that pairs or groups of anthroposophists offer moral technology training (substack.com/home/post/p-153027360). At the 2020 MysTech conference, I showed the central importance of overcoming antisocial forces in the context of the threefold social organism's history and the

* Rudolf Steiner, *The Temple Legend,* lecture 20, Jan. 2, 1906 (my emphasis).

conscious development of *manas:* selfless/group love (*Rosemary's Substack*, substack.com/home/post/p-153040959).

"Individuation isn't the end, but the ongoing accompaniment to a next step: group spiritual capacity-building." This is what Harlan Gilbert of the Threefold Education Center called for on February 15, 2022 in the concluding talk of his series "The Karma of Covid": "...we need to act together in new ways. Probably spiritual paths are the only way to lift up beyond immediate self-interest." I will add a caveat to his last sentence: Outside formal spiritual paths I experienced "pilot"—perhaps proto-spiritual—forms of applied agape "working together in new ways." Inside the anthroposophical movement many of these trends seem to be gathering steam. Several anthroposophical Annual General Meetings online and other initiatives have brought isolated people together in heart-warming social encounters of spiritual refreshment and grateful reception—agape events. For me this was particularly important because my local anthroposophic community was dormant during the pandemic.

From 2023 to the present, I have co-founded and participated in several circles of Michael School meeting regularly online and sometimes in person to witness and support each other in our individual and social journeys. We experience attending these "warm circles" open heartedly, reverently, faithfully as nourishment for our souls, healing from the social evils working around us, and as laboratories creating social "sacramental" forms. Something like a "group soul" dedicated to Michael, Christ, Sophia comes into play rhythmically week to week. Such spiritually formed relational events might be seen as a 21st-century version of medieval monastics dedicating their days and years together.

I am heartened by anthroposophists and dozens of "Michaelic" initiatives outside of formal anthroposophy practicing social arts where new forms of agape arise to inspire people to tap into the warm regenerative social field together to transform difficult situations. May the consciousness, the skill sets and applications gain constant momentum!

Note: A memoir by Ludwig Graf Polzer-Hoditz backs me up (see page 250):

> The tragedy of Middle Europe is, therefore, not economic poverty, which is perhaps more beneficial than wealth, but the conscious, systematic ruin of the faculties of soul and spirit in the individual. True, the complete extermination of such faculties is no longer possible. *Rudolf Steiner has preserved humanity from this fate.* In the last resort, even if only after many catastrophes, the needs of a group of younger people will show the way of the spirit and its consequences in life....
>
> Rudolf Steiner saw through all this ['dark powers at work in the various political camps'] and endeavored to oppose the materialistic and agnostic lack of ideas with thoughts suited to the real needs of the present and future. Practice which so often boasts of its successes had led humanity into material and spiritual misery which even today is manifesting in the most terrible form.
>
> From anthroposophy, those who were willing to hear had learned that it was not only a question of war among men, but that what happened during the war and continued to happen after the so-called "Peace" was a war of spiritual beings in human souls. The souls of individual men had become the theatre of war. But the groups which were fighting one another were ruled by the powers of darkness, and it was just because demonic powers were opposing each other that the war on earth became so bitter and is getting more and more so. The spiritual beings of Light must first of all be victorious in individual souls before man can unite in a spiritual community which will put an end to the wholesale slaughter now sanctioned by the bodies politic. In other words, only true spiritual individualism which can develop in a free life of the Spirit can lead without force and compulsion to a new culture and put an end for always to the old herd-life.*

---

* Ludwig Graf Polzer-Hoditz, *Memories of Rudolf Steiner: Reminiscences of an Austrian* (my emphasis, pp. 69–70; written at the request of Walter Johannes Stein and published in German in 1937; English translation: St George, Spring Valley, NY, 1987).

My Path to International Peacebuilding

Olivia Stokes Dreier

On a hot afternoon on the eastern coast of Sri Lanka in 2012, I whispered to my Sri Lankan co-facilitator, "I have no idea what we should do next." We had recently launched a USAID-funded reconciliation program in the country for 80 Hindu, Buddhist, Muslim, and Christian religious leaders. This was just one year after the end of Sri Lanka's brutal 17-year civil war. The Sinhala Buddhist-led government had claimed victory through military force, leaving thousands of Tamils dead or "disappeared," regardless of whether they were fighters. Our program focused on Eastern Sri Lanka, one of the country's most ethnically mixed regions. Mutual mistrust ran deep. Blame and bitter resentment simmered just below the surface, and violence threatened to resurface at any moment. Except for Christians, religious identities and loyalties aligned with ethnic ones; Hindus were all ethnically Tamil, Buddhists were ethnically Sinhalese, and Tamil-speaking Muslims had been caught in the crossfire, accused by both sides of being collaborators. In our work with the religious leaders, we had asked them to share what they could bring from their respective spiritual traditions to contribute to the reconciliation process and to develop ethnically mixed projects in their communities. Progress in rebuilding trust between these leaders had been slow and that afternoon we had taken a risk.

After some initial exercises focused on the principles of dialogue, emphasizing the importance of speaking authentically from one's own lived experience and listening with openness, we had invited each religious group to take turns sitting in the center of the room, speaking with each other about their biggest concerns for their identity group, while the other groups formed a circle around them, simply listening (through translation on their headphones) without comment. What unfolded was not what we expected. One by one, each group shared horrific stories of the violence they had personally experienced or witnessed, while the others listened in rapt silence. Preexisting beliefs about who had suffered the most had clearly been challenged, and now it was time for a tea break. How could we process what was just spoken without further exacerbating tensions? Then, to my utter surprise, I saw a Buddhist monk, a Hindu priest, and a Muslim Imam, who had only some broken English as a common language, head for tea, arm-in-arm and smiling from ear-to-ear. What had just happened?

Intuitively, I knew. It was something I had experienced before in my peacebuilding work, where in a moment of seeming grace participants had a deep experience of their common humanity across the deepest divides. When it happened, it was palpable and profound shifts occurred. And for our Sri Lankan religious leaders it was a turning point. Tensions still emerged over the course of our next year and a half of work together, but the religious leaders became deeply committed to the reconciliation process, launching over 50 community projects in intentionally visible, multi-faith teams. Tamil and Sinhalese youth enrolled in language classes to be able to speak to each other, war damage to mosques and Hindu temples was repaired by villagers from all ethnic groups, and women in a mixed group basket-making cooperative decided to share rumors of brewing violence and plan steps to calm tensions before they exploded.

I have often asked myself the question posed by the editor of this volume: how has my interest in anthroposophy and the work of Rudolf Steiner shaped my peacebuilding and other work in the social domain? It is not an easy question to answer, as I have not set out to apply anthroposophy to my work in a prescriptive manner. But since my early twenties, it has imbued how I understand every aspect of human life and whatever work I have felt called to do in the world, whether as a psychotherapist, a peacebuilder, or more recently on defending democracy. So, what are the pathways that led me to that moment in tension-ridden post war Sri Lanka and to trust in the transformative power of human connection, even in the aftermath of war? Some relate to the many ways anthroposophy has inspired me, others to various biographical influences.

I was born in Paris, where my father worked for the Marshall Plan, which was arguably the most successful large-scale, postwar peacebuilding effort to date. My career shift into international peacebuilding, after years as a psychotherapist, occurred after he died in his early nineties, and I have often wished I had entered this work while he was still alive. There is so much I would have asked. But no doubt, the theme of societal recovery from the devastation of war was in the air I first breathed and who knows what influence my father has had on me from the other side (quite a bit, I like to think). When I was growing up, my father worked as a lawyer in New York City, after losing his presidentially appointed position when Eisenhower took office. His hopes of getting back into international work were further dashed by McCarthy-era politics. I suspect I unconsciously internalized his longing to be involved once more.

I would date my spiritual quest to the sudden loss of my mother to heart failure when I was 14. We had attended the local Episcopal Church, which, to my adolescent self, seemed merely for convention's sake. Nothing in the way Christianity was presented made sense to me, nor did it seem meaningful to my parents, though that was never discussed. But the thought that my mother had simply ceased to exist or that my own existence and sense of beingness was the product of pure chance made no sense either. My mother had a deep love for the natural world and had shared it in ways that hinted at the unseen. I can still feel her hand on my shoulder, alerting me to a particular bird call on one of our early morning walks.

As a teenager, the seeker in me grew interested in Eastern philosophies, and through a college program that funded me to work in a non-Western county between sophomore and junior years, I set off to work with the Gandhian movement in rural India. Stranded en route in England as I awaited my Indian visa, I chanced upon Emerson College and ended up working on its biodynamic farm for six weeks. And so began my initial acquaintance with and resistance to anthroposophy. I loved the work on the farm but heard various anthroposophical ideas and maxims uttered with great certainty and no context, which dampened my curiosity. Besides, my heart was set on getting to India.

As for my spiritual quest, I was soon in for a rude awakening. Wanting to learn how to meditate, I had met with a devotee of an Indian guru, who passed through my college some months earlier. I had little interest in having a guru but figured I needed a technique. Out of curiosity, upon landing in Delhi, I reached out to a contact and learned that the guru had also just arrived from his home state and would deliver his most spiritually significant annual ceremony the next day. Through my experience of that event and subsequent encounters at the guru's home ashram, I discovered that the movement was a cult with a very dark side. The guru believed that the world needed to be ruled by a spiritual elite and that violence might be required to get there. Several devotees who tried to leave had been found dead, leading to national headlines and the guru's eventual arrest. What had appeared to be about peace and love back in the US was anything but. My supposedly personalized mantra contained an honorific name for the guru, and I felt almost infected. With good intention and youthful naiveté, I had stumbled upon something seemingly evil. I would not leap so easily into the world of spirit again. I had brought Steiner's *Knowledge of the Higher Worlds* with me from my time at Emerson, but for my next one and a half years in rural India, the book sat on a shelf unread, even though I was often starved for reading matter. (Three years later I read it over the course of a couple of days, unable to put it down.) Fortunately, at the Gandhian school where I worked, the lead teacher, a humble self-taught Sanskrit scholar, guided me through the teachings of the

Vedas. The experience felt pure and healing. The school was close to Bodhgaya, where the Buddha is said to have reached enlightenment. Sitting now in the shade of what is believed to be a seedling of the original Bodhi tree, watching the Tibetan Buddhist monks perform prostrations on boards worn smooth by those repeated acts of reverence, and listening to their deep throated chants was profoundly soothing. But after a week-long silent Buddhist meditation retreat, I knew that Buddhism, with what I understood at the time to be a negation of the self, was not my path.

A year after my return to the US, I met my husband, Alexander Dreier. I was immediately drawn to him but not to the fact that he was deeply interested in anthroposophy. However, given his lack of dogmatism and wonderful sense of humor, I was willing to explore what I had previously resisted, and together we spent two years at Emerson College. This time it stuck. I had the experience that so many describe when first fully meeting anthroposophy. Suddenly, life made sense, what I had vaguely intuited felt elucidated, and the content, while new, seemed somehow familiar.

In our second year we joined the "Social Development Course." My husband had been studying biodynamics but we both felt drawn to work in the social realm, to work that would take us outside of anthroposophical communities and demand fresh approaches. During my last year of college, I had been a live-in volunteer in a halfway house for people coming out of both mental hospitals and prisons (a bold and questionable experiment). I was struck by the sensitive souls I met there. One man told me that he was first hospitalized and medicated when he reported an encounter with an uncle who had recently died. When I read Steiner's description of how over the course of the 20th century people would start unconsciously crossing the threshold into experiences of the spiritual world, I wondered whether some of those suffering from various forms of "mental illness" might in fact be having spiritual experiences for which neither they nor those around them were prepared. With youthful enthusiasm, my husband and I decided we would start a therapeutic community based on a biodynamic farm. To gain experience, my husband took a job running the farm at Gould Farm, a therapeutic community founded in the early 1900s in western Massachusetts and the closest thing we had found to what we hoped to start. After several years of living and working in that community, I then got a degree in clinical social work, following the path we had laid out for ourselves. We soon realized, however, that our vision would require enormous resources, especially for it to operate without just serving the wealthy, which held little interest for me. With two young children, we soon transferred our entrepreneurial energy to helping start the Hartsbrook Waldorf School in Hadley, Massachusetts. I then began work as a psychotherapist, first at the local university and then at a local medical clinic, work I continued for the next 15 years. I saw clients from a wide variety of backgrounds and around issues ranging from everyday life challenges to more serious psychological conditions.

I found being a psychotherapist—accompanying people in their darkest moments or as they addressed their most difficult life questions—to be an extraordinary privilege. Friends and acquaintances connected to anthroposophy often asked me how I applied anthroposophy to my work as a therapist. I remember feeling that I ought to be able to answer that question, and I tried a couple of times to present on the topic, quite unsuccessfully in my estimation. In truth, while anthroposophical insights about adult development, our threefold nature, and the unfolding of karma were embedded in my view of the human being and the forces that shaped the struggles and aspirations of my clients, I did not want to impose those frames of reference too readily. Any preconceived notions seemed to be in the way of authentic human-to-human encounter, especially when those seeking psychotherapy presented themselves in their most vulnerable states. Over time, I observed that my clients found the discernment, direction, and inner strength they sought when they felt fully heard and seen by me. Most importantly, they sensed my confidence that they would find their way through whatever obstacles were causing their distress. On one level, it was quite simple. I realized that transformation began with my own presence. When I truly opened myself to the person in front of me, seeing them as a spiritual being with prebirth intentions, something shifted. When I fully appreciated their distinct gifts, acknowledged their flaws, and honored their struggles to navigate life, I created an environment where healing could emerge naturally. The quality of my attention became the foundation for therapeutic change.

Whereas I loved my work, I felt a pull to return to international work, and as our children grew more independent, that felt more possible. In India, I had worked in the country's poorest state with children who came from families who were at the very bottom of the caste hierarchy and had endured a recent famine. They were the first from their communities to be educated and arrived at the school with all the gifts and potential that children are born with everywhere. The school had grown out of the Sarvodaya movement, founded in the 1950s by Vinoba Bhave, a follower of Gandhi who spent years walking from village to village, persuading landlords to donate land for the landless who worked their fields, often for slave wages. Extraordinarily, over two million acres were collected and redistributed to the landless, including to the families of the children at the school. The movement fell short of its many lofty goals, but my involvement with it left me with an indelible impression of both the impact of exploitation and the potential of grassroots social movements.

During the mid-1990s I was also learning of the horror stories coming out of the Bosnian war and the Rwandan genocide. The fall of the Berlin Wall had seemingly failed to launch an era of global peace. The mid-1990s saw an explosion of inter-ethnic and inter-religious conflicts, in which civilians were caught in the crossfire, resulting in massacres, sexual violence and massive displacement. Despite how much I valued my life and work in my community, I was conscious at the same time of America's insularity and felt the urge to step beyond its privileged spaces. I was also intrigued by the sprouting of local NGOs and grassroots movements around the world. It reminded me of Bhave's pioneering experiment in 1950s India. Attending an anthroposophical conference in the Philippines convened by Nicanor Perlas on the potential for social renewal led by civil society inspired me further. One morning as I entered the clinic where I worked as a therapist, I experienced a profound moment of clarity. With news of ethnic conflicts regularly in the headlines, I felt a deep inner knowing that it was time to shift careers, to apply what I'd learned about human healing to communities torn apart by violence. The skills I'd developed over those years, deep listening, creating safe spaces for vulnerability, recognizing patterns of trauma, suddenly seemed urgently needed beyond the therapy room. My question was: how to proceed?

As part of my exploration, I attended a two-week peacebuilding institute initiated by Paula Green, a local psychologist and peace activist. The participants included people from around the globe and different sides of violent conflicts, and I witnessed how the opportunity to bridge and reconcile across deep divides can promote healing from the trauma of war. This was confirmed for me when I traveled with Paula to Bosnia to witness her work on the ground. Bosnian Serb and Bosnian Muslim educators had been engaging in a carefully constructed series of workshops and dialogues over the last couple of years. Slowly, and often with two steps forward and one step back, mutual trust had been restored, and they were working together to make their schools welcoming environments for the "other side," as refugees were returning to their home communities.

I was awed by Paula's facilitation, her capacity to surface underlying tensions in ways that could be safely addressed. The Bosnian Serbs in the group came from the region that held the most notorious concentration camps for Bosnian Muslims and "rape camps" for Bosnian Muslim women. The Bosnian Serbs easily expressed hopes for peace and reconciliation but to the frustration of the Bosnian Muslims avoided acknowledging what had in fact transpired and tended to equalize the suffering of both sides. As a result, the process became frozen. At a key moment, Paula turned to me and her American co-facilitator and suggested we sit in the center and speak with each other about the harm done in our country and in the world "in our name" as Americans. The list was long and our shame real. Then after a period of silence, one of the Serb participants spoke to how terrible she felt about what was done in her name as a Serb. The others followed suit and the whole dynamic shifted. Paula's intuitive action in that moment, when all seemed stuck, was just what was needed. For me, it was a courageous example, and close approximation, of what Steiner describes as moral intuition. And its impact was palpable.

After a year attending a mid-career graduate program to familiarize myself with current theories of conflict resolution, peacebuilding, and international relations, I joined Paula to help her develop the small nonprofit she had recently established, the Karuna Center for Peacebuilding, which I eventually directed.*

Over the next two decades, this work took me to more than twenty conflict-affected countries, working with local partners at all levels of society from the grassroots to the halls of parliament. Our efforts focused on social healing. While postwar political settlements and economic reconstruction are critical, they do not in and of themselves bring social healing in situations where the entire social fabric has been torn apart by violence and enmity, leading all too often to repeated cycles of violence. This was evident to me on that first trip to Bosnia. A young Bosnian Muslim educator told me that the principal of his school, a man he had grown up admiring, had led the Serbian militia that committed a massacre in his village, in which over 50 members of his extended family died. He returned to his village after three years as a refugee with hatred toward all Serbs and desire for revenge. At first a reluctant participant in the Karuna workshops, he eventually found the experience transformative. He now directs his own

* *Karuna* comes from the Sanskrit word for compassion.

peacebuilding NGO in Northern Bosnia, leading workshops for Bosnian Muslim and Bosnian Serb youth who then traverse the country with "peace caravans."

Depending on the needs perceived by local partners and available funding, Karuna's projects have varied in scope and duration, but common threads include: tailoring programs to fit local culture and context; working with each side separately at first to establish trust; joint workshops that develop a common language around the dynamics of conflict and pathways toward peace; facilitated dialogues to understand the lived experience of the other side; joint projects that solidify mutual trust and have ripple effects in divided communities; work with media to lift up positive stories of reconciliation that show what's possible and counter narratives that fuel cycles of revenge; and advocacy with policy makers to support reconciliation and change policies that perpetuate residual tensions.

As in my work as a psychotherapist, I have resisted applying preconceived anthroposophical ideas to peace-building in a prescriptive manner. Indeed, part of what has always resonated for me in anthroposophy is Steiner's fundamental commitment to human freedom. I thus find it essential to draw inspiration from anthroposophy without reifying it into doctrine. As Steiner's close collaborator Ita Wegman stated emphatically in a 1933 lecture, "Evil would result if dogma were to enter anthroposophy and unfree, established ideas were to be laid down instead of an unfettered spiritual life being allowed."*

Still, Steiner's concept of "social threefolding" quietly informed my approach in Rwanda and elsewhere. Without explicitly naming it as such, our work addressed all three spheres: cultural healing through community-based trauma work, political engagement through dialogue with local and national leaders, and economic cooperation through community projects. The balance of these

* Ita Wegman, *The Mysteries* (compiled and translated by Crispian Villeneuve, Temple Lodge, 1995).

elements, which took different forms in different country contexts, seemed essential to lasting reconciliation.

In my work as a therapist, I recognized that I had to be careful of my power in the encounter, to be sure that my biases, framing, or potential suggestions would not interfere as clients opened deep emotional wounds. They needed the safety and freedom to explore their own responses to their challenges. Similarly, societies recovering from the ravages of war are at their most vulnerable and need encouragement to find their own pathways toward cultural and spiritual resilience and revitalization, whether building on age-old traditions or developing new forms. I was often dismayed to see simplistic conflict resolution frameworks, techniques, and exercises exported by Western experts and implemented in ways that ignored cultural context.

The value of understanding and honoring local traditions became especially clear through Karuna's involvement over many years with peacebuilding efforts in the Casamance region of southern Senegal, home to Africa's longest war of secession. We worked with political leaders, civil society, and the political wings of the fractured rebel groups, but we had the biggest impact when we took seriously some local advice that had been ignored by other international organizations. We were told that the rebels, who had grown weary from decades of struggle, would not lay down their arms unless the sacred oaths they had taken to fight to the end were lifted by the priestesses of the sacred forests of each community. We raised funds for the ceremonies to take place at a fraction of the cost of previous programs in the region. Families called their rebel sons home, including the rebel commander, for the oaths to be ceremonially lifted, along with the removal of magic spells for protection from bullets as well as cleansing rituals for those who had killed. A peace process remained elusive, but in the regions where the ceremonies were held, violence ceased, confirming my conviction that the more deeply I listened without bias to what was needed in any given situation, the more effective I could be.

I have worked on various reconciliation efforts in post-genocide Rwanda, where I also brought peacebuilding students from across the globe for field seminars as part of a graduate program I led. I developed our largest and most impactful program in collaboration with local partners to support the reintegration of ex-perpetrators, who had completed prison or community service sentences. They were returning to their home communities, the very places where they had killed. Dialogue has been a core component of all my peacebuilding work, but in Rwanda its potential for healing was dramatically evident. One of our Rwandan partners trained community dialogue facilitators, and another held trauma healing sessions for ex-perpetrators and survivors together. These two efforts worked in tandem, and the participants, whether they had committed atrocities or survived them, formed deep bonds. Remarkably, they then worked together to rebuild trust in their communities and to advocate with local and national political leaders to support their efforts.

The word dialogue has a wonderful origin in Greek: *dia*, meaning through and *logos,* with its range of multiple meanings, including Heraclitus' divine creative principle and the divine Word in the Gospel of John. With the right preparation, people can gather to dialogue across the deepest divides, even in the aftermath of genocide, and experience what exits in all of us as universally human. For me, this possibility embodies something that Steiner describes especially clearly in his lectures on *Awakening to Community.* In each encounter with another human being, when we are capable of fully listening to the other, even to those who hold opposite views to our own, we become each other's "awakener," and something of the divine is revealed.

Out of his research on the evolution of human consciousness and culture, Steiner describes in various lectures how in the late 19th century a new sense of individualism emerged—but accompanied by new impulses for cosmopolitanism and a yearning to find what is universally human. Witnessing the growing nationalism and enmity that led to World War I, he also spoke during and after the war years of the resistance to this call toward the universal, a resistance that harkened back to blood ties and rigid belief systems. This reactionary tendency to cling to the illusory security of group identities is perhaps even more pronounced today. As Steiner suggested, we need to find a counterforce to grow beyond the limits of every kind of *given* community and create new, *voluntary* associations and communities out of choice. Belief in this potential has guided my peacebuilding work and allowed me to project confidence in its possibilities.

Steiner also spoke to the importance of preparing for a far distant future when, as human consciousness continues to evolve, we will find ourselves not only pained by the sight of poverty and hunger but feel such suffering as our own, another's hunger as a physical sensation in our own body.* A glimmer of this possibility comes to mind as I recall a peacebuilding workshop in Macedonia, where the violence in Kosovo had spread, initiated by Albanian Macedonians who complained of decades of discrimination. An Albanian man had listened to a Macedonian woman describe the deep fear she felt while giving birth as violence raged outside the hospital. He said he suddenly felt her fear inside himself. It became his fear, and in that moment, he no longer experienced Macedonians as the oppressor.

Five years ago, I retired as director of Karuna Center, but I remain active in peacebuilding projects. Two years ago, I was asked by a peacebuilding colleague in New Zealand to be a senior research fellow for a Japanese peace research institute. My area of focus was to be "global challenges to democracy." Although given little time to deliberate on this offer, on instinct I said yes and then wondered what I had gotten myself into, given my lack of expertise in the field.

* "Preparing for the Sixth Epoch," lecture on June 15, 1915, in Düsseldorf; currently available in *The Mystery of Death: The Nature and Significance of Central Europe and the European Folk-Spirits,* lecture 13, "Community above us—Christ within us" (Rudolf Steiner Press, Forest Row, UK, 2023).

Uncertain as to how to proceed, I created an international working group of democracy experts and peacebuilders to give guidance. Our joint work is now gaining momentum with a focus on democratic resilience.

With democracies under pressure worldwide, I've found that the same principles that heal divided communities after war can strengthen democratic institutions during polarized times. In both contexts, people must learn to dialogue across differences, build trust through joint efforts, and develop narratives that overcome dehumanization. The Democracy Lighthouse platform we've created connects over 300 institutes globally that are reimagining democracy for the 21st century. Like our work with religious leaders in Sri Lanka, we're creating spaces where people with vastly different worldviews can recognize their common humanity and shared stake in democratic systems. I believe that there is a growing global desire to cultivate spaces of human freedom rooted in appreciation of our common humanity. It is a cosmopolitan impulse, a "Michaelic impulse," in the face of growing polarization. And dialogue, dia-logos, or "the logos" itself, lies at its heart.

The older I get, the more grateful I am for the insights of anthroposophy, both from Steiner and the many who have carried forward his ideas with fresh perspectives and new applications. At the same time, I am evermore aware of the importance of reaching beyond our existing anthroposophical circles. The truths we strive to understand are larger than any of us can comprehend, and we live in an increasingly complex world. To become full participants in a new cosmopolitan age will require both radical openness and a strong moral compass, the very essence of Steiner's ethical individualism.

About the Authors

Benjamin Bingham is a Class Holder in the School of Spiritual Science and the CEO/Founder of 3Sisters Sustainable Management, Inc. (3SSM), a Delaware Benefit Corporation managing 100% impact portfolios across private and public asset classes (www.scarabfundsllc.com). Educated at Groton School, Yale, and Emerson College (UK), his writing and work draw on broad experience as an artist, biodynamic farmer, and teacher. His pioneering book published in 2015, *Impact Investing: Making Money Matter*, is an important contribution to this expanding movement and will be republished this fall in a revised and updated version. Currently, in addition to his work at 3SSM, Ben is the Founding Chair of iWorkflow, a technology platform for integrating the delivery of services to the un- and under-insured in partnership with the United Way and MDC (www.iworkflow.org).

Robert M. Burnside's background is in three domains: leadership, learning, and life. He has been providing leadership development for others beginning with his 15 years at the Center for Creative Leadership. He has been helping humans learn how to learn, beginning with his role as Chief Learning Officer for fifteen years at Ketchum Public Relations followed by seven years as Senior Learning Advisor for Nomadic Learning. Currently Robert is focusing on understanding the impact of generative artificial intelligence on leadership, learning and life, writing about this in https://roborobert.substack.com/archive. He has been developing his overall understanding of the life of the human being since 1985 through study of Rudolf Steiner's spiritual science, known as anthroposophy.

Gordon Collins is an executive coach, consultant and facilitator. He specializes in developing the leadership capability required to lead individuals, align teams, and create high performing work cultures. His approach enables his clients to produce greater levels of clarity, confidence and commitment toward their vision and goals. Gordon is the president and founder of The Coaching Network, based in Victoria, British Columbia. Gordon is also a member of The Association for Social Development, a network of international consultants inspired by the work of Bernard Lievegoed.

Olivia Stokes Dreier is a Senior Research Fellow on Global Challenges to Democracy at the Toda Peace Institute and a Senior Peacebuilding Advisor to Karuna Center for Peacebuilding, where she served for many years as executive director. In collaboration with local partners, she has developed and led peacebuilding programs in over 20 conflict-affected countries. She is a longtime student of anthroposophy and was involved in the founding and development of the Hartsbrook Waldorf School in Hadley, Massachusetts.

Bart Eddy is an educator, entrepreneur, and community development advocate who has worked in Detroit for more than forty years. During that time, he co-founded the Barnabas Youth Opportunities Center (1983), Detroit Community Schools (1997), and the Sunbridge International Collaborative (2012). He currently directs the "Brightmoor Makers" program for youth employment and advocacy and is passionately committed to helping young people find their sense of vision, mission, and purpose in the global community. Bart was a class teacher at the Detroit Waldorf School from 1988 to 1996.

Karen Gierlach was born in England, grew up in Germany and attended Waldorf Schools in both countries. Since retiring from Waldorf teaching 25 years ago, she has facilitated biography and social art workshops for Waldorf teachers and parents, both here and abroad. She also enjoys bringing workshops to adults in other settings, like classes for seniors at the local university, in workshops at the local library and recently for the Sisterhood of Salaam Shalom.

Paul Gierlach has, for the past 45 years, been involved in Waldorf communities, primarily as a teacher in grade schools, high schools and teacher training programs in the US and China. As a history teacher he has been primarily interested in the manner in which individuals through the ages have created the societies they inhabit. As an anthroposophist, he uses the teaching curriculum and its formative wisdom to prepare those individuals to create sensible, spirit-oriented communities now and for the future.

Neil H. Golder, PhD, lives in Ithaca, New York, and in the Hudson Valley. He has worked for many years with the Ithaca Catholic Worker, is a fellow of the School of Spiritual Psychology, and does some eurythmy, speech formation, and biography work at the Threefold Community in Spring Valley, New York.

Alice Groh lives on a small biodynamic farm in Wilton, New Hampshire. She and her late husband Trauger Groh, with two other farmers and community families, established one of two pioneer Community Supported Agriculture (CSA) farms in the US in 1986. She remains active in the agricultural, educational, and anthroposophical life in her community.

Joan Jaeckel (editorial assistance) met anthroposophy at age 21 and ever since has felt moved to find and connect with "others seeking the same goals." Part of the founding team of Ocean Charter School, she currently serves on the board of The Source School: Creating Cultures of Connection using the transformational listening practices of Otto Scharmer's Theory U. Previous projects include consulting producer on the CINE Golden Eagle Award-winning documentary, *The Waldorf Promise*. She lives in Los Angeles and is a mother, stepmother, and grandmother. Through caregiving of her stroke-recovering husband, she is learning about the need for greater social awareness at the other end of life, too.

Gary Lamb is currently the director of the Hawthorne Valley Center for Social Research in Upstate New York. He is a former Waldorf teacher and administrator, and has written and edited several books on social threefolding, Waldorf education, technology, and freedom and funding of education. Together with Joel Kobran, he was a co-editor of the *Threefold Review* journal for 14 years.

Lisa Mahar served as school administrator at Monadnock Waldorf School in Keene, New Hampshire, from 1991 to 2018. She is a founding member of the Administrators Network of the Association of Waldorf Schools of North America (AWSNA), is a trained meeting facilitator, and advises and consults with Waldorf schools on governance, community building, administrative review, meeting facilitation, mentoring, visioning, and administrative planning. She has a deep interest in the social mission of Waldorf education and the human relationships that inspire, form, and support our schools. Her mentoring is guided by the needs of the individual, posing questions and lines of inquiry that lead to meaningful insights and practical action.

Rosemary McMullen completed her PhD in English literature in 1971 and taught several decades at the college level, with certification in poetry therapy, family constellations, Waldorf education, and biodynamic agriculture. Rosemary has published essays, poetry, and fiction, and facilitated group work in many of the these fields.

Davina Muse, M.Ed., LMHC USA (ret.), returned to her native land, England, following 35 fulfilling years in the US. She is a mother and grandmother hoping to offer continuity among past, present, and future, between here and there wherever they are. She endeavors to be a promising and humorous wise elder.

Pierre Noack was born and raised in Belgium. He graduated as a mechanical and electrical engineer. Hired by a German machinery manufacturer, Aerzen, he soon accepted a management position as CEO in the United States, which he occupied for three decades before transferring back to Germany until retirement. He is active with anthroposophy, gardening, and being with his children and grandchildren.

Joseph Rubano lives in Oceanside, California. In addition to what he said about himself in his article on being a counselor, he loves to dig in the dirt, plant seeds, watch plants grow, make fire, write poetry, fix broken things, make things out of wood, and be outside as much as possible. Both poems in his article are from his recent book, *This Crazy Love Life: Meetings along the Way* (True Meetings Press, 2025).

Christopher Schaefer, PhD, is a retired adult educator and organization development consultant living in the Berkshires. He has taught at both Emerson College, where he co-founded the Centre for Social Development and at Sunbridge College in Spring Valley, New York. He is a father and grandfather. His books include: *Vision in Action: Working with Soul and Spirit in Small Organizations* (coauthored with Tÿno Voors); *Partnerships of Hope: Building Waldorf School Communities;* and *Re-Imaging America: Finding Hope in Difficult Times.*

Signe Eklund Schaefer directed Foundation Studies at Sunbridge College for over twenty years and was a founding member of the Center for Biography and Social Art after having initiated the biography training program in 1998. In recent years, she has been writing: *She was Always There: Sophia as a Story for our Time* (2023); *Why on Earth? Biography and the practice of Human Becoming* (2013); *I Give You My Word: Women's Letters as Life Support, 1973–1987* (2019); and *Elder Flowering: Lived Experiences of Growing Older*

(2024, co-edited with Karen Gierlach). A mother, grandmother, and great-grandmother, she lives with her husband Christopher in Great Barrington, Massachusetts.

Carrie Schuchardt, M.Ed., has spent most of her life in community, especially in Camphill, with people of diverse needs and gifts. Since 1980 she is also involved nationally and internationally in refugee resettlement and advocacy. With her husband John, Carrie founded the community of the House of Peace in 1990 in Ipswich, Massachusetts (houseofpeaceinc.org).

John Schuchardt, J.D., co-director of the House of Peace, was co-initiator of the Plowshares Movement in 1980 (see www.wagingnon-violence.org and Wikipedia: Plowshares Movement). He is known for his leadership in the movement to abolish war and nuclear weapons.

Michael Soulé has worked over the past 40 years in the Waldorf movement as a class teacher, administrator, AWSNA executive, teacher trainer, and consultant advisor to many schools and individuals. He is a semi-retired co-director of Leading with Spirit, supporting the Waldorf movement through workshops, school advising, and individual coaching. He lives with his wife in a co-housing community on Whidbey Island, Washington.

Marti Stewart is the current Administrative Director at City of Lakes Waldorf School, where she has served for the past 23 years. Marti is a founding member of Leading with Spirit, created to enhance administrative and board leadership in Waldorf schools across the continent through support and professional development activities such as coursework, mentoring, and school consulting. She resides in Minneapolis, where she enjoys drawing, painting, gardening, reading, attending cultural events, and spending time with her partner and adult children. She is currently pursuing a master's degree in Integrative Health and Wellbeing Coaching through the University of Minnesota.

Chiaki Uchiyama, M. Ed., was born and raised in Yokohama, Japan, and began her journey into anthroposophy in 1996. She has since dedicated her career to Waldorf education, serving as a teacher, pedagogical director, and now school director at Portland Waldorf School in Milwaukie, Oregon. She has led annual language teacher conferences and presented widely through Waldorf Early Childhood Association of North America (WECAN), Association of Waldorf Schools of North America (AWSNA), Center for Anthroposophy, other teacher training institutes, and National Association of Independent Schools (NAIS) conferences. Chiaki holds an Ed.D. in Waldorf education from Antioch University in Keene, Hew Hampshire, with her dissertation, *Heart-Thinking Leadership*, exploring diversity, equity, and inclusion through the lens of anthroposophy.